Mental Illness, Due Process
and the Criminal Defendant

Special Committee on the Study of
Commitment Procedures
and the Law Relating to Incompetents

THE COMMITTEE

J. Kenneth Campbell, *Chairman*
John N. Marden, *Secretary*
Alfred Berman
Henry DeVine
Sol Gelb
The Honorable Abraham N. Geller
Melvin Glass
Richard A. Green
W. Cecil Johnston, M.D.
The Honorable Jacob Markowitz
Commissioner Paul D. McGinnis
The Honorable John M. Murtagh
Francis J. O'Neill, M.D.
Simon Rosenzweig
The Honorable Joseph A. Sarafite
Commissioner Christopher F. Terrence, M.D.
Gray Thoron
Arthur Zitrin, M.D.

Russell D. Niles, *President of the Association* (*ex officio*)
David S. Worgan, *Liaison Member with the
Executive Committee of the Association*

THE STAFF

Malachy T. Mahon, Director*
Francis J. Devlin, Student Assistant †
Frank T. D'Onofrio, Student Assistant †
Rita H. Quasman, Student Assistant †
Shaun S. Sullivan, Student Assistant †

* Associate Professor, Fordham University School of Law
† Summer, 1965, while at Fordham University School of Law

MENTAL ILLNESS
DUE PROCESS
and
THE CRIMINAL DEFENDANT

A Second Report and Additional Recommendations
by the Special Committee on the Study of Commitment
Procedures and the Law Relating to Incompetents
of the
ASSOCIATION OF THE BAR
OF THE CITY OF NEW YORK
in cooperation with
FORDHAM UNIVERSITY SCHOOL OF LAW

New York
FORDHAM UNIVERSITY PRESS
1968

First published 1968 by FORDHAM UNIVERSITY PRESS

© Copyright 1968 by the Association of the Bar
of the City of New York Fund, Inc.
Library of Congress Catalog Card Number: 68–19789

PRINTED IN THE UNITED STATES OF AMERICA
BY THE COLONIAL PRESS INC.
CLINTON, MASSACHUSETTS

CONTENTS

Foreword by J. Kenneth Campbell   ix

SUMMARY AND RECOMMENDATIONS   1

CHAPTER I. MENTALLY ILL PRISONERS UNDER
         SENTENCE   13

1. Admission Procedures (RECOMMENDATION
     NO. 1)   15
2. Periodic Review (RECOMMENDATION NO. 2)   22
3. Discharge Prior to Expiration of Sentence
     (RECOMMENDATION NO. 3)   26
4. Discharge Upon Expiration of Sentence
     (RECOMMENDATION NO. 4)   28

CHAPTER II. FORMER PRISONERS AND THE
         ALLEGEDLY DANGEROUSLY
         MENTALLY ILL   32

1. Background   33
2. Situation as of February, 1966
     a) Former Prisoners Retained at Matteawan
         (N.Y. Correc. Law §§ 408, 409)   37
     b) Former Prisoners Retained at Danne-
         mora (N.Y. Correc. Law § 384; N.Y.
         Mental Hygiene Law § 87[3])   39
     c) Former Prisoners Hospitalized after
         Release from Prison (N.Y. Correc. Law
         § 412)   41

d) Allegedly Dangerously Mentally Ill
Patients (N.Y. Mental Hygiene Law
§ 85)   44
e) Need for Revision   48
3. The *Baxstrom* Case   52
4. For Further Improvement
(RECOMMENDATIONS NOS. 5–8)   59

CHAPTER III. THE MENTALLY ILL DEFENDANT   72

1. Legislative History   73
2. The Standard (RECOMMENDATION NO. 9)   79
3. Place and Duration of Examination
(RECOMMENDATION NO. 10)   86
4. Hospitalization Procedures
a) The Statutes   91
b) The Need for Revision
(RECOMMENDATION NO. 11)   98
5. Automatic Periodic Judicial Review
(RECOMMENDATION NO. 12)   102
6. Disposition of the Criminal Charge
a) Present Procedures   107
b) Proposed Revisions (RECOMMENDATIONS
NOS. 13–17)   115

CHAPTER IV. PERSONS ACQUITTED OF CRIME BY
REASON OF INSANITY   125

1. The Statutes   125
2. Administration   128
3. Proposed Revisions (RECOMMENDATIONS
NOS. 18–19)   133

APPENDICES

APPENDIX A. A *History of Matteawan State
Hospital*   139
1. Antecedents: 1788–1858   139

2. Auburn Asylum: 1859–1892   142
3. Matteawan State Hospital: 1892–1966   145

APPENDIX B. *New York Legislation Affecting
Mentally Ill Prisoners: 1842–1965*   191

1. Utica Asylum: 1842–1858   191
2. Auburn Asylum: 1858–1893   192
3. Prisoners at Matteawan: 1893–1965   196
4. Prisoners at Dannemora: 1899–1965   201

APPENDIX C. *Tables*   207

1. Matteawan State Hospital, Annual
Population 1925–1966   207
2. Types of Commitments to Matteawan State
Hospital, 1940–1966   208
3. Matteawan State Hospital, Census,
1962–1966   210
4. Matteawan State Hospital, Prisoners Under
Sentence and Time-expired,
by Type of Crime   211
5. Matteawan State Hospital, Disposition of
Patients Discharged 1960–1966   212
6. Matteawan State Hospital, Disposition of
Patients Discharged 1940–1964   213
7. Matteawan State Hospital, Condition of
Patients Discharged 1940–1965   213
8. Matteawan State Hospital, Length of
Residence by Year and Type of Admission,
October 1, 1965   214
9. Matteawan State Hospital, Length of
Residence by Year and Type of Admission,
September 16, 1966   216
10. Dannemora State Hospital, Annual
Population 1925–1965   218
11. Dannemora State Hospital, Source of
Admission 1955–1965   218

12. Dannemora State Hospital, Releases
    1955–1965   219
13. Dannemora State Hospital, Classification of
    Patients by Crime, November 1965   220
APPENDIX D. *Operation Baxstrom After One Year*
    (Robert C. Hunt and
    E. David Wiley)   221
APPENDIX E. *Selected Statutes*   229

FOREWORD

The report which follows deals with the procedures for admission, retention and discharge of the various classes of mental patients who are involuntarily confined and treated at Matteawan and Dannemora State Hospitals, the two hospitals operated by New York State's Department of Correction. That department is, of course, charged with the responsibility for operating the state's prison system and the patients in those hospitals are, by and large, those who have had a "brush with the law."

The latter phrase is intended to embrace (1) those who have been charged with (but never convicted) of a crime and found to be unable to stand trial, (2) those who have become mentally ill while serving a prison sentence after conviction, and (3) those who have been tried but acquitted by reason of insanity. Matteawan has also been the repository for those patients in the civil hospital system found to be so dangerously mentally ill that their presence in a civil hospital endangers the safety of others.

While the number of patients in these hospitals has been relatively small (never as many as 3,500 in any year), their fates have been governed by an incredible patchwork of laws which are not only incongruous and inconsistent but often seem to defeat their very purpose. In these pages the reader will find, for example, that a law designed to insure justice by saving a mentally incompetent defendant from the risk of wrongful imprisonment on a charge he does not understand, can result in having that defendant—untried, unconvicted and presumed innocent under the law—spend the rest of his life in a maximum-security institution such as Matteawan.

This report is an outgrowth of this committee's earlier report *Mental Illness and Due Process*, published by Cornell University Press in 1962, which led to the enactment of a full-scale revision of so much of New York State's Mental Hygiene Law as relates to procedures for the admission, retention, and discharge of those "civil patients" treated in hospitals operated or supervised by New York State's Department of Mental Hygiene.

The committee's first report included a chapter entitled "Admissions in Criminal Cases" (pp. 220–57) which disclosed the hodgepodge of laws governing what were called "criminal law patients." It described how existing laws established procedures for admission and discharge according to such accidents as the geographical place where proceedings were begun, such irrelevant considerations as whether the patient was male or female, and circumstances as fortuitous as whether the patient's hospitalization was sought before or after indictment. While that single chapter contained some few recommendations for changes in the law, it did not purport to be a study in depth.

When, in 1964, the legislature wholly revised the procedures governing civil patients, it became apparent that there had been a great widening of the already existing gap between the legal protections afforded to civil patients and those afforded patients in the custody of the Department of Correction at Matteawan and Dannemora. It was equally apparent that there was need for a comprehensive study of all the laws relating to Matteawan and Dannemora patients—a study which could form the basis for recommendations looking toward the removal of certain glaring inequities and the enactment of an intelligent, cohesive legislative program to provide justice where opportunities for injustice had flourished for more than a century.

We are deeply grateful to the New-Land Foundation for providing the funds to enable us to undertake our study. That foundation had provided part of the funds which financed our initial study from 1960 to 1962, and its willingness to finance our current project has enabled us to complete an important segment of the work which we were unable to complete in 1962.

Our current project was undertaken in the summer of 1965. At that time the membership of the committee was reorganized in an effort to obtain representation from a cross-section of the various agencies and instrumentalities familiar with and concerned about the problems with which we were to deal. The committee, as reconstituted, counts among its members New York State's Commissioner of Correction, a deputy commissioner of the Department of Mental Hygiene, four Supreme Court justices, the Director of Matteawan State Hospital, the Director of Central Islip State Hospital, the Director of Psychiatry at New York City's Bellevue Hospital, two assistant district attorneys, the Director of the Mental Health Information Service for the First Judicial Department, a professor of law and a number of practicing attorneys, including some exceptionally well versed in the practice of criminal law. My personal thanks are extended to each of these distinguished gentlemen for the untold hours and days which they have taken from their other important endeavors to devote to the work of this committee.

A special word must be said in praise of those representatives of the Department of Correction who sat on the committee or assisted us in our work. A thread which runs through the committee's recommendations is that all of the patients now in Matteawan and Dannemora, other than prisoners under sentence, should be removed from the jurisdiction of the Department of Correction and be retained and treated in hospitals under the supervision of the Department of Mental Hygiene. Although it became evident at an early stage of our work that the committee was trending toward proposals which would all but empty Matteawan and Dannemora, these representatives of the Department of Correction continued to make the fullest disclosure to us of all data relevant to the department's institutions, whether favorable or unfavorable, and continued to make effective and valuable contributions to the development of recommendations which, if adopted, will have a profound effect upon the operations of their department.

A word must also be said about the degree to which each member of the committee takes responsibility for the text of the report and the recommendations which we put forward. The committee operated on the principle that all would be bound by a majority vote and there were some few instances where some few committee members failed to concur in certain of our recommendations. The report itself was prepared by our committee's staff director and was revised and approved by action of the full committee. It should be regarded as a product of the collective judgment of all members of the committee rather than the deliberately chosen words of any individual member.

The committee's research and deliberations extended over a period of almost two years and during that time we found that the laws which we were studying were changing under our very feet. The result was that certain of our recommendations have or will have become law, either by statute or judicial decision, even before our report is released.

An outstanding example is the United States Supreme Court's decision in *People ex rel. Baxstrom v. Herold*, 383 U.S. 107, decided in 1966. Early in our deliberations we determined to recommend that mentally ill prisoners who had completed serving their sentences should be removed from Correction Department hospitals and treated as civil patients in hospitals under the jurisdiction of the Department of Mental Hygiene. The Supreme Court held that Baxstrom, a prisoner held in Dannemora beyond the expiration of his sentence, had been denied equal protection of the laws in that he had been denied certain rights to which civil patients were entitled under New York law. The Department of Correction and the Department of Mental Hygiene immediately cooperated to remove from Dannemora and Matteawan and admit to civil hospitals more than nine hundred patients believed to be covered by both the letter and spirit of the *Baxstrom* decision and at this writing the practice of retaining time-expired prisoners in Correction Department hospitals has been terminated.

Other statutory changes, consistent with the committee's recommendations, have been made while our work was in progress and still further statutory changes are in prospect. New York State's Temporary Commission on Revision of the Penal Law and Criminal Code has been actively working on proposed revisions of certain sections of the Criminal Code which govern the hospitalization of mentally ill defendants and, by the time this report is released, that commission is expected to have published its recommendations for revision of those statutes. We have endeavored throughout to maintain close liaison with that commission's staff and a draft of this committee's report was made available to that staff in the spring of 1967. We hope and expect that the legislation to be proposed by that commission will be consistent with a number of our own recommendations.

We would have preferred to append to our report a draft statute to carry out our recommendations. However, the prospective proposals of the Temporary Commission, which involve significant changes in nomenclature and terminology in the Criminal Code, have made it impractical for us to do so.

At the inception of our project we thought we were embarking on a relatively simple task and that the fruits of our work could be recorded in a relatively short report. It is perhaps not surprising that the task turned out to be much more complicated than we had imagined and, of necessity, the report longer than we had wished. I know I speak for the entire committee in according the highest credit to our Staff Director, Professor Malachy T. Mahon, who guided us through these complexities with the aid of a bright creative talent and a firm grasp of the manifold ramifications of each of the laws which came under our scrutiny. His mastery of the subject matter and his devoted dedication to the task at hand will be evident to all those who read our report.

There are many others who gave the committee invaluable aid in the course of this project and to whom we are deeply indebted. Our sincere thanks are extended:

To Presiding Justice Bernard Botein of the New York Supreme Court's Appellate Division, First Department, for his indispensable assistance in the launching of this project and for the guidance and inspiration which he has afforded to this committee from the time of its organization in 1960.

To E. David Wiley, Counsel to the State's Department of Mental Hygiene, and to Manuel T. Murcia, Counsel to the State's Department of Correction, who sat with the committee at every meeting and gave unstintingly of their time and considerable talents.

To the more than thirty district attorneys throughout the state who found the time and took the trouble to respond to the lengthy questionnaires which we submitted to them.

To Peter J. McQuillan, Counsel to the Temporary Commission on Revision of the Penal Law and Criminal Code and a former member of the staff of this committee, who gave us many hours of his valuable time.

To Frank J. Duval, Assistant Attorney General of the State of New York, who was extremely helpful to us in developing data relating to the existing practices for judicial review of the retention of Correction Department patients.

To Messrs. David N. Fields and Arthur Snyder, two New

York attorneys, active and experienced in the areas which we studied, who supplied us with much valuable material.

To all those in the New York State Department of Mental Hygiene who cooperated so fully in providing much needed information to us, and to Howard Mantel of the Institute of Public Administration for his helpful assistance.

Our most earnest hope is that the efforts of this committee, and of all who contributed to those efforts, will lead to the reforms in the law which we have proposed.

New York, N.Y.
August 1, 1967

J. KENNETH CAMPBELL
Chairman

Mental Illness, Due Process and the Criminal Defendant

Summary and Recommendations

The committee has reviewed the New York State laws and procedures regulating the hospitalization of mentally ill persons at Matteawan State Hospital and Dannemora State Hospital, the two mental hospitals operated and staffed by the State Department of Correction. The patients at these two hospitals included (1) prisoners serving sentences; (2) prisoners whose sentences had expired; (3) allegedly dangerously mentally ill civil patients transferred or committed from civil state hospitals; (4) defendants accused of crime who are found incompetent to stand trial, and (5) persons acquitted of crime by reason of insanity.

The committee has studied the history of the laws governing these patients, and has gathered a great deal of information on their practical administration. The result of these efforts is the following series of recommendations for revision of the laws and procedures affecting each class of patients. Some have already been enacted. The considerations supporting each proposal are set forth in the balance of the committee's report.

The basic and unifying thread which runs throughout our recommendations is a rejection of the notion that the mere fact of a criminal charge or conviction is a proper basis upon which to build other unnecessary, unprofitable, and essentially unfair distinctions among the mentally ill.

I. MENTALLY ILL PRISONERS UNDER SENTENCE

General Principles

Mentally ill prisoners serving sentences should continue to be hospitalized in institutions under the jurisdiction of the Department of Correction. However, the procedures governing their hospitalization should be modified to provide to such persons some of the rights accorded to civil patients. Safeguards against unnecessary and possibly harmful confinement among the mentally ill are as necessary and important for prisoners as they are for anyone else.

RECOMMENDATION NO. 1 (*Admission procedure*). The Correction Law (sections 383, 408) should continue to provide for hospitalization of mentally ill prisoners under sentence in an institution within the Department of Correction upon judicial order entered after notice, examination by two examining physicians, and an opportunity to be heard. In addition, however, these statutes should be amended to provide that the Mental Health Information Service should receive notice of such applications, and should have the same powers and perform the same services as set forth in Article 5 of the Mental Hygiene Law as to civil patients.

RECOMMENDATION NO. 2 (*Periodic review*). The procedures for the involuntary retention and periodic judicial review of ordinary civil patients, including on the occasions of such review the assistance of the Mental Health Information Service, should apply to prisoners hospitalized while serving a sentence.

RECOMMENDATION NO. 3 (*Discharge prior to expiration of sentence*). Those sections of the Correction Law (sections

2

386, 410) which at present provide for the return to prison of patients at Dannemora and Matteawan who have "recovered" before the expiration of their sentence should be amended to eliminate the requirement of full recovery, and to substitute therefor a criterion that the prisoner "has recovered or has improved to the degree that he no longer requires hospitalization."

RECOMMENDATION NO. 4 (*Discharge upon expiration of sentence*). The Correction Law (sections 385, 409) at present provides for the discharge by the hospital director of any prisoner whose sentence has expired if, in the opinion of the director, such prisoner is recovered or "is reasonably safe to be at large." However, the criteria for discharge in these sections are not uniform since section 409 also requires that there be relatives or friends willing to maintain the discharged Matteawan patient without further public charge. The statutes should be amended uniformly to authorize discharge of any patient who is recovered or who is "no longer in need of hospitalization."

II. FORMER PRISONERS
AND THE
ALLEGEDLY DANGEROUSLY MENTALLY ILL

General Principles

Mentally ill prisoners whose sentences have expired should thereafter have the same legal rights and services and the same medical treatment to which all other citizens of the state are entitled. If further hospitalization of such prisoners is required after their sentences have expired they should be hospitalized in institutions under the jurisdiction of the Department of Mental Hygiene under the procedures regulat-

3

ing the hospitalization and continued retention of civil patients.

Responsibility for the care and treatment of *all* civil mental patients must be vested in the Department of Mental Hygiene. Existing authorization to hospitalize civil patients in correctional institutions should be abolished. Because certain patients, whether former prisoners, defendants, or ordinary civil patients, may be shown to be dangerous to others, there should be established at one or more institutions within the Department of Mental Hygiene a facility or facilities designed to care for such patients.

RECOMMENDATION NO. 5 (*Hospitalization of former prisoners*). If, in the opinion of a correctional hospital director, a prisoner whose term of sentence is about to expire is in need of continued hospitalization, the director should be empowered to apply for his admission to a hospital under the jurisdiction of the Department of Mental Hygiene under the procedures established in the Mental Hygiene Law for the admission of ordinary civil patients (N.Y. Mental Hygiene Law §§ 72–74).

RECOMMENDATION NO. 6 (*Civil hospitalization of dangerously mentally ill patients*). Dangerously mentally ill patients, except prisoners still under sentence, should be hospitalized under appropriate conditions within the Department of Mental Hygiene. Existing authorization to hospitalize such patients at an institution within the Department of Correction (N.Y. Mental Hygiene Law § 85) should be abolished.

RECOMMENDATION NO. 7 (*Old-law patients in Matteawan and Dannemora State Hospitals*). Within six months after the effective date of the proposed new law, (*a*) all time-expired prisoners retained under sections 384 and 408 of the Correc-

4

tion Law at either Dannemora or Matteawan, and (*b*) all patients retained at Matteawan under section 85 of the Mental Hygiene Law, or under former section 412 of the Correction Law, must be discharged therefrom. In the cases of all such patients the respective hospital directors of such institutions would be entitled within that six months to make application for hospitalization of such patients in accordance with recommendations 5 and 6.

RECOMMENDATION NO. 8 (*Old-law patients transferred to civil hospitals*). Within six months after the effective date of the proposed new law, hospital directors holding former prisoners in civil hospitals (under sections 384 and 409 of the Correction Law) would be obliged to cause such patients to be readmitted to the hospital under the procedures regulating the new admission and subsequent retention of ordinary civil patients.

III. THE MENTALLY ILL DEFENDANT

General Principles

Ancient and respected principles of fundamental fairness forbid the conduct of criminal proceedings against a defendant whose mental condition precludes him from understanding those proceedings or assisting in his own defense. However, the present statutes governing the examination and disposition of such defendants, and the policies they have come to embody, provide opportunity for great unfairness and prejudice. They must be revised.

Because the defendant, even when *indicted*, has merely been accused of crime, he should not be hospitalized as a criminal in a correctional institution. He should be hospitalized as a civil patient in a civil institution, and should receive the same protections and be eligible for the same programs as are available to other civil patients—subject, however, to such supervision as may be required to assure his continued availability for prosecution upon recovery.

Steps must be taken to assure that the standard of mental capacity to be tried is correctly understood and uniformly administered throughout the state. To avoid unnecessary and unfair burdens upon the accused, his family, the hospitals, and the courts, examinations for this purpose should be permitted to be conducted on an out-patient basis in appropriate cases. The rule which requires that the criminal proceeding be suspended for the duration of the defendant's disability, and thereafter resumed, should not continue to prohibit the defendant's counsel from meanwhile having access to the court to make necessary motions and to preserve evidence. Limitations must be imposed upon the maximum time a prosecution may be suspended and the charges left hanging. No prosecution should be allowed to be postponed indefinitely—64 years is known to be possible—or for any period so lengthy as to be manifestly unjust.

Hospitalization of a defendant should not be mandatory if it would not be required for an ordinary civil patient suffering the same type of disability, unless it would provide opportunity for or assurance of a more prompt recovery and resumption of the proceedings than would any appropriate alternative forms of treatment, or unless the interests of justice would require it. In these probably few cases, courts should be vested with discretion to order such suitable alternatives to hospitalization as would be consistent with the public interest and which would include safeguards against the possibility of malingering. Where no sacrifice of public protection or of the interests of justice is involved, to insist upon mandatory hospitalization in every case is to demand the surrender of an accused's liberty as the price of what is justified as a protection of his rights.

RECOMMENDATION NO. 9 (*Uniform application of the standard of competence to be tried*).

(*a*) The Commissioner of Mental Hygiene and the Administrator of the State Judicial Conference should jointly develop, establish, and supply to every examining psychiatrist a uniform form of the report of the results of the examination required to be completed by the examiners and filed with the court. It should contain a reasonably detailed explanation of the legal criteria of capacity to be tried.

(*b*) The examiners' report should specify the nature and extent of the examination, a diagnosis and prognosis, and an opinion as to whether the defendant is dangerously mentally ill. So far as practicable, it should state the reasons for its findings, by making particular reference, for example, to those aspects of the proceedings which the defendant is not able rationally to understand, or by stating in reasonable detail, and in light of the particular circumstances of his own case, why he is believed not sufficiently able rationally to consult with his counsel.

(*c*) When an order of examination is made, the services of the Mental Health Information Service should be made available to the defendant to inform him of his rights and to report to the court in connection with its consideration of the results of the examination. Before confirming or rejecting the report of the examination the court should hold a hearing if demanded by the defendant or the people, or whenever there is sufficient doubt as to the validity of the report, upon the court's own motion. At any such hearing the defendant should be represented by counsel.

RECOMMENDATION NO. 10 (*Out-patient examination*). Psychiatric examinations ordered by courts should expressly be allowed to be conducted on an out-patient basis without mandatory incarceration or hospitalization in any case in which there is no reason to suspect the defendant to be dangerously mentally ill or in need of immediate hospitalization, providing the director of the examining hospital or clinic or other appropriate official agrees, and providing the defendant is otherwise entitled to release on bail. The period of remand for observation at the place of incarceration or in a hospital should be limited to thirty days, subject to extension for cause where necessary.

RECOMMENDATION NO. 11 (*Civil hospitalization*). Any defendant accused of a misdemeanor or a felony, who is judicially determined to be incompetent to be tried, whether or not indicted, should be hospitalized for treatment, under such security as is necessary to assure his continued availability to prosecution, in an appropriate institution under the jurisdiction of the Department of Mental Hygiene, to be returned to court when he is again fit to proceed unless otherwise lawfully discharged.

The order of hospitalization shall authorize the hospital director, under such conditions of bail or parole as the court deems necessary, to permit the defendant to participate in such therapeutic programs (including open-ward and home visits) as the director in his discretion deems appropriate, unless for good cause the court decides to withhold such permission until further order of the court. Such an order may be made at any time thereafter upon the application of the hospital director, the defendant, or the Mental Health Information Service.

RECOMMENDATION NO. 12 (*Automatic periodic judicial review*). The procedure for the involuntary retention and periodic judicial review of ordinary civil patients, including the assistance of the Mental Health Information Service, should apply to defendants hospitalized as at present unfit to stand trial (*a*) except that the issues considered upon review should be whether the defendant is at present fit to proceed as well as whether he is in need of continued hospitalization, and (*b*) except that a determination that a defendant is unfit to be tried should not be subject to a jury trial review, and a determination of need for continued hospitalization should be subject to a jury trial review.

RECOMMENDATION NO. 13 (*Partial suspension of proceedings*). The proceedings against a defendant judicially found to be unfit to be tried should, as at present, be suspended during the period of his disability, but the suspension should not operate to disadvantage the defendant unnecessarily. Only those aspects of the proceedings requiring the participation of the defendant should be postponed. Counsel should be permitted to make pre-trial motions otherwise available to the defendant and, in the circumstances, not requiring his assistance. Denial of relief should be without prejudice to renewal after defendant's recovery. There should also be provision to take and preserve essential evidence that might otherwise be unavailable at trial.

RECOMMENDATION NO. 14 (*Prompt and uniform prosecution*).

(*a*) Felony cases. If a defendant charged with a felony is examined and hospitalized before an indictment is

9

filed, the district attorney should be required to secure an indictment within 12 months or during such additional period as the court may grant. If an indictment is filed before or during such period, a warrant should be lodged at the institution in which the defendant is hospitalized, and when sufficiently recovered to proceed, he should be returned to court. If the formal charge is not timely filed, the proceedings should be dismissed and further prosecution permanently barred, and the defendant should be discharged by the hospital unless within 30 days a new order is obtained authorizing his retention as an ordinary civil patient until he is no longer in need of hospitalization.

(*b*) Misdemeanor cases. Similar provisions should be applied to defendants charged with any misdemeanor anywhere in the state who are hospitalized prior to the filing of an information or indictment in the trial court except that the period within which the district attorney must act should be six months.

(*c*) The proceedings against any defendant accused of any misdemeanor, and against whom an information or indictment has been filed prior to (or timely, after) the order of hospitalization, should be "suspended" as in all felony cases.

RECOMMENDATION NO. 15 (*Dismissal of prosecution*). If a defendant charged with a felony or misdemeanor against whom proceedings are left "suspended" is hospitalized for so long a period as to render it unjust in the court's opinion thereafter to resume the proceedings, the court should expressly be allowed to dismiss the prosecution in the interest of justice, and the defendant should thereafter be hospitalized as an ordinary civil patient under a new court order.

RECOMMENDATION NO. 16 (*Discretionary alternatives to hospitalization*). Courts should be granted discretion, where appropriate, to order suitable alternatives to hospitalization of defendants mentally unfit to be tried. The decision should be based upon a complete evaluation of the defendant's circumstances and the public interest, and should contain such terms and conditions as are necessary to protect against malingering.

RECOMMENDATION NO. 17 (*Old-law patients*). The benefits of each of our proposed revisions (recommendations nos. 11–16) should be expressly extended to apply to all patients previously admitted to state mental hospitals under these procedures.

IV. PERSONS ACQUITTED OF CRIME BY REASON OF INSANITY

General Principles

Any person who is acquitted of crime by reason of mental illness should, in his own interest and for the protection of the public, automatically and immediately be examined as to his current mental condition. If he is determined to be in need of hospitalization, it should be accomplished by the procedures established for the hospitalization of ordinary civil patients, and he should thereafter be treated for all purposes as a civil patient.

RECOMMENDATION NO. 18 (*Persons acquitted of crime by reason of mental illness*). Any person acquitted of crime by reason of insanity must automatically and immediately be ordered examined as to his present mental health and possible need for hospitalization. The procedures governing observation and examination of mentally ill defendants should apply. Incarceration or hospitalization for such purpose should not exceed thirty days, except that the court may extend the period to a maximum of sixty days.

If, following a hearing upon the results of such examination, the acquitted defendant is determined to be in need of hospitalization for mental illness, the court should commit him to the custody of the Commissioner of Mental Hygiene for care and treatment at an institution within the Department of Mental Hygiene under the procedures regulating other civil patients, including periodic review, notice of applications to retain the patient, jury trial review of orders authorizing retention, assistance of the Mental Health Information Service, and eligibility for transfer and release.

RECOMMENDATION NO. 19 (*Old-law patients*). Defendants who have been hospitalized automatically upon acquittal should receive the benefits of the proposed new law within six months of its effective date.

CHAPTER I

Mentally Ill Prisoners
Under Sentence

Each year over 200 persons who are being imprisoned in New York State after conviction of crimes ranging from vagrancy to murder are diagnosed mentally ill and are then hospitalized at either Matteawan State Hospital or Dannemora State Hospital.[1] Matteawan is the lineal descendant of the "State Lunatic Asylum for Insane Convicts" organized at Auburn in 1858 to hospitalize mentally ill prisoners convicted of felonies. Over the years both convicted misdemeanants and untried defendants were added. Patient overcrowding led to erection of a new facility at Beacon in Dutchess County where the Auburn institution was then reorganized in 1893 as Matteawan State Hospital. Once again, however, overcrowding led to new buildings, but this time they were erected adjacent to Clinton Prison at Dannemora, and a new, separate facility for male felons was organized there in 1900 as Dannemora State Hospital.[2] Both hospitals are operated by the Department of Correction which has complete jurisdiction and control over them, subject only to visitation and inspection by the Commissioner of Mental Hygiene.[3] Matteawan and Dannemora are the only state-operated mental hospitals that are not part of the

[1] See Tables 2, 11.
[2] The origin of the two institutions is traced in Appendix A, *infra.*
[3] N.Y. Correc. Law §§ 375, 400; N.Y. Mental Hygiene Law § 11.

Department of Mental Hygiene. In November 1965 there were 84 prisoners under sentence at Matteawan and 456 at Dannemora.[4]

The procedures governing the admission, release and retention beyond expiration of sentence of mentally ill prisoners at Matteawan and Dannemora have had a long and tortuous legislative history.[5] It would be gross understatement to characterize more than a century of legislative action on these matters as inconsistent patchwork. Latter-day procedural reforms can in most instances be traced directly to the need immediately to accommodate an adverse judicial decision in a habeas corpus proceeding brought by one of the patients.

In this chapter we review the admission and discharge procedures. The major recommendations for revision dealt with here would extend to a mentally ill prisoner the same minimum legal assistance and other assurances that protect an ordinary citizen against unnecessary and possibly harmful confinement among the mentally ill. Other changes recommended would encourage increased psychiatric care in prisons and discourage prolonged hospitalization in those cases where the patient is likely to receive greater benefit from participation in rehabilitative prison programs. While the committee accepts the need to maintain separate institutions in the Department of Correction for mentally ill prisoners, we reject, here and in the following chapter, the notion that the mere fact of a criminal charge or conviction is a proper basis upon which to build other unnecessary, unprofitable and essentially unfair distinctions among the mentally ill.

[4] See Table 13.
[5] See Appendix B, *infra*.

1. ADMISSION PROCEDURE

RECOMMENDATION NO. 1. The Correction Law (sections 383, 408) should continue to provide for hospitalization of mentally ill prisoners under sentence in an institution within the Department of Correction upon judicial order entered after notice, examination by two examining physicians, and an opportunity to be heard. In addition, however, these statutes should be amended to provide that the Mental Health Information Service should receive notice of such applications, and should have the same powers and perform the same services as are set forth in Article 5 of the Mental Hygiene Law as to civil patients.

Hospitalization of mentally ill prisoners was accomplished by administrative decision of the prison warden as early as 1818, when the New York Asylum's limited facilities were made available to prisoners at Newgate Prison in New York City.[6] Prior court approval of a decision to hospitalize a prisoner at Utica State Hospital or later at the Auburn Asylum was required in only scattered instances[7] before 1896 when court orders were made prerequisite to transfers of prisoners to Matteawan.[8] When Dannemora was organized only three years later, however, its admission procedure was placed on a purely administrative-transfer basis.[9] The statutes did not provide for notice and a hearing on the

[6] N.Y. Laws 1818, ch. 211, § 9.
[7] E.g., N.Y. Laws 1842, ch. 135, § 32 (prisoners to Utica on court order); N.Y. Laws 1847, ch. 460, §§ 14, 96–100 (prisoners from county jails to Utica under 1842 court order procedure, but now state prisoners to Utica by administrative order); N.Y. Laws 1858, ch. 130 (male felons to Auburn by administrative order); N.Y. Laws 1874, ch. 446, tit. 1, art. 2 (county penitentiary prisoners to Auburn on court order).
[8] N.Y. Laws 1896, ch. 545, art. IV, § 97.
[9] N.Y. Laws 1899, ch. 520, § 9.

15

question of need for hospitalization until 1943,[10] and even then did so only in connection with admissions to Matteawan. Not until 1962 were Dannemora admissions put upon a judicial hearing basis,[11] and the rate of admissions immediately declined.[12]

At present the admission procedures at both Matteawan and Dannemora require the warden of the penal institution to apply to a court of record (or, in New York City, to make an administrative transfer to a city hospital) for an examination of an inmate by two physicians not connected with the institution whenever the prison physician certifies the inmate as mentally ill. If the examining physicians also certify the inmate to be "mentally ill," the warden then applies to the court, on three days written notice to the inmate and to a member of his family or to a friend, for an order committing the inmate to either Matteawan or Dannemora. The inmate, any friend or relative, or the court on its own motion, may require a hearing on the application. If the court finds the inmate to be "mentally ill," he is committed (*a*) to *Dannemora* if he is a male prisoner (either a felon or a mentally defective misdemeanant[13]) in a state penal or correctional in-

[10] N.Y. Laws 1943, ch. 382 (amending N.Y. Correc. Law § 408). See People ex rel. Greenwell v. McNeill, 262 App. Div. 912, 28 N.Y.S. 2d 839 (2d Dep't 1941) (per curiam).

[11] N.Y. Laws 1962, ch. 393 (amending N.Y. Correc. Law § 383). See People ex rel. Brown v. Johnston, 9 N.Y. 2d 482, 174 N.E. 2d 725, 215 N.Y.S. 2d 44 (1961) (for first time holding patient administratively transferred to Dannemora entitled to writ of habeas corpus to test commitment even though still under sentence).

[12] Annual admissions to Dannemora dropped from 216 in 1960 and 267 in 1962, to 169 in 1963 and 151 in 1965. See Table 11.

[13] Persons convicted of felonies or misdemeanors or adjudicated youthful offenders, juvenile delinquents or wayward minors, and found to be mentally defective, may be confined at Eastern Correctional Institution at Napanoch. N.Y. Correc. Law §§ 60, 438-a, 438-b,

stitution (N.Y. Correc. Law §§ 375, 383), or (*b*) to *Mattea-wan* if the inmate is (i) a female prisoner in a state penal or correctional institution, or (ii) a prisoner of either sex in a state or local penal or correctional institution convicted of a misdemeanor or undergoing a sentence of one year or less, or (iii) persons committed to any penal institution as youthful offenders, juvenile delinquents or wayward minors (N.Y. Correc. Law §§ 400, 408).

Both statutes (N.Y. Correc. Law §§ 383, 408) provide that if there are no relatives or friends within the state, the written notice to the prisoner alone will suffice. Neither statute requires the court to advise the prisoner of his right to retain counsel,[14] and neither authorizes appoint-

---

439. (But see Chapter III, note 71, *infra*.) Should there later be need for hospitalization for mental illness, all patients go to Matteawan under N.Y. Correc. Law § 408, except felons and misdemeanants who go to Dannemora under N.Y. Correc. Law § 383. Prior to 1950 all non-felons at Napanoch were sent to a civil hospital, but to avoid the "considerable expense and inconvenience" involved the law was amended that year to allow all classes to be transferred to Dannemora. N.Y. Laws 1950, ch. 229; New York Legislative Annual 51 (1950). In 1961, however, the statutes were again amended to cure the "obvious defect" of requiring youthful offenders, wayward minors and juvenile delinquents "to be thrown with hardened insane felons, while other insane adults serving shorter sentences receive the quite different treatment of being sent to [Matteawan] an institution more conducive to recovery." New York Legislative Annual 41 (1961); N.Y. Laws 1961, ch. 157. At present, therefore, the only misdemeanants not hospitalized at Matteawan are those becoming mentally ill at Napanoch. There would appear to be no reason for this except the 1950 considerations of "expense and inconvenience."

As of May 20, 1965, there were 151 mentally defective patients at Dannemora State Hospital, including 99 "indeterminates," 15 time-serving felons, and 37 time-expired patients recommitted under N.Y. Correc. Law § 384 (Letter to staff director from Dr. W. Cecil Johnston, Sup't M.S.H., June 1, 1965).

[14] Cf. 1961 Op. N.Y. Att'y Gen. 180, 181. Compare Mental Hygiene Law §§ 77, 88(c); note 15, *infra*.

ment of counsel. Whether appointed counsel will some day be constitutionally required remains an unanswered question.[15] It is well to note here that the committee learned that in 1965 some 60 percent of the inmates (of all classes) at Dannemora had less than $10 in their accounts, and many had "no funds or only pennies." [16]

[15] As noted in Chapter II, the U.S. Supreme Court avoided the issue in Baxstrom v. Herold, 383 U.S. 107 (1966). The New York Court of Appeals has recently held that Baxstrom and other equal protection cases require appointment of assigned counsel in habeas corpus proceedings instituted by indigent mental patients. People ex rel. Rogers v. Stanley, 17 N.Y. 2d 256, 217 N.E. 2d 636, 270 N.Y.S. 2d 573 (1966). See also People ex rel. Williams v. LaVallee, 19 N.Y. 2d 238, 279 N.Y.S. 2d 1 (1967).

Effective July 1, 1966, a new section 35 of the Judiciary Law (as added by N.Y. Laws 1966, ch. 761, § 6) authorizes any court holding a habeas corpus hearing involving an inmate of any state institution, or a "hearing in a civil proceeding to commit or transfer a person to or retain him in a state institution when such person is alleged to be mentally ill" to "assign counsel to represent such person, if it is satisfied that he is financially unable to obtain counsel." N.Y. Judiciary Law § 35(1)(a). The court may also appoint no more than two psychiatrists to examine and testify. N.Y. Judiciary Law § 35(3). Fees are authorized to be paid and are a state expense. N.Y. Judiciary Law § 35(4). As of December 13, 1966, there had been 103 claims for compensation under this section certified to the Judicial Conference by the State Comptroller on behalf of 81 attorneys and 22 psychiatrists. The limited available information indicated that 71 of the counsel claims were for habeas corpus proceedings and only 1 was definitely for assistance in a proceeding under Section 383 (Letter to staff director from Harold Taylor, Assoc. Adm. Analyst, State Jud. Conf., December 14, 1966.).

[16] Information supplied by Dr. R. E. Herold, Director of Dannemora State Hospital, indicated that as of May 20, 1965, the hospital's population included 20 patients with committees, 49 receiving Social Security benefits, 33 receiving Veterans' benefits, and "over 60% of our patients have less than $10.00 in their accounts. Many have no funds or only pennies."

In these circumstances it is questionable, to say the least, whether there is adequate opportunity for the confined prisoner to understand his rights or to seek assistance in opposing the application, or for the court to be guided by as complete an investigation of the need for hospitalization as would be available in civil cases. In accordance with prior recommendations of this committee,[17] a Mental Health Information Service has been established as an arm of the court in each of the four judicial departments in the state.[18] Staffed partly with lawyers, the service has been assigned the duty to inform involuntary civil patients of their rights under the law, and to investigate and provide the court with relevant information concerning the patient's case.[19] We believe that it may provide a workable device to assure adequate protection of the rights of a proposed patient who cannot afford to retain counsel.[20] For these reasons the com-

---

At Matteawan the "patients' deposit account" has grown from $3,274.07 in 1918 to $468,871.00 (M.S.H. Ann. Rep., March 31, 1966). Dr. W. Cecil Johnston, Director of Matteawan, advised the committee that as of May 1, 1965, 142 patients had committees appointed, 167 received Social Security benefits, 112 received Veterans' benefits, 925 had "other money" but only 165 earned "interest on their money (at least $500)."

[17] Mental Illness and Due Process 20–1, 150–51 (1962).

[18] N.Y. Mental Hygiene Law § 88 (eff. Sept. 1, 1965).

[19] See e.g., 1965 Rep. N.Y. Jud. Conf. 78–83, N.Y. Leg. Doc. No. 90 (1966), (Regulations Governing the Mental Health Information Service of the First Judicial Department).

[20] See note 15, *supra*. Sections 383(7) and 408(7) of the Correction Law allow the court "forthwith" to commit to the correctional hospitals any prisoner proposed for commitment who "is in need of immediate treatment." We are advised that the availability of tranquilizing drugs and staff consultants at every penal institution should make such precipitate action unnecessary in most cases. Moreover, we are advised that such prisoners as are "forthwith" committed rarely

mittee recommends that the statutes, N.Y. Correc. Law §§ 383, 408, be amended to provide that notice of all applications to examine and commit prisoners under sentence be required to be served upon the Mental Health Information Service, and that its powers and services (N.Y. Mental Hygiene Law § 88) expressly be extended to include this class of involuntary patients.

Although these patients may be mentally ill and in need of hospitalization, they are also prisoners who are not yet entitled to their freedom. The history of Matteawan is replete with instances in which those patients who were under sentence have tried to escape from custody. Whether or not the nature of an individual prisoner's illness requires a high degree of security, his obligation upon recovery to continue

---

exercise their right to demand a hearing on the need for hospitalization, perhaps because of the apparent futility of challenging a fait accompli. Nor do their relatives exercise this right. The committee expects that the Mental Health Information Service, through its authority to investigate and report to the court, will serve as a check upon applications for needless and burdensome resort to emergency procedures.

The committee considered the possibility of recommending that hospitalization procedures for prisoners be amended to conform in their entirety to those established for civil patients by N.Y. Mental Hygiene Law §§ 72–74 (as added, N.Y. Laws 1964, ch. 738, § 5, eff. Sept. 1, 1965) (involuntary admission upon certificates by two examining physicians, rights to notice, hearing, assistance of Mental Health Information Service, periodic automatic judicial review). It appears, however, from experience with the "forthwith" commitments just discussed that if the hearing procedures were revised so as to follow hospitalization (as with civil patients) there is a genuine possibility they would be even less effective. Friends, relatives and other prisoner-witnesses whose presence might be necessary for a complete hearing might not be readily available to the patient after he is removed to the Canadian border or to Dutchess County. The hearings could of course be sent back to the county of origin, but that is where they are now held under the present system.

to serve out the sentence imposed by the court does require it. New York is among a minority of states which provide separate hospitals for criminal law patients,[21] but we are not satisfied that the therapeutic value of segregated or unsegregated hospitalization in a civil institution outweighs society's legitimate interest in demanding secure custody of persons convicted of crime and sentenced to a term of imprisonment. It is possible, moreover, that civil hospitalization would unduly impede the further development of open-door civil institutions. The committee recognizes, however, that the fewer than 100 individuals convicted of petty misdemeanors or minor offenses who each year became mentally ill while serving short jail terms of several months or less (and perhaps also the few female felons) could be treated differently from those convicted of dangerous crimes or sentenced to long prison terms. Although it may be desirable to maintain mental hospital facilities within the Department of Correction for the limited purpose of maximum security, we would urge that, consistent with such security, the hospitals be placed on an equal basis with civil state hospitals. As discussed below,[22] with respect to programs and staffing there have long been pronounced and unjustified budgetary distinctions drawn between civil and correctional mental hospitals.

[21] Weihofen, Disposition of the Mentally Ill, in Rubin, The Law of Criminal Correction, ch. 14 (1963); Weihofen, Institutional Treatment of Persons Acquitted by Reason of Insanity, 38 Texas L. Rev. 849 (1960). See generally Magleby, Should the Criminally Insane Be Housed in Prisons?, 47 J. Crim. L., C. & P.S. 677 (1957). Professor Weihofen's analysis indicates that the "criminal insane" are placed (a) in civil hospitals in 32 states (5 unsegregated, and 27 in separate wards); or (b) in a penal institution's ward in 2 states; (c) in either (a) or (b) in 3 states, and (d) in separate institutions in 9 states. Weihofen, op. cit. supra at 850–51 & nn. 8–12.

[22] See Chapter II, infra, and Appendix A.

2. PERIODIC REVIEW

RECOMMENDATION NO. 2. The procedures for the involuntary retention and periodic judicial review of ordinary civil patients, including on the occasions of such review the assistance of the Mental Health Information Service, should apply to prisoners hospitalized while serving a sentence.

Under sections 73 and 74 of the Mental Hygiene Law no civil patient may be retained in a hospital against his will except for specific periods of time authorized by court orders (at intervals of six months, one year, then every two years) granted after notice and an opportunity to demand a hearing and jury trial review. Courts have repeatedly held that prisoners are not entitled to civil review procedures,[23] and it may at first appear that there is no compelling reason why they should be, since hospitalized prisoners are not entitled to their freedom upon recovery. Moreover, during hospitalization they suffer no disadvantage with respect to the running of their sentence, nor, as of 1966, will hospitalization deny them the possibility of earning a "good time" reduction of their maximum sentence to advance their mandatory parole date.[24] The committee believes, however, that

[23] People ex rel. Brunson v. Johnston, 15 N.Y. 2d 647, 204 N.E. 2d 200, 255 N.Y. 2d 867 (1964); People ex rel. Kamisaroff v. Johnston, 12 N.Y. 2d 66, 192 N.E. 2d 11, 242 N.Y.S. 2d 38 (1963); People ex rel. Conover v. Herold, 24 App. Div. 2d 773, 263 N.Y.S. 2d 858 (3rd Dep't), leave to app. denied, 16 N.Y. 2d 488 (1965); People ex rel. Carroll v. Herold, 27 App. Div. 2d 958 (3rd Dep't 1967).

[24] N.Y. Correc. Law § 230(4) (as amended by N.Y. Laws 1966, ch. 652). The bill was recommended by the Governor's Special Committee on Criminal Offenders and is expected to provide "an additional incentive for rehabilitation" during hospitalization and to "aid in the rehabilitation of inmates who have recovered and, despite the length of their illnesses, can look forward to the same parole release

substantial rights are indeed at stake, and that to protect them it is necessary to afford the hospitalized prisoner under sentence the same opportunity to seek judicial review of his commitment as is available to civil patients.

First, there is always present the possibility that a prisoner who has initially been judicially determined to be mentally ill (N.Y. Correc. Law §§ 383, 408) is no longer mentally ill, or at least not in need of further hospitalization, and that the hospital staff either has not recognized the patient's improvement or has arbitrarily delayed acting upon it. The Court of Appeals implied in 1961 that hospitalization of a sane prisoner among the mentally ill may present issues of cruel and unusual punishment under the New York State Constitution.[25] *Second,* the only recently recognized right of a prisoner under sentence who claims recovery to seek discharge from the hospital and return to a prison on a writ of habeas corpus appears once again to be in doubt,[26] and

---

date they would have had if they had not been transferred to a special institution." Governor's Memorandum of Approval, 1966 McKinney's Session Laws 3003.

[25] People ex rel. Brown v. Johnston, 9 N.Y. 2d 482, 468 n. * 174 N.E. 2d 725, 726 n. *, 215 N.Y.S. 2d 44, 46 n. * (1961).

[26] In People ex. rel. Carroll v. Herold, 27 App. Div. 2d 958 (3rd Dep't 1967), and People ex rel. Conover v. Herold, 24 App. Div. 2d 773, 263 N.Y.S. 2d 858 (3rd Dep't), leave to app. denied, 16 N.Y. 2d 488 (1965), the court affirmed orders dismissing writs of habeas corpus obtained by time-serving patients at Dannemora. Noting that the patients had been admitted upon judicial determinations that they were mentally ill (under section 383 of the Correction Law as it had been amended in obvious response to People ex rel. Brown v. Johnston, *supra* note 25) the Appellate Division said that the prisoners' return to prison was governed by statute, N.Y. Correc. Law § 385, and that since the basis for the Brown decision had been changed by statute a patient is no longer entitled to a writ of habeas corpus. Although the possibility of arbitrary administrative transfer is in fact no longer a basis for making habeas corpus available, such

if it were no longer available prisoners under sentence would be the only class of mental patient in the state with absolutely no right to judicial review of the need for continued hospitalization over the years or decades it may take to serve out a sentence. *Third,* the Court of Appeals held subsequent to *Baxstrom* that a mentally ill prisoner hospitalized at Dannemora has no right to seek to vacate an erroneous conviction (even if it led to his imprisonment and hospitalization) by *coram nobis* proceedings until his "sanity is restored." [27] *Fourth,* the Court of Appeals has also recently suggested [28] that a patient in a state hospital who concedes

---

an approach would appear to ignore the possibility of arbitrary administrative refusals to discharge a patient as a continuing basis for the writ.

[27] People v. Booth, 17 N.Y. 2d 681, 216 N.E. 2d 615, 269 N.Y.S. 2d 457 (1966): "Order affirmed. In our opinion the trial court was correct in denying the writ or error coram nobis until petitioner's sanity is restored (see People v. Cossentino, 14 N.Y. 2d 750)." Fuld, J., dissented: "I do not believe that a defendant's mental condition disables him from seeking coram nobis relief (Cf. Baxstrom v. Herold, 383 U.S. 107). I would reverse and remand for a hearing on the merits." The Appellate Division, First Department, which had affirmed dismissal on the ground that the petition was insufficient and therefore did not reach the question of petitioner's sanity, 24 App. Div. 2d 436, 260 N.Y.S. 2d 824, appears to have recognized in an earlier case, People v. Hensler, 23 App. Div. 2d 651, 257 N.Y.S. 2d 457 (1965), a distinction between mere mental illness and mental illness which normally constitutes incapacity to participate in legal proceedings. See N.Y. Code Crim. Proc. §§ 658, 870. The Court of Appeals apparently would draw no such distinction, at least so far as postconviction proceedings are concerned. Cossentino, cited by the Court of Appeals, was a judgment appeal in a capital case, and indefinite postponement of argument thereon was a disposition sought by and agreeable to the appellant who subsequent to conviction was found mentally ill.

[28] People ex rel. Anonymous v. La Burt, 17 N.Y. 2d 738, 217 N.E. 2d 31, 270 N.Y.S. 2d 206, cert. denied, 87 Sup. Ct. 299 (1966); Compare Rouse v. Cameron, 373 F. 2d 451 (D.C. Cir. 1966); Note, 80

his mental illness but complains of inadequate medical care should turn, not to a court, but to the Mental Health Information Service, or should attempt to induce the Commissioner of Mental Hygiene administratively to exercise his investigative powers (which, in the case of a patient at Matteawan or Dannemora, would mean investigating the affairs of a separate state department). *Fifth,* judicial review procedures designed to protect a sane or recovered patient's right to personal freedom necessarily protect him as well against confinement among the mentally ill where he may be subjected to mental, emotional or physical injury.[29] Even a prisoner who is not entitled to personal freedom is still entitled to the latter protection. In that respect his rights, and his needs for protection, are indistinguishable from those of any civil patient. Thus, as the Supreme Court held on an analogous issue,[30] although for purposes of designating the place of hospitalization and type of custody the state may reasonably classify prisoners separately, the state should

---

Harv. L. Rev. 898 (1967); cf. Birnbaum, The Right to Treatment, 46 A.B.A.J. 499 (1960).

[29] The possibility has been mentioned. People ex rel. Brown v. Johnston, 9 N.Y. 2d 482, 217 N.E. 2d 636, 270 N.Y.S. 2d 573 (1961); see Dennison v. New York, 49 Misc. 2d 533, 267 N.Y.S. 2d 920 (Ct. Cl. 1966), reversed 28 App. Div. 2d 608 (3rd Dep't 1967). As to the possibility of physical injury in civil hospitals see discussion of N.Y. Mental Hygiene Law § 85, Chapter II, at note 45, *infra.*

[30] Baxstrom v. Herold, 383 U.S. 107, 111–12 (1966): "Classification of mentally ill persons as either insane or dangerously insane of course may be a reasonable distinction for purposes of determining the type of custodial or medical care to be given, but it has no relevance whatever in the context of the opportunity to show whether a person is mentally ill *at all.* For purposes of granting judicial review before a jury of the question whether a person is mentally ill and in need of institutionalization, there is no conceivable basis for distinguishing the commitment of a person who is nearing the end of a penal term from all other civil commitments." (Emphasis in original.)

not classify them separately for purposes of providing protection against confinement of sane persons among the mentally ill.

For these reasons, therefore, the committee believes that there is genuine need to extend to prisoners under sentence the right to every "substantial review proceeding [which is] generally available" [31] on the issue of the need for hospitalization, including the right to periodic judicial review and the right to demand a jury trial. It cannot lightly be assumed that every prisoner will demand such review,[32] but even if they did the total number of prisoners still under sentence at any one time is insignificant when compared to the number of involuntary patients in civil state hospitals.[33] Moreover, many of the lesser offenders hospitalized at Matteawan are under such short sentences that there will not be need for proceedings beyond the initial determination.

3. DISCHARGE PRIOR TO EXPIRATION
OF SENTENCE

RECOMMENDATION NO. 3. Those sections of the Correction Law (sections 386, 410) which at present provide for the return to prison of patients at Dannemora and Matteawan who have "recovered" before the expiration of their sentence should be amended to eliminate the requirement of full recovery, and to

[31] Id. at 111.

[32] We are advised by Dr. R. E. Herold (Director, D.S.H.) that prior to Baxstrom (see Chapter II) 62 out of 477 time-expired patients declined consideration for transfer to civil hospitals. See also Appendix D (noting that 454 post-Baxstrom patients chose voluntary-status hospitalization).

[33] There were 85,279 resident patients in the civil state hospitals on April 1, 1964, when there were fewer than 2,971 patients of all classes in both Matteawan and Dannemora combined. State of N.Y., Dep't of Mental Hygiene, Official Directory of State and Licensed Mental Institutions (1965), p. 176.

substitute therefor a criterion that the prisoner "has recovered or has improved to the degree that he no longer requires hospitalization."

At least since 1842 it has been the statutory policy of this state not to return a patient to prison until he has fully recovered from his mental illness. The statutory criterion has been expressed differently over the years, at various times requiring the patient to be "restored to his right mind," [34] or "returned to reason," [35] or, as at present, simply "recovered." [36]

Correctional hospital directors should be permitted to return patients to *state* penal and correctional institutions when their illness is in remission, or as soon as their degree of improvement, short of recovery, renders further hospitalization unnecessary. This recommendation reflects the fact that the Division of Forensic Psychiatry of the State Department of Mental Hygiene at present provides psychiatric and psychological services to those institutions. In most cases, however, the 53 psychiatrists and 33 psychologists listed [37] by the Division for 1965 merely "render regular part-time service." It is desirable, of course, to increase the prison psychiatric services both to reduce the number of cases requiring hospitalization simply because other less drastic treatment is not available, and to facilitate prompt return to participation in correctional and rehabilitative pro-

[34] N.Y. Laws 1842, ch. 135, § 32.
[35] N.Y. Laws 1858, ch. 130, § 10.
[36] N.Y. Correc. Law §§ 386, 410.
[37] State of N.Y., Dep't of Mental Hygiene, Official Directory of State and Licensed Mental Institutions 12–17 (1965). During the 1965–1966 budget year only 23 full-time positions were authorized in the department for "psychiatric services to correctional institutions and division of parole" and no increase was recommended for the next year. State of N.Y., Executive Budget 1966–1967, 488.

grams. It would also be desirable to make a broader distribution of discharged patients among the various institutions than has been the practice. Most patients discharged from Dannemora as recovered have been transferred to adjacent Clinton Prison[38] for which the services of only one full-time psychiatrist and four part-time psychologists are listed.

The prisoners who are to be returned to *county* jails and penitentiaries from Matteawan are in a different situation, however. There is no organized state-wide psychiatric service available upon which to rely for any aftercare that might be necessary. We believe, however, that if the statutory criterion with respect to returns from Matteawan (section 410) is stated permissively, the hospital director can decide each case on the basis of the medical facilities known to be available to inmates of the particular jail or penitentiary involved.[39]

4. DISCHARGE UPON EXPIRATION OF SENTENCE

RECOMMENDATION NO. 4. The Correction Law (sections 385, 409) at present provides for the discharge by the hospital director of any prisoner whose sentence has expired if, in the opinion of

[38] See Tables 11 and 12. Most releases are made to Clinton Prison and most admissions are from the same prison. We were advised by Dr. R. E. Herold (Dir., D.S.H.) that "a great many admissions from Clinton Prison are re-admissions," and that the hospital medical staff "renders practically no service to inmates at Clinton Prison" (Letter to staff director, August 19, 1965). The practice goes back to 1858 when releases from the original Auburn Asylum were required to be sent to the adjacent Auburn Prison (see Appendix B). The practice results in a savings of transportation costs.

[39] See, e.g., Rep. N.Y. Comm'n of Correc. (1961). N.Y. Correc. Law § 501 (each county jail must be staffed with at least one physician). See generally, State of N.Y., Comm'n of Investigation, a Report on County Jails and Penitentiaries in New York State (Nov. 1966).

the director, such prisoner is recovered or "is reasonably safe to be at large." However, the criteria for discharge in these sections are not uniform since section 409 also requires that there be relatives or friends willing to maintain the discharged Matteawan patient without further public charge. The statutes should be amended uniformly to authorize discharge of any patient who is recovered or who is "no longer in need of hospitalization."

Both Matteawan and Dannemora may discharge prisoners to the community upon expiration of sentence if they are "reasonably safe to be at large," even if still mentally ill. However, the Matteawan patient must in addition have friends or relatives willing and able to support him, whereas the Dannemora patient need not.[40] This distinction is archaic and discriminatory. It can be traced back to 1858 when in the era of county poorhouses the legislation organizing Matteawan's predecessor, the Auburn Asylum, authorized discharge of a prisoner upon expiration of sentence even if he were still mentally ill, so long as some friend or family would execute a written indemnification against his becoming a public charge.[41] The qualification was retained in one form or another in all subsequent legislation governing the Auburn–Matteawan institution.[42] A similar qualification was contained in the original 1899 Dannemora legislation,[43] and it survived until 1961.[44]

We have elsewhere[45] recommended that upon expiration

[40] The first part of our recommendation has since been adopted by an amendment of N.Y. Correc. Law § 409 (N.Y. Laws 1966, ch. 891, § 5), eliminating the need for friends or relatives.

[41] N.Y. Laws 1858, ch. 130 § 8.

[42] E.g., N.Y. Laws 1863, ch. 139, § 2; N.Y. Laws 1884, ch. 289, § 9.

[43] N.Y. Laws 1899, ch. 520, § 11.

[44] N.Y. Correc. Law § 385 (prior to its amendment by N.Y. Laws 1961, ch. 429, § 2).

[45] See Chapter II, *infra*.

of his sentence a prisoner should in all respects be treated as a civil patient. He should not be hospitalized unless his illness requires it. For the sake of consistency therefore the criteria for discharge should be stated in similar terms.

Special mention should be made of post-release parole supervision of male felons at Dannemora and female felons at Matteawan. All are now entitled to release upon expiration of their maximum sentence as *reduced* (under N.Y. Correc. Law § 230) by any allowance they may have received for good behavior while in prison, or for cooperation to the limit of their capacity while in the hospital. For the unexpired balance of their maximum term they will be under the jurisdiction of the State Board of Parole. At the time of eligibility for release under these provisions, if still in need of hospitalization, they should be treated as civil patients in the manner covered in succeeding recommendations. For those who have already been returned from hospital to prison, or who, although still in the hospital on the release date, are no longer in need of hospitalization, there will be supervision in the community by a parole officer. In New York City the parole officer may in some cases be able to provide at least minimum psychiatric follow-up through the Division of Parole's Mental Hygiene Unit. The unit was established in New York in 1959 to provide mental hygiene services to parolees, and to orient parole officers to the behavioral problems encountered in their casework. It is presently staffed by five part-time psychiatrists, one psychologist, and five parole officers.[46] This unit, although obviously of very limited scope at present, could serve as the nucleus of an expanded aftercare system for patients who have been

[46] State of N.Y., Div'n of Parole, Facts and Figures Concerning the Division of Parole (1965); 1963 Rep. Div'n Parole (108–112), N.Y. Leg. Doc. No. 107 (1964).

hospitalized during a prison sentence, but in our opinion these patients should be integrated into the state's network of Community Mental Health Clinics.[47]

[47] See N.Y. Mental Hygiene Law §§ 190–191-b (Community Mental Health Services Act). Within the Department of Mental Hygiene itself, five aftercare units are operated in the Metropolitan area where patients on convalescent care report at regular intervals rather than returning to the institution where they were hospitalized. The department's aftercare program in the upstate area is operated in the institutions. State of N.Y., Executive Budget 1966–1967, 500.

CHAPTER II

Former Prisoners and the Allegedly Dangerously Mentally Ill

In this chapter we discuss the laws and procedures applicable to four types of patients: (1) prisoners who are hospitalized at Dannemora while serving a sentence and who are still in need of hospitalization when their sentences expire; (2) prisoners in the same situation except that they are hospitalized at Matteawan at expiration of sentence; (3) prisoners who, whether or not they were hospitalized as mentally ill while they were serving a sentence, were released from a jail or prison when their sentences expired and who sometime *thereafter* are hospitalized for mental illness, and (4) any patient admitted by civil proceedings to a civil hospital who is thereafter committed to Matteawan on the ground that he is "dangerously mentally ill."

These four classes of patients are treated together because, although their medical needs and legal rights are essentially alike, the procedures which have evolved respecting them are not uniform. Moreover, although all four classes are civil patients, they have been set apart as a group from all other civil patients, not only with respect to procedural matters, but also with respect to their eligibility for care and treatment in a civil hospital rather than in a correctional institution.

To demonstrate the genuine complexity of the problems involved in this area of the law, as well as to give some idea of the full scope of the obvious inequities that have existed, in some cases for as long as a century, the discussion is presented in four parts: *first,* a brief background of the problem; *second,* a summary of the procedures governing, and the people involved in, each of the four classes as of February 23, 1966, when *Baxstrom v. Herold,*[1] a case involving some of these problems, was decided by the United States Supreme Court; *third,* an analysis of the arguments, decision and effects of the Baxstrom case, and *fourth,* the committee's recommendations for further improvement in this area.

In essence the committee recommends that former prisoners should be treated as civil patients when their penal sentences have expired; that any person, with or without a past criminal conviction, who requires hospitalization in a high-security facility as "dangerously mentally ill" should be cared for by the Department of Mental Hygiene whose responsibility it is to operate mental hospitals, and not by the Department of Correction whose proper responsibility is to operate prisons and reformatories, and that the benefits of these proposed changes be extended to the hundreds of individual patients who have been hospitalized under the present discriminatory procedures.

1. BACKGROUND [2]

Prisoners believed to be still mentally ill on the day their sentences expired have never been able to anticipate easy

[1] 383 U.S. 107 (1966).

[2] For a more detailed history of the various statutes see Appendix B.

33

separation from the prison authorities. They were retained at Utica State Hospital in the period 1842–1858 until it was "safe, legal and right" to release them, or until the hopelessness of their illness led the hospital to send them to a county poorhouse.[3] No court order was required to justify retaining them, and in fact a court order was at first required before they could be released.[4] From 1858 to 1966 [5] (with the exception of the period 1863–1875 [6]) no court order was required in order to retain a time-expired prisoner at the Auburn Asylum or its successor at Matteawan. Oddly, however, just as Matteawan has required a court order for admission (but not retention) ever since 1896,[7] Dannemora had required a court order for retention (but not admission) ever since 1899.[8] The time-expired prisoner's right to a hearing on the question of his need for continued hospitalization was not recognized until 1948 and, predictably, even then it applied only to the administratively admitted patient at Dannemora,[9] and not until 1966 was it extended to the

[3] E.g., N.Y. Laws 1842, ch. 135, §§ 32, 42; N.Y. Laws 1846, ch. 324, §1; N.Y. Laws 1848, ch. 294.

[4] N. Y. Laws 1842, ch. 135, §§ 32, 42.

[5] See, e.g., N.Y. Laws 1858, ch. 130, §§ 8, 10; N.Y. Laws 1861, ch. 63, § 1; N.Y. Correc. Law, § 409 (prior to repeal and replacement by N.Y. Laws 1966, ch. 891, § 5).

[6] Compare N.Y. Laws 1863, ch. 139, § 2, and N.Y. Laws 1875, ch. 574.

[7] N.Y. Laws 1896, ch. 545, art. IV, § 97; N.Y. Correc. Law § 408.

[8] N.Y. Laws 1899, ch. 520, § 10; N.Y. Correc. Law § 384 (prior to repeal by N.Y. Laws 1966, ch. 891, § 1).

[9] See Troutman v. State of N.Y., 273 App. Div. 619, 79 N.Y.S. 2d (3rd Dep't 1948); N.Y. Laws 1948, ch. 377; cf. N.Y. Legislative Annual 37 (1948). Section 384 was amended to require the Dannemora *retention* procedure to follow that provided in section 408 for *admission* to Matteawan which, since 1943, had required notice and opportunity to demand a hearing. See Appendix B.

judicially admitted patient at Matteawan as one of the effects of the *Baxstrom* decision.[10]

Quite apart from the question of the adequacy of the procedural protections afforded to time-expired prisoners, a more significant question is raised by the century-old practice of denying these patients the right to hospitalization in ordinary civil institutions. The Utica Asylum, New York's first state mental hospital, could receive all classes of civil and criminal patients, after opening in 1842, but even before the special "Auburn Asylum for Insane Convicts" was built, male prisoners had been removed from Utica in 1855 [11] because (according to a later explanation by the Lunacy Commission) their "presence was very objectionable to the ordinary inmates." [12]

Time-expired patients were removed from Utica to Auburn in 1861,[13] two years after Auburn had opened its doors. Then female prisoners were removed in 1865.[14] In 1874 penitentiary inmates were made transferrable from the civil hospitals to Auburn, and after 1893 they were committible directly to Auburn's larger successor at Matteawan.[15] The 1893 Matteawan legislation also authorized transfers of time-expired prisoners to civil hospitals, but in 1894 the Lunacy Commission noted that transfers had been "discontinued," mainly because "their presence in the other state hospitals would be objectionable." [16]

10 See text accompanying notes 51–60, *infra*.

11 N.Y. Laws 1855, ch. 456.

12 1894 Lunacy Comm'n Rep., 18 N.Y. Ass. Doc. No. 97, at 71 (1895).

13 N.Y. Laws 1861, ch. 63, § 1.

14 N.Y. Laws 1865, ch. 353, § 2.

15 N.Y. Laws 1874, ch. 446, tit. 1, art. 2, § 24; N.Y. Laws 1893, ch. 81, § 8.

16 1894 Lunacy Comm'n Rep., 18 N.Y. Ass. Doc. No. 97, at 73 (1895).

At least equally important, however, was the fact that the 1890 State Care Act,[17] which marked the assumption by the State of New York of full responsibility for the care and treatment of its mentally ill, required the removal from county poorhouses to state mental hospitals of some 2,000 patients in three years,[18] and created a tremendous demand for bed space in those hospitals. To help make room, prisoners and ex-prisoners were denied entry, and mentally ill defendants in criminal cases were transferred to Matteawan.[19] Then Dannemora State Hospital was opened in 1900 to care for mentally ill convicted felons who were still under sentence.[20] It was at first believed that as their sentences expired they would be sent to Matteawan for further care,[21] but Matteawan's perennial overcrowding made that impossible. Dannemora began a sixty-year climb to a population exceeding 1,300 patients.[22]

During all these years the civil hospitals doubtless had a number of difficult patients admitted on ordinary civil process whose illness posed a danger to other patients, to staff, or, if they should elope, to the community at large. Greater security was available at Auburn and later at Matteawan, but the only legal bases for placing such patients in those institutions appear to have been (1) arraignment on a criminal charge based upon a particular act of violence, followed by commitment to Auburn or Matteawan as unable to stand trial, and (2) simple administrative transfer, under a 1904 statute, if the patient had previously been imprisoned on a conviction and had either been previously at Matteawan or

---

[17] N.Y. Laws 1890, ch. 126, § 3.
[18] 1894 Lunacy Comm'n Rep., N.Y. Ass. Doc. No. 97, at 70 (1895).
[19] Id. at 71.
[20] N.Y. Laws 1899, ch. 520, §§ 8–9.
[21] 1894 Lunacy Comm'n Rep., N.Y. Ass. Doc. No. 97, at 73 (1895).
[22] See Table 10.

still manifested "criminal tendencies."[23] That statute survived (as N.Y. Correc. Law § 412) until it was repealed in 1965.[24] In 1932, when new construction had temporarily relieved the overcrowding at Matteawan,[25] the civil hospitals were given new authority to apply to courts for orders transferring to Matteawan even the ordinary civil patient who had no criminal record if his illness posed special dangers.[26] That authority is presently continued as section 85 of the Mental Hygiene Law.

Thus, four types of individuals who were mentally ill and who had no present involvement with the criminal law were by 1932 set aside by law from other patients in the state hospital system and were placed in hospitals operated by the prison authority. The procedures governing each of them were constantly revised, but never was there made any discoverable effort to make revisions uniformly. As a result, the statutes applicable to the various patients on February 23, 1966 were markedly different.

2. SITUATION AS OF FEBRUARY 1966

a) Former Prisoners Retained at Matteawan
(N.Y. Correc. Law §§ 408, 409)

As of February 1966, a prisoner whose sentence expired while he was still considered by the hospital director to be

[23] N.Y. Laws 1904, ch. 525, § 2.
[24] N.Y. Laws 1965, ch. 524, § 1 (eff. June 28, 1965).
[25] See Appendix A.
[26] N.Y. Laws 1932, ch. 574, § 1 (adding a new section 83-a to the N.Y. Mental Hygiene Law, later amended and renumbered as section 85 by N.Y. Laws 1933, ch. 395, § 24; see note 43, *infra*.

mentally ill could be retained at the hospital by a simple administrative decision of the director not to release him. The law required no court order, no notice, no hearing. Once retained, the patient might possibly look forward to eventual discharge upon full recovery, or perhaps earlier if release to his relatives or friends would be reasonably safe. The law also authorized the commissioner of correction, with the consent of the commissioner of mental hygiene, to transfer a time-expired patient to a civil state hospital where he would then become eligible for trial release, convalescent status, and for any other benefits and procedures available to civil patients.

Historically consisting largely of vagrants and petty misdemeanants with relatively few female felons in their number,[27] many of the prisoners transferred to Matteawan while serving short jail or penitentiary sentences would not be long there before their time would be up. Until very recently, with not even one social worker to make investigations, the criterion for "safe" releases, that there would be relatives or friends willing and able to assist the patient, would have been quite difficult to administer properly. There has never been a system of aftercare facilities available to these patients. Because they were "objectionable," it has until recently been extremely difficult to transfer significant numbers of them to civil hospitals. Finally, far from their home counties, unaided by counsel, and unable to secure independent psychiatric opinion, their applications for writs of habeas corpus rarely were successful.[28]

For all of these reasons the number of time-expired pa-

[27] See Appendix A and Table 4.
[28] See Tables 5, 6, 12. As to counsel, see Chapter I, *supra*, at note 15.

tients at Matteawan has always been large. In November 1965, the 233 time-expired patients outnumbered the 84 patients still serving time by almost three to one, and with them constituted almost twenty percent of the hospital population.[29] One patient had been there since 1921, and 56 had been there twenty years or longer.[30]

b) Former Prisoners Retained at Dannemora (N.Y. Correc. Law § 384; N.Y. Mental Hygiene Law § 87[3])

As of February 1966, a prisoner-patient at Dannemora could be retained beyond expiration of his sentence only by a court order issued after notice and an opportunity to demand a hearing. If the court believed that the patient needed institutional care, it would commit him to the custody of the Commissioner of Mental Hygiene to be placed in an appropriate institution in the Department of Correction or in the Department of Mental Hygiene. Moreover, although he might be "placed" at Dannemora, and although there might be no physical change in his circumstances reflecting his new status, the procedure was "deemed a civil commitment." Once retained, the patient could later be transferred back and forth between departments by administrative order. He could be discharged by the Commissioner of Mental Hygiene when fully recovered, or when discharge would not be "detrimental to the public safety or welfare, or injurious to the patient." He might also be released on convalescent status.

If the Commissioner of Mental Hygiene refused to grant

[29] See Table 3.
[30] See Table 8.

39

discharge, the patient was expressly given the right to apply to a court (N.Y. Mental Hygiene Law § 87[3]) for an order absolutely discharging him, or for an order conditionally releasing him subject to revocation for five years. As an aid in deciding the application, the court was vested with authority to appoint two qualified and disinterested psychiatrists to examine him, and could "call for the presentation of such other evidence written or oral, as it may consider necessary for the proper disposition of the application."

By November 1965, more than half of the 918 patients at Dannemora had finished their sentences.[31] In 1962 a sizable number had been transferred to civil hospitals, but the volume of transfers soon slackened until the pace was revived in 1965.[32] It is obvious that relatively few were being "placed" in appropriate civil hospitals by the Commissioner of Mental Hygiene into whose custody they were committed. Between 1960 and 1965, there were 429 habeas corpus applications by patients at Dannemora, and it has been estimated that no more than five or six of these were successful.[33] In 1964, the New York Court of Appeals held that time-expired patients at Dannemora were not entitled to apply for habeas corpus relief until they had first exhausted the judicial review procedures detailed in Mental Hygiene

[31] See Table 13.

[32] See Table 12.

[33] Letter to staff director from Dr. R. E. Herold, Director, Dannemora State Hospital, August 19, 1965. But see Table 12. (Releases "by court order" in 1965 might include applications under N.Y. Mental Hygiene Law § 87[3].) As to judicial willingness carefully to weigh claimed denials of equal protection on such writs, see People ex rel. Kamisaroff v. Johnston, 13 N.Y. 2d 66 (1963) (". . . there *probably* is a rational basis for saying that even after such persons finish their sentences they may be kept in a separate mental hospital"). (Emphasis added.)

Law section 87(3), discussed above.[34] To many of them, it would appear, that decision was their first notice that buried in the supplement to the Mental Hygiene Law there was a statute dealing solely and expressly with them. There was no reference to that statute in the Correction Law where the retention procedure itself was spelled out.

With little or no resources to oppose retention, with no advice as to their limited rights, "deemed" civil patients but kept in a maximum-security facility among prisoners serving sentences for felonies, the patients could do little more than await monthly visits[35] by a representative of the Commissioner of Mental Hygiene and hope, first, that he would interview them, and, second, that he would recommend to Albany at least that they be transferred, if not released. The hospital would make recommendations based principally upon the patient's behavior; those with violent, assaultive and paranoid tendencies were not usually recommended.[36] The staff's own recommendations were not determinative, however. For example, of 222 patients recommended to be interviewed for transfers, as of May 20, 1965, only two had in fact been transferred as of August 19, 1965.[37]

c) *Former Prisoners Hospitalized after Release from Prison (N.Y. Correc. Law § 412)*

The authority to make administrative transfers to Matteawan based solely upon clinical judgment that former prisoners who had been admitted to a civil hospital on ordinary process still possessed "criminal tendencies" was first

[34] People ex rel. Brunson v. Johnston, 15 N.Y. 2d 647, 204 N.E. 2d 200, 255 N.Y.S. 2d 867 (1964).
[35] Letter to staff director, note 33, *supra.*
[36] Ibid.
[37] Ibid.

enacted in 1904 and more recently was contained in section 412 of the Correction Law until it was repealed in 1965.[38]

[38] The State Care Act of 1890 (N.Y. Laws 1890, ch. 126) marked the assumption by the State of New York of full responsibility for the care and treatment of the mentally ill. It required the removal from county poorhouses to state hospitals of some 2,000 patients in three years, and created a tremendous demand for bed space (1894 Lunacy Comm'n Rep., N.Y. Ass. Doc. No. 97 [1895]). In the Matteawan organic act, the Lunacy Commission was given authority (traceable to 1884 and ultimately to 1869) to transfer any criminal order patient to Matteawan (N.Y. Laws 1893, ch. 81, § 12). By 1894 that authority had been used, apparently solely to create much needed space, to transfer all criminal order patients to Matteawan (1894 Lunacy Comm'n Rep., supra, at 71). Having been continued on enactment of the 1896 Insanity Law (N.Y. Laws 1896, ch. 545, § 101) the transfer authority was considerably broadened only four years after completion of Dannemora had relieved some of the strain on Matteawan.

In 1904, and until June 28, 1965, administrative transfer from civil hospitals was authorized in the case of (1) any criminal order patients, (2) "any patient who has previously been sentenced to a term of imprisonment in any penal institution, [a] and who still manifests criminal tendencies or [b] any such patient who has previously been an inmate of" Matteawan (N.Y. Laws 1904, ch. 525, § 2).

The statute was carried through the 1909 Consolidated Laws, the 1927 Prison Law, and emerged in 1929 as Section 412 of the Correction Law.

Although the statute did not expressly authorize retransfer to a civil hospital after a period of treatment at Matteawan, that appears to have been the practice. However, Matteawan could not release such patients to the community. In 1959 the superintendent of Matteawan was given authority by an amendment of Section 412 recommended by the Department of Mental Hygiene (N.Y. Laws 1959, ch. 264; N.Y. Legislative Annual 187 [1959] to discharge a patient who (1) had recovered, or (2) was at least no longer "dangerous to himself or others"; disposition was no longer limited merely to retransfer to civil hospitals. In 1963 the section was amended to give the Commissioner of Correction authority to reject proposed transfers to Matteawan (N.Y. Laws 1963, ch. 147). After further changes in phrasing,

The statute had narrowly survived repeated attacks made in federal and state courts.[39] Seventy-four patients had been transferred to Matteawan under section 412 between 1904 and 1925,[40] and another 132 were so transferred during the period between 1940 and 1965.[41] Despite the repeal, on No-

---

Section 412 was repealed in 1965 on the recommendation of the Department of Mental Hygiene due to its "possible unconstitutionality." (N.Y. Laws 1965, ch. 524, eff. June 28, 1965; Memorandum to Governor, Dep't Mental Hygiene, May 19, 1965.)

[39] The constitutionality of administrative transfers of civil patients to Matteawan had been upheld by a memorandum decision of the New York Court of Appeals in 1949, People ex rel. Monaco v. McNeill, 299 N.Y. 605, 86 N.E. 2d 176 (memorandum decision). In 1961, however, the United States Court of Appeals for the Second Circuit held such transfers unconstitutional because Section 412 did not provide, and could not be read as impliedly providing, for a hearing. Because other civil patients in civil hospitals could be transferred to Matteawan (under N.Y. Mental Hygiene Law § 85) only after "detailed judicial proceedings" which find them "dangerous," and because there is "nothing to demonstrate that ex-convicts who . . . become mentally ill, are inherently more dangerous," the distinction between the procedures governing their respective transfers were "repugnant to the equal protection clause of the Fourteenth Amendment." (United States ex rel. Carroll v. McNeill, 294 F. 2d 117 [2d Cir. 1961].) After the Supreme Court had agreed to review the case, but while it was still pending, the patient died. The Second Circuit's decision was then vacated and remanded with directions to dismiss the cause as moot. (369 U.S. 149 [1962].) Thereafter, another patient challenged his Matteawan transfer in a state court, but was unsuccessful, because, although agreeing with the rationale of the vacated federal court decision, the New York court was bound by the earlier decision of the state's own highest court rejecting the constitutional claim. (People ex rel. Aronson v. McNeill, 19 App. Div. 2d 731, 242 N.Y.S. 2d 427 [2d Dep't], appeal dismissed, 13 N.Y. 2d 1043, 195 N.E. 2d 316, 245 N.Y.S. 2d 609 [1963].)

[40] 1924 Ann. Rep. Sup't State Prisons 345–350, N.Y. Leg. Doc. No. 111 (1925).

[41] See Table 2.

vember 1, 1965, there were still 54 patients at Matteawan who had been admitted under section 412, including one who arrived in 1921 and six who had been there twenty years or longer.[42] Their ultimate release was authorized by section 409 of the Correction Law, whenever they had recovered or were reasonably safe to be at large. The statute also authorized their transfer back to a civil hospital. These 54 patients were still there on the day *Baxstrom v. Herold* was decided. They would not be there long after it.

*d) Allegedly Dangerously Mentally Ill Patients
(N.Y. Mental Hygiene Law § 85)*

As of February 1966, section 85 of the Mental Hygiene Law, first enacted in 1932,[43] still permitted courts to commit

[42] See Table 2.

[43] N.Y. Laws 1932, ch. 574, § 1 (enacted as § 83-a and renumbered § 85 by N.Y. Laws 1933, ch. 395, § 24). In 1921 the governor had vetoed a bill which "would have authorized the transfer [to Matteawan] of any patient who committed an act that would be interpreted as a criminal offense if committed by a sane person." 1921 Ann. Rep. Sup't State Prisons 345, N.Y. Leg. Doc. No. 12 (1922). Although he did not claim credit, the likely reason for the governor's veto was the objection of the superintendent of Matteawan: "When a patient is transferred from a civil hospital his history shows criminal tendencies and usually the patient is dangerous or homicidal. Unfortunately there are no facilities available for the care and treatment of such cases owing to the usual overcrowding and it simply means that we are compelled to treat these cases on all of our wards and the problem of safely guarding our patients is increased. . . . Fortunately the bill did not meet with executive approval and we are indebted to the chief executive for his action on this bill. Such a law would have authorized the indiscriminate transfer of cases and it would have been absolutely impossible to safely care for any of the transfers which would have been legally made." (Ibid.)

By 1931, however, the superintendent could report that the over-a patient of a civil hospital to Matteawan if he (i) committed or were liable to commit an act which, if he were sane, would constitute homicide or felonious assault, or (ii) if he were so "dangerously mentally ill that his presence in

---

crowding at Matteawan had been largely eliminated by new construction. (1931 Ann. Rep. Comm'n Correc., N.Y. Leg. Doc. No. 85, at 307 [1932].) The very next year, section 83-a was added to the Mental Hygiene Law authorizing judicial commitment of dangerous civil patients to Matteawan after examination by a commission of "three disinterested persons." Such commitments, initiated by the district attorney upon the certificate of a superintendent of a hospital within his county, were not to be deemed as evidence of any criminal conduct, nor were they to be considered as punishment for a crime. The patient was to be kept at Matteawan until he became "no longer dangerous," at which time he could administratively be transferred by the Commissioner of Mental Hygiene to a civil hospital.

After renumbering as section 85 (N.Y. Laws 1933, ch. 395, § 24), the criteria for removal to Matteawan were broadened in 1953 to include patients dangerous "to the community" because of eloping tendencies, as well as those dangerous to patients and staff. N.Y. Laws 1953, ch. 699, § 1; N.Y. Legislative Annual 208 (1953). The procedure and discharge rules were also amended. Briefly stated, the civil hospital was now to institute the proceeding so that district attorneys would not have to act in cases involving patients resident in other counties. The reference in amended section 85 to the "correction law" was apparently intended to refer to section 409 which allowed release of time-expired prisoners at Matteawan who had recovered or were "reasonably safe to be at large."

In 1963 the section was repealed, and a new section 85 was substituted. (N.Y. Laws 1963, ch. 704.) The new statute made no change in the discharge language, but adopted the hearing rules and procedures (enacted in 1943 and amended in 1960) used to commit mentally ill prisoners to Matteawan, i.e., section 408 of the Correction Law. Those procedures were adopted because they "have been perfected in recent years and have been found to be highly suitable for commitment of mental patients who are dangerous or potentially dangerous from whatever source to correctional institutions." N.Y. Legislative Annual 282 (1963). By the 1963 substitution, the "very

such a hospital" was dangerous to other patients, to staff, or, if he should escape, to the community. By this date, however, the statute required notice to the patient and his family or friends, an examination by independent psychiatrists, an opportunity to demand a hearing, and the right to assistance of retained [44] counsel. Fewer than 400 patients had

cumbersome and slow" commission of three disinterested persons was replaced by two physicians not connected with the applicant hospital; to avoid the administrative difficulty and detriment to the patient involved in keeping him "in close confinement" at the civil hospital during the proceedings, the court was authorized to order an interim transfer to Matteawan. (Ibid.) Notice of the application to the patient and his family or friends was required, and the right to demand a hearing was expressly given to "any relative or near friend."

In 1965 the legislature clarified the release procedures for section 85 patients at Matteawan. The reference in section 85 to release "as provided in the correction law" (as amended in 1953) appeared to authorize discharge on recovery or when the patient was reasonably safe to be at large, the criteria in section 409 of the Correction Law. But because there was no "explicit authority," and because Matteawan's superintendent believed he did not "have the power" to release section 85 patients, the Department of Mental Hygiene proposed an amendment to section 409 aimed at "the problem of the 'forgotten patient' at Matteawan." Memorandum to Gov., Dep't Mental Hygiene, May 19, 1965. As amended, section 409 expressly applies to prisoners (as previously) and to "any other patients who are neither prisoners nor charged with crimes," including, among others, patients transferred to Matteawan under section 85.

[44] In Application of Sullivan, 297 N.Y. 190, 78 N.E. 2d 467 (1948) the New York Court of Appeals modified a court order so as to reverse it, to the extent that it granted $150 to an attorney assigned in a section 85 proceeding as beyond the power of the court even though the statute authorized as charges upon the county of patients' original admission the fees of examiners and medical witnesses and "other necessary expenses." See also In re Sullivan, 85 N.Y.S. 2d 251 (Sup. Ct. 1948) (denying motion for appointment of an independent psychiatrist because "no authority" authorizing it was shown).

been admitted to Matteawan under section 85 since its
enactment in 1932,[45] and there were 199 patients still there

[45] In an address to the Dutchess County Psychiatric Society in September 1956, Dr. W. Cecil Johnston, present Superintendent of Matteawan and a member of this committee, reviewed the history of admissions to Matteawan under section 85. The total number of patients so admitted between September 1933 and September 1956 was 204 (including 50 from Kings Park Hospital and 52 from Pilgrim State Hospital). The "basic reasons for commitment" were reported to be Murder of an attendant, 2; Murder of a visitor, 1; Murder of other patients, 37; Escape and Murder, 2; Fracture of skull of attendant, 2; Fracture of skull of patient, 3; Assaults on employees, 84; Assaults on other patients, 47; Threats, 8; Escapes, 16; Escape and rape, 4. It was noted that "on many occasions the patient was considered to be dangerously mentally ill for multiple reasons and quite often these patients were assaultive but they also attempted to escape from the hospital. It is interesting to note that escape as a reason for their commitment to this hospital under section 85 was only occasionally mentioned prior to 1946."

The superintendent also reported that as of 1956, 140 of the patients were still at Matteawan, 31 having died and 33 having been transferred to civil or Veterans Administration hospitals, released to relatives, etc. Among those remaining, 52 were in seclusion wards, 69 were in close supervision wards, and 19 were in minimal supervision wards. It was also noted that the hospital staff were "more aware" of the presence of section 85 patients because of frequent "inquiries of relatives" and the "relative difficulty in effecting their release." According to Dr. Johnston: "Since there is no provision for convalescent status at Matteawan . . . , we are very reluctant to discharge into the community a patient committed as dangerously mentally insane without the supervision and observation provided patients on convalescent status. Likewise, after patients have shown a period of improved behavior under the closer supervision furnished at this hospital, their return to a civil hospital is understandably weighed very carefully by the representatives of the Department of Mental Hygiene who evaluate their condition and pass judgment upon their condition and pass judgment upon their suitability for transfer to a civil hospital." As an example, the superintendent noted that 10 patients proposed for transfer back to civil hospitals had been "disapproved."

on November 1, 1965,[46] shortly before the decision in *Baxstrom*. Some 33 patients had been there twenty years or longer.[47] Over the years the occasions for successful section 85 applications reportedly included homicide in 42 cases and assault in 136 cases.[48]

e) *Need for Revision*

The disparities in treatment among the various types of patients are obvious. All were civil patients and yet all were in correctional hospitals. Only one class (section 85) was entitled to a judicial hearing with notice and an impartial examination to determine the need for hospitalization in a

---

In addition to reporting his impressions that civil hospitals "not infrequently kept [these patients] on their usual ward until more serious behavior becomes manifest" because of the complicated procedures required by section 85 at that time (prior to 1963), Dr. Johnston suggested an alternative procedure for the disposition of dangerous patients in civil hospitals: "The only difference in the care and treatment of this group of patients as compared to civil hospitals is that Matteawan provides more strict supervision and greater security. It might be speculated that if one of the civil hospitals, for example, in the metropolitan areas, had a ward or annex equipped with the same means of supervision and security provided at Matteawan, cases that would be eligible for commitment according to section 85 might be transferred to such a ward or annex and remain there until their condition warranted transfer or release under convalescent care. . . . The reason the metropolitan district was suggested as a possibility is that according to our statistics, a somewhat larger number of patients are sent from that district and those hospitals are grouped within a smaller area so that the difficulty of visitation is not an objectionable feature."

From April 1, 1956, to March 31, 1966, another 136 patients were admitted to Matteawan under section 85. See Table 2.

[46] See Table 3.

[47] See Table 8.

[48] See note 45, *supra*.

maximum-security hospital. The others were placed or retained there on the basis of clinical judgment and administrative decision. Among the former prisoners, after repeal of section 412 of the Correction Law in 1965, the sole test of whether a patient could be placed administratively in a correctional hospital was whether his need for hospitalization was discovered before or after his sentence expired.

Even between the two classes of prisoners retained after expiration of sentence (those at Dannemora and those at Matteawan) there were vast differences. A prisoner could be retained at Dannemora only after extensive court proceedings involving notice, examination, and an opportunity to be heard. At Matteawan, however, no court proceedings at all were required. Discharge from Matteawan was by order of its director, but discharge from Dannemora was by order of an official in Albany with no resident representative at Dannemora. Convalescent status release was available to the patient "placed" at Dannemora and not to the patient retained at Matteawan (but there is no evidence that such releases were ever made). No form of independent examination and judicial review (except habeas corpus) was available at Matteawan, but a special proceeding could be instituted at Dannemora. The court entertaining the Matteawan habeas corpus application had jurisdiction to order discharge, but the court hearing the Dannemora proceeding had conditional release as an available alternative in difficult cases.

There was neither rhyme nor reason for these distinctions. More importantly, however, some of these protective devices existed more in theory than in practice. Finally, the respective procedures in no way reflected the advances that had been made in devising enlightened hospitalization procedures for the ordinary civil mental patient.

In 1964, new procedures for the involuntary hospitalization and retention of the mentally ill were enacted in article 5 of the Mental Hygiene Law, to become effective on September 1, 1965.[49] The new statute had been recommended by this committee.[50] Under the new procedures an involuntary patient may be hospitalized up to 60 days upon the certificates of two physicians (N.Y. Mental Hygiene Law § 72). Promptly advised of his rights by the new Mental Health Information Service (N.Y. Mental Hygiene Law § 88), the patient can demand a judicial hearing, and in any event involuntary patients may not be retained longer than 60 days without judicial orders (entered after notice and an opportunity to be heard and subject to jury trial review) authorizing further hospitalization, first for six months, then for one year, and thereafter at two-year intervals (N.Y. Mental Hygiene Law §§ 73, 74). Notice of all such applications is also required to be served upon the Mental Health Information Service which is authorized to demand a hearing thereon. Although these statutes applied to involuntary civil patients, they made no reference to the various classes of "civil" patients at Matteawan and Dannemora. As a result, those patients continued to be governed by the special statutes regulating their admission or retention and stating the conditions for their release or transfer to civil hospitals.

It was in the context of these considerations that the present committee tentatively decided to recommend that all former prisoners should be treated the same way as any other citizen of the state. The committee could find no valid reason, legal or medical, historical or current, for denying

[49] N.Y. Mental Hygiene Law §§ 70–88, as amended by N.Y. Laws 1964, ch. 738 (eff. Sept. 1, 1965).
[50] See generally, Mental Illness and Due Process (1962).

these patients as a class exactly the same legal rights and services that any one else could demand. We considered recommending that the only basis for separate hospitalization in a secure central facility such as Matteawan should be a full-dress judicial determination of dangerous mental illness, rather than an administrative decision based upon clinical judgment alone. We also considered recommending that wherever dangerous civil patients were to be hospitalized—in a correctional institution or in an appropriately secure civil hospital—they should be granted the same rights to periodic judicial review as they would enjoy if not transferred, except that the scope of the review might be enlarged to consider the continued need or not for separate hospitalization.

A crucial issue upon which even tentative agreement was difficult to reach involved the place of hospitalization for the dangerously mentally ill. Possibilities that were considered for recommendation included: (i) continuing the status quo, i.e., admission to Matteawan operated by the Department of Correction and subject only to inspection by the Department of Mental Hygiene; (ii) transfer of jurisdiction over Matteawan to the Department of Mental Hygiene; (iii) establishment of a new hybrid institution subject to the divided jurisdiction of the Department of Correction (security aspects) and the Department of Mental Hygiene (medical aspects); (iv) a series of regional facilities operated by the Department of Mental Hygiene, perhaps most likely to be accomplished by increasing existing security wards in civil hospitals to accommodate any such patient as may require closer supervision and for a longer period than is usual in the "open-door" facilities.

The committee decided to pass on to other matters and to postpone further discussion of this issue until after the

51

Supreme Court of the United States rendered its decision in *Baxstrom v. Herold,* a case involving a time-expired prisoner at Dannemora, which the court had agreed to review a few months after the committee began its work. It seemed at the time likely that the court would have something to say about the validity of confining civil patients in a correctional institution, and that its decision might determine the scope of the alternatives available to the state in dealing with these patients.

3. THE BAXSTROM CASE

According to the brief filed in the Supreme Court by his counsel,[51] Johnnie K. Baxstrom had been convicted of a felonious assault on a policeman in April 1959, and had been sentenced to a term of two and one-half to three years in state prison. On June 1, 1961, or about six months before his sentence would have expired, Baxstrom was administratively transferred from Attica Prison to Dannemora State Hospital. In November of that year the hospital director applied to court, as required, for an order of commitment which would authorize Baxstrom's continued hospitalization after December 18th, the day his sentence would expire. While the application was pending, Baxstrom was interviewed by a representative of the Commissioner of Mental Hygiene to determine his suitability for placement in a civil hospital in the event the court should commit him under section 384. He was "disapproved," because the examining doctor did not consider him "to be suitable for care in a civil hospital."

[51] Brief and Appendix for Petitioner, Baxstrom v. Herold, 383 U.S. 107 (1966).

Notice that a commitment proceeding was to be held on December 6, 1961, had been served upon two relatives who lived in Maryland, and upon Baxstrom himself, but on the day of the hearing Baxstrom was alone. The court accepted certificates by two independent physicians that Baxstrom was mentally ill, and then heard the hospital director testify that Baxstrom was still in need of hospitalization with a diagnosis of "psychosis due to epileptic deterioration." Baxstrom, who was "indigent" and without counsel "was accorded a brief opportunity to ask questions." Baxstrom was not advised that he had any right to retained or assigned counsel, or that he was entitled to call witnesses on his own behalf. The court committed him to the custody of the Commissioner of Mental Hygiene pursuant to section 384, regretting that it had no power to order a transfer to a civil hospital since the director of Dannemora said he saw no objection to a transfer. That, however, was a matter for administrative decision by the commissioner. Baxstrom of course remained at Dannemora, but now somewhat magically he was deemed a "civil" patient in the "custody" of a civil authority.

In May 1962 and again in May 1963, Baxstrom sought release on writs of habeas corpus, but each time he was unsuccessful. Apparently he never made any application to a court under section 87(3) of the Mental Hygiene Law. On the first writ he had been ordered examined by an independent psychiatrist who found him still mentally ill, but who saw "no reason why he could not be treated in a civil mental hospital." Once again, no one had any objection to his transfer to a civil hospital, but the court was powerless. The second writ was dismissed without a new independent examination because Baxstrom had no evidence that his condition had changed since he was last examined. As to transfer, the hospital director told the court how Baxstrom had been rejected by the commissioner's representative back in 1961 and, once again, the court was powerless to act.

Dismissal of the second writ was appealed to the Appellate Division, but that court affirmed the dismissal without opinion, and the New York Court of Appeals refused to hear a further appeal.[52] Persistent, however, in a manner for which Clarence Earl Gideon became famous, Baxstrom himself wrote to the United States Supreme Court and to the Legal Aid Society in New York City.[53] An attorney entered the case, and, on June 7, 1965, the Supreme Court agreed to review the order dismissing his second writ of habeas corpus. Then, for only the second time since he had been committed to the custody of the Commissioner of Mental Hygiene in December 1961, and almost four years later, Baxstrom was again examined and found unsuitable for transfer by a representative of the commissioner.

In his brief Baxstrom attacked the procedure by which his 1961 commitment had been accomplished. He argued that at the time of his "civil" commitment to the custody of the Commissioner of Mental Hygiene in 1961 he was entitled to the assistance of assigned counsel. He contended that counsel could have demanded the attendance of the physicians upon whose certificates that he was still mentally ill the court relied. He argued that counsel could have cross-examined these physicians, and could have suggested to the court a way in which it could effect a transfer to a civil hospital despite the administrative decision of the Com-

[52] People ex rel. Baxstrom v. Herold, 14 N.Y. 2d 490, 202 N.E. 2d 159, 253 N.Y.S. 2d 1028, denying leave to appeal in 21 App. Div. 2d 754, 251 N.Y.S. 2d 938 (3d Dep't 1964).

[53] Information supplied by Leon B. Polsky, New York Legal Aid Society, counsel for Baxstrom in the United States Supreme Court.

missioner of Mental Hygiene.[54] Baxstrom's second point was that the retention procedure under section 384 was an unconstitutional denial of the equal protection of law in that it did not provide time-expired "civil" patients with the same right to demand a jury-trial review of the decision to commit as was afforded to all other "civil" patients. His third and last point was that section 384 denied him the equal protection of the law by permitting the hospitalization of one class of "civil" patient in a correctional facility based upon the administrative determination by the Commissioner of Mental Hygiene that they are not suitable for care in a civil hospital, while all other "civil" patients were entitled to a judicial determination (under N.Y. Mental Hygiene Law § 85) that they require such care because of dangerous mental illness. Baxstrom did not directly raise the question whether any civil patients could be hospitalized in a correctional facility; the attack was directed against the discriminatory procedures by which such hospitalization was accomplished.

The attorney general's brief[55] attempted to demonstrate that Dannemora was indeed a hospital and not a prison or part of a prison; that one or more criminal convictions in a patient's record constitutes a rational basis for treating the patient as one of a class of patients called "insane criminal" while still under sentence, and "criminally insane (one with dangerous or criminal propensities)" upon expiration of sentence; that the state may rationally establish separate

[54] The court "could have refused to commit the Petitioner under section 384 and required the state to proceed under the Mental Hygiene Law rather than the Correction Law." Brief and Appendix for Petitioner, p. 16.

[55] Brief and Appendices for Respondent, Baxstrom v. Herold, supra, n. 51.

hospital facilities for such classes because "to commingle this group with the civilly insane would serve only to inflict harsh and unreasonable discrimination on the civilly insane"; and that procedural safeguards adequate to insure fundamental fairness in the commitment procedure were supplied by the notice that was served, the opportunity of the patient himself to speak and to cross-examine, and the subsequent availability of petitions for judicial review under the special proceedings authorized by Mental Hygiene Law section 87(3), or in habeas corpus proceedings to which Baxstrom had in fact twice resorted.

The attorney general's brief also mentioned as being "of importance" the various safeguards available to "retained involuntary patients" including access to the Mental Health Information Service and automatic periodic judicial review, but the brief could not have intended to imply that these were available to time-expired patients at Dannemora (or Matteawan), because in practice they had not been. Contending that Baxstrom had no right to assignment of counsel, the attorney general distinguished civil commitments in which "avarice, hatred, self interest" and the possibility of a "frame" might be involved, from "the case of an alleged criminally insane" in which "the risk of a miscarriage of justice is remote, if not totally absent" because the "sanity hearing is held in vacuum" and the examining psychiatrists "can hardly be suspected of ulterior motives in the case of the criminally insane already in a state hospital." Because the proceedings were neither accusatory nor penal, and involved only "searching out of a condition of the mind," the patient had no right to assignment of counsel or to jury trial review. Finally, Baxstrom's demands were "simply and totally unrealistic."

Each side appended non-record material to its brief, reflecting perhaps their evaluation of the important issues in the case. Counsel for Baxstrom offered some random statistics and reports on the relative success of assigned counsel in opposing commitment proceedings. The attorney general presented a chart of the Dannemora hospital staff, various institutional budgets showing the great sums expended yearly at the correctional hospitals, Baxstrom's lengthy criminal record, a copy of a second transfer evaluation report made while the case was pending in the Supreme Court, and an aerial photograph of the hospital showing its physical separation from adjacent Clinton Prison.

The opinion for a unanimous court was handed down by the Chief Justice on February 23, 1966, Mr. Justice Black concurring in the result. The court did not hold that Baxstrom was entitled to assignment of counsel; it relegated that issue to a footnote which merely flagged the fact that those who could afford to retain counsel could do so, but that Baxstrom who was "indigent" had no counsel.[56] On the other hand, although it noted Dannemora's "striking dissimilarities" from civil hospitals, and that "certain privileges of patients at Dannemora are restricted by statute," [57] the court did not say that time-expired or other civil patients could not be hospitalized at Dannemora, a decision the attorney general's arguments appear to have been framed to forestall. Baxstrom did win his case, however.

The Supreme Court held that a prisoner who is civilly committed upon expiration of sentence (1) is entitled to the same jury-trial review of that commitment decision as is available to anyone else who is civilly committed, and (2) is entitled to the same judicial determination of dangerous mental illness as is required before any other civil patient

[56] 383 U.S. at 109 n. 1. See Chapter I, note 15, *supra*.
[57] 383 U.S. at 113 (citing N.Y. Correc. Law § 388).

can be hospitalized in an institution in the Department of Correction.[58] The court made no reference to the right to automatic periodic review, but since it held Baxstrom entitled to any "substantial review proceeding generally available" to civil patients, it was clear that he would be entitled to that as well. It was also clear that the availability of such review had to survive a patient's commitment to Matteawan under M.H.L. section 85.

The effects of the *Baxstrom* decision were immediate and profound. A situation that had been allowed to exist since 1861 was in part relieved overnight. In compliance with the clear mandate of the decision the state promptly[59] instituted a crash program to have all time-expired patients at Dannemora admitted to civil hospitals. The procedure adopted was that used for the involuntary hospitalization of any ordinary civil patient, admission to a civil hospital upon the certificates of two physicians. Thereafter they would in all respects be treated as ordinary civil patients. The staff at Dannemora supplied the required certificates. The same procedures were adopted for the time-expired patients at Matteawan. In addition, the small group of civil patients who had been administratively transferred to Matteawan under section 412 of the Correction Law as being former prisoners with "criminal tendencies" were also admitted to civil hospitals, since they too had been hospitalized in a correctional institution without a judicial determination of dangerous mental illness.

Since the court did not forbid hospitalization of dangerous patients in a correctional hospital, any of the transferred former prisoners who could be proved to a court to be dangerously mentally ill might still be sent to Matteawan under

[58] 383 U.S. at 110–11.
[59] N.Y. Times, March 23, 1966, p. 96, col. 1.

section 85 of the Mental Hygiene Law. One might expect that the number of such returns would be large, since most of the patients had already been administratively rejected for civil hospital care on the basis of clinical judgment. We are advised, however, that, as of one year later, of 969 "*Baxstrom* patients" who were removed from Dannemora and Matteawan, only *seven* had been returned to Matteawan under section 85.[60]

4. RECOMMENDATIONS
FOR FURTHER IMPROVEMENT

Some of the recommendations upon which the committee had tentatively agreed prior to the decision in *Baxstrom* have now become constitutional doctrine. However, although the case itself accomplished much, much more remains to be done.

RECOMMENDATION NO. 5 (*Hospitalization of former prisoners*). If, in the opinion of a correctional hospital director, a prisoner whose term of sentence is about to expire is in need of continued hospitalization, the director should be empowered to apply for his admission to a hospital under the jurisdiction of the Department of Mental Hygiene under the procedures established in the

[60] See the narrative of "Operation Baxstrom" in Appendix D. The Utica Observer-Dispatch, June 8, 1966, reported that Baxstrom died on June 7 "in Baltimore, Md., of epileptic seizures." He had been admitted to a civil hospital, but had obtained his release through a jury-trial review (under N.Y. Mental Hygiene Law § 74).

On April 22, 1966, Dr. Christopher H. Terrence, Acting N.Y. State Commissioner of Mental Hygiene, noted that "with few exceptions" some 700 "supposedly angry, hostile, acting-out people who would destroy the very roots of our society" had been removed to civil hospitals from Matteawan and Dannemora and "they adjusted very well. At this moment only five or six have had to be returned to Dannemora." Governor Rockefeller's Conference on Crime 201 (1966).

Mental Hygiene Law for the admission of ordinary civil patients (N.Y. Mental Hygiene Law §§ 72–74).

This recommendation states what has become the practice since the *Baxstrom* decision. The former prisoner is now treated in all respects as an ordinary civil patient admitted under the Mental Hygiene Law. Appropriate notices and opportunities to be heard are provided to the patient, to certain persons designated by the patient and to the Mental Health Information Service; periodic review is required; and orders authorizing retention are subject to review in the form of a jury trial. A provision reflecting these procedures should be substituted for the existing provisions in the Correction Law (section 384) concerning the retention of mentally ill prisoners whose terms of sentence have expired. Likewise, the provisions in Correction Law section 409 which permit the retention at Matteawan of a prisoner whose term has expired should also be replaced. The provision in the Mental Hygiene Law (section 87[3]) which deals with procedures for obtaining the discharge and judicial review of certain patients whose sentences have expired should be repealed, since those matters are now governed entirely by the general discharge and review provisions of the Mental Hygiene Law.[61]

RECOMMENDATION NO. 6 (*Civil hospitalization of dangerously mentally ill patients*). Dangerously mentally ill patients, except prisoners still under sentence, should be hospitalized under appropriate conditions within the Department of Mental Hygiene.

[61] These three statutes (N.Y. Correc. Law §§ 384, 309; N.Y. Mental Hygiene Law § 87[3]) have since been repealed, and new provisions in accord with recommendation no. 5 have been added to section 385 and new section 409 of the Correction Law making the ordinary civil hospitalization procedures applicable to time-expired prisoners at Dannemora and Matteawan. N.Y. Laws 1966, ch. 891, §§ 1, 4, 5.

Existing authorization to hospitalize such patients at an institution within the Department of Correction (N.Y. Mental Hygiene Law § 85) should be abolished.

The committee recognizes that certain mental patients, whether former prisoners or ordinary civil patients, pose special dangers to their fellow patients, to the staff, and to the community. Their capacity to cause serious physical injury is amply demonstrated by the homicides and assaults committed by those patients who have in the past been sent from civil hospitals to Matteawan.[62] Fortunately, however, their number has never been large when compared to the total population of the civil hospitals. On April 1, 1964, there were 85,279 resident patients in twenty-one civil state hospitals operated by the Department of Mental Hygiene.[63] In the course of the year ending on that date only 22 of those patients had to be committed to Matteawan under section 85 of the Mental Hygiene Law as "dangerously mentally ill," and the following year only 15 patients were moved.[64] As of November 1, 1965, the total number of patients still in residence at Matteawan (having been admitted either under section 85 as "dangerously mentally ill" or under section 412 of the Correction Law as having "criminal tendencies") was still only 253.[65] Their numbers have not significantly increased since former prisoners removed to civil hospitals under the *Baxstrom* decision have been eligible for return under section 85. In fact, as of January, 1967, it appeared that the total would be reduced to approximately 70 patients

[62] See note 45, *supra.*

[63] State of N.Y., Dep't of Mental Hygiene, Official Directory of State and Licensed Mental Institutions 176 (1965).

[64] See Table 2. In the year ending March 31, 1966, there were only 18 admissions under N.Y. Mental Hygiene Law § 85. Ibid.

[65] See Table 3.

as a result of new review procedures.[66] However, patients who are hospitalized as not mentally fit to stand trial, or upon acquittal by reason of insanity, should also be considered in defining the scope of this problem, since many of them may be dangerously mentally ill. For reasons discussed in the next chapter, the committee believes these patients should also be hospitalized in civil institutions. Obviously, therefore, the number of patients in civil institutions who may require secure custody at any one time may number several hundred.

As mentioned previously, one of the most difficult questions faced by the committee was whether to recommend that hospitalization of dangerously mentally ill civil patients in a correctional hospital, Matteawan, should be terminated, and, if so, what substitute should be proposed. The decision of the United States Supreme Court in the *Baxstrom* case noted the "striking" dissimilarities[67] between correctional and civil hospitals, but did not pass upon the validity of hospitalization of civil patients at Dannemora or at Matteawan.

The committee's study[68] of annual reports of Matteawan State Hospital from its opening to 1966 demonstrates that the problems of operating a mental hospital in the Department of Correction have changed very little since the first patients were moved from Auburn to Beacon in 1892. Over the decades the problems have included constant overcrowding, vacancies, turnover, and unlicensed physicians on the medical staff; inadequate personnel recruitment devices; lack of aftercare and convalescent status facilities; lack of social workers and psychologists, and serious and repeated doubts as to the propriety of assigning the administration of a mental hospital to the correctional authorities. In original concept

[66] See Table 3, and note 74, *infra*.
[67] Baxstrom v. Herold, 383 U.S. at 113.
[68] See Appendix A (History of Matteawan State Hospital).

something less than a prison but more than a hospital, Matteawan was an experiment that was proudly announced, but which, despite the sustained efforts of its administrators, was allowed to falter. Unflattering publicity, repeated escapes, a costly error in overtaxed judgment, economic pressures, personnel shortages, and obviously favored attention to civil hospitals—all combined to cause Matteawan to drift into decline as a pioneer mental hospital and into constantly improved status as a security institution. Operated by a prison authority, inspected by a hospital authority, and usually ignored by the budget and the legislature, Matteawan has become at best a stepchild whose proper parent has long been in doubt. At least three times it has been proposed [69] to transfer Matteawan from the Department of Correction to the Department of Mental Hygiene, and on one occasion the transfer was effected, but only for a period of months.

Occasional sensational publicity has aroused public interest every now and then, but *seventy years* of annual reports ranging in temper from polite requests to outright threats have seldom aroused anyone. Expensive new security devices have been authorized hard on the heels of various escapes,[70] but an educational program that was needed in

[69] By Governor Odell in 1902 as an economy measure, 10 Messages from the Governors 342–43 (Lincoln ed. 1909); by the 1926 Hughes Comm'n on Reorganization of State Government, State of N.Y., Public Papers of Gov. Smith 597, 638 (1926); and by the 1954 Blain Commission, N.Y.S. Mental Hygiene Council, Report on Study of Release Procedures for Mental Patients in N.Y.S. (Dec. 7, 1954). Only the 1926 effort bore fruit, and even then only temporarily. See generally Appendix A.

[70] See generally Appendix A. On March 31, 1965 there were 1,809 patients at Matteawan. For the 1965–1966 fiscal year the N.Y. State Director of the Budget approved a total expenditure of $6,458,745 for personal services by 1,010 employees including 14 psychiatrists, 2 psychologists, 1 psychiatric social worker, 10 occupational thera-

1894 was still a problem in 1964. Social workers were requested in 1922, but the first position was not authorized until almost forty years later. Aftercare was requested in 1919, but it is not available even today. Unlicensed physicians have long been a staple in its diet.

For these reasons the committee believes that the responsibility for the care and treatment of *all* civil mental patients must be vested in the Department of Mental Hygiene. Nowhere else can there be any assurance that, absent general economic disaster, they will timely benefit from the full range of available modern treatment programs. No amount of new spending, or program expansion, or administrative changes in security, visiting and correspondence regulations at Matteawan could give assurance against isolated retrenchment in future budgets or under future administrations.

If adopted, our recommendation could be implemented upon the basis either of a single, central institution, or of a series of regional facilities.

Central High-security Facility

Such a facility could be established in several ways. *First,* the existing plant, facilities and personnel at Matteawan might simply be transferred to the Department of Mental Hygiene. However, such a transfer might pose new problems in hospitalizing misdemeanants and female felons under sentence, and might interfere with the new uses to which space made available by the *Baxstrom* decision is being devoted.[71] Moreover, a serious personnel problem might result

---

pists, and 774 custodial and security personnel. State of N.Y., Exec. Dep't (Div'n of Budget), Certificate of Approval for Personal Services, Dep't Corr., Matteawan State Hospital (April, 1965).

[71] There were several interesting collateral effects of the Baxstrom decision. With half of its population gone, the hospital at Dannemora had sufficient surplus facilities to surrender control of an area to

since correctional hospital officers assigned to Matteawan are not on the same pay scale as civil state hospital attendants.

A *second* possibility, reorganizing Matteawan as a hybrid institution subject to the divided jurisdiction of the Departments of Correction (security aspects) and Mental Hygiene (medical aspects), would not likely work, since correctional officers are becoming increasingly more involved in treatment programs at Matteawan and Dannemora. It might prove extremely difficult to maintain in practice a theoretical demarcation of authority. What works at a hospital prison ward, such as Bellevue, designed for temporary custody and observation, might not work at a state hospital.

A *third* possible solution, similar to the others, would be to use existing or expanded facilities within the Department

---

adjacent Clinton Prison for use in cooperation with Canada's nearby McGill University as the Clinton Prison Diagnostic Center at which experimental psychiatric research and intensive pre-parole evaluation of normal inmates could be conducted by a specially recruited staff under conditions assuring complete segregation from the hospital's own population (N.Y. Correc. Law § 71-a, as added by N.Y. Laws 1966, ch. 653 § 1, eff. June 21, 1966).

There was extra space made available at Matteawan as well, and it was also authorized to be put to novel use. Mental defectives who are not mentally ill, but for whom greater psychiatric and therapeutic facilities would now be available at Matteawan, were authorized to be removed from Eastern Correctional Institution at Napanoch to a new "Beacon Institution for Defective Delinquents" which was established in vacant facilities at Matteawan, again under separate administration and with complete segregation from the hospital's mentally ill population. (N.Y. Correc. Law § 420, as added by N.Y. Laws 1966, ch. 819, § 1, eff. July 28, 1966.) Both bills were recommended by the Governor's Special Committee on Criminal Offenders, N.Y. Legislative Annual 348 (1966).

Subsequently, in N.Y. Times, Dec. 14, 1966, p. 51, col. 1, it was reported that the New York State Narcotic Addiction Control Commission (N.Y. Mental Hygiene Law, art. 9) expected to use for its patients 350 beds made available at Matteawan State Hospital.

of Mental Hygiene for establishment of a new central institution.

Each of these possibilities presupposes a central institution accepting patients on a statewide basis. Each would impede visiting and social work, and would be inconsistent with the localized approach to hospitalization within the Department of Mental Hygiene. High-security custody in a central institution, moreover, would involve severe restrictions upon the patient's freedom, and no matter what its name, location, or parent department, it can also be expected to carry with it in the public eye a stigma of dangerousness not easily overcome. If our recommendation were implemented on any basis involving central hospitalization, it should be understood as also proposing that special safeguards be provided to protect against arbitrary admission or retention of patients who are not so dangerously mentally ill as to require maximum-security custody. The decision to admit a patient to such an institution should not be left to administrative judgment. Whereas very few such patients are admitted to Matteawan under present section 85 of the Mental Hygiene Law (requiring a judicial determination), the mass exodus and negligible returns of former prisoners following the *Baxstrom* decision appear to indicate that administrative placements occur in many cases in which the evidence to obtain a judicial order is lacking.[72]

The *Baxstrom* case does not of itself require that these admissions be based solely upon a judicial determination of dangerous mental illnesses.[73] In our opinion, however, the

[72] See also the similar statistical experience with administrative placements of mentally ill defendants discussed in Chapter III; see note 74, *infra*.

[73] The court there assumed that "transfer among like mental hospitals is a purely administrative function," but went on to note that,

importance of so significant an event in the life of an individual patient is sufficient warrant to recommend that no person be admitted to a central high-security facility except upon a judicial determination that it is necessary for the protection of others. New York's 35-year-old policy of requiring judicial action should be continued even though such a new institution would be entirely within the same hospital system. Patients proposed for admission should be given the assistance of the Mental Health Information Service, and should continue to receive the benefits of automatic periodic judicial review, but the scope of review should be expanded to include the question of continued dangerous mental illness.[74]

Regional Facilities

Another reasonable basis upon which the state could implement our recommendation that dangerously mentally ill patients be hospitalized only within the Department of Mental Hygiene would be a series of regional facilities established as high-security wards at civil state hospitals. Existing

where the hospitals are "functionally distinct," the "classification of patients for involuntary commitment to one of these institutions may not be wholly arbitrary." 383 U.S. at 114.

[74] This aspect of our recommendation has already been implemented. Section 85 of the Mental Hygiene Law has been amended by addition of a new subdivision 4-a providing for automatic periodic judicial review of dangerous mental illness. N.Y. Laws 1966, ch. 891, § 3. Also, the Mental Health Information Service must now receive notice of applications made under this section. N.Y. Laws 1966, ch. 891, § 2. Interestingly, we are informed by Dr. W. Cecil Johnston that in October 1966 there were 176 patients at Matteawan under section 85, and that by December 20, 1966, the number was reduced to 107 patients. We are further advised that as of January 1967, the staff proposed to seek retention orders (on the occasions of periodic review) for only 70 of these patients. The rest would be returned to civil state hospitals as no longer dangerously mentally ill.

facilities designed for the care and custody of patients only temporarily dangerously mentally ill could be adapted to the needs of longer-term patients. This solution would avoid the geographic drawbacks of a central institution, as well as the probable stigma associated with it. It is possible, moreover, that gradual reintegration of the patient into the rest of the hospital population might be more easily accomplished for patients recovering from long-term dangerous mental illness than would be possible by retransfer to an "open door" hospital from a central institution with maximum security throughout. We recognize that the need for sustained security, even though only partial, would be generally out of character for "open door" institutions. However, if the department is properly to be charged with full responsibility for the hospitalization of *all* civil patients, an accommodation suiting the medical and custodial needs of all its patients must be reached.

The movement of a patient from ward to ward within a single institution is essentially a medical matter. As in the case of inter-institutional transfers, however, where a particular ward is functionally distinct from all others, and placement there involves added risks and increased restraints upon personal liberty, the patient should be protected against arbitrary transfers. However, we consider it neither necessary nor appropriate at this time to suggest that such inter-ward movement be conditioned upon prior court approval. It appears likely that internal administrative review procedures (on either a hospital or department level)[75]

[75] E.g., under existing hospitalization procedures, the N.Y. Dep't Mental Hygiene, Policy Manual § 505 (March 20, 1964), provides that "protective restraint or seclusion is to be employed only for satisfactory surgical or medical reasons, or to prevent a patient from injuring himself or others." They may be used only on order of a

could provide the necessary protection, especially since they would be supplemented by access to the continuing assistance of the Mental Health Information Service and periodic judicial review.

RECOMMENDATION NO. 7 (*Old-law patients in Matteawan and Dannemora State Hospitals*). Within six months after the effective date of the proposed new law, (*a*) all time-expired prisoners retained under sections 384 and 408 of the Correction Law at either Dannemora or Matteawan, and (*b*) all patients retained at Matteawan under section 85 of the Mental Hygiene Law, or under former section 412 of the Correction Law, must be discharged therefrom. In the cases of all such patients the respective hospital directors of such institutions would be entitled within that six months to make application for hospitalization of such patients in accordance with recommendations 5 and 6.

RECOMMENDATION NO. 8 (*Old-law patients transferred to civil hospitals*). Within six months after the effective date of the proposed new law hospital directors holding former prisoners in civil hospitals (under sections 384 and 409 of the Correction Law) would be obliged to cause such patients to be readmitted to the hospital under the procedures regulating the new admission and subsequent retention of ordinary civil patients.

The thrust of recommendations 7 and 8 is that the benefits of the proposed new laws should be extended to all patients who were hospitalized under the former statutes and who are still at Matteawan and Dannemora, or who have been administratively "placed" in civil hospitals under statutes (e.g., N.Y. Mental Hygiene Law, section 87[3]) that provide special procedures for only limited judicial review.

---

physician which states the reasons therefor and which must be included in a "full" daily record thereof. Only a camisole or restraining sheet may be used to restrain a patient, and then only for two-hour periods. Seclusion in a room alone with closed door which cannot be opened from the inside may not "exceed three hours in the daytime and the patient shall be visited every hour, day and night."

After *Baxstrom* was decided the Department of Correction promptly caused all former prisoners retained at Matteawan (N.Y. Correc. Law §§ 408, 412) and Dannemora (N.Y. Correc. Law § 384) to be admitted to civil hospitals under the normal procedures for effecting involuntary civil hospitalization. For the most part, therefore, recommendation no. 7 has already been implemented. However, there are almost 200 patients[76] still hospitalized at Matteawan as "dangerously mentally ill" under section 85 of the Mental Hygiene Law. Under the proposed new law these patients should be removed from Matteawan and, if necessary, admitted to a civil hospital. If at such time these patients are believed not only to be in need of continued hospitalization but are also alleged to be still dangerously mentally ill, their hospitalization as such may be accomplished at a facility and in the manner proposed in recommendation no. 6, discussed above. Furthermore, in light of *Baxstrom,* and whether or not the committee's recommendations for hospitalization within the Department of Mental Hygiene are adopted, all patients presently hospitalized at Matteawan under section 85 are immediately[77] entitled to the review procedures currently available to other civil patients.

Finally, in the years before *Baxstrom,* many former pris-

---

[76] As this report is undergoing final revisions the number of section 85 patients is constantly being revised downward. The latest available figure is 107 as of December 20, 1966. See note 74, *supra.*

[77] This aspect of our recommendation has been enacted into law, N.Y. Mental Hygiene Law § 85(4-a) (as added by N.Y. Laws 1966, ch. 891, § 3, eff. July 29, 1966). "Old-law" patients at Matteawan under section 85 cannot be retained longer than six months after the effective date of the subdivision without application for a new court order issued in accordance with and subject to the hearing and review procedures provided by N.Y. Mental Hygiene Law §§ 73, 74. See also note 74, *supra.*

oners retained at Matteawan (Correc. Law section 408) or Dannemora (Correc. Law section 384, M.H.L. section 87 [3]) were transferred to civil hospitals.[78] These patients were hospitalized (upon expiration of sentence) and then transferred under procedures which have since been declared unconstitutional. Therefore, any such patients still in civil state hospitals should be discharged and readmitted as new civil patients, if still in need of hospitalization, and should in all respects be treated as civil patients.

[78] See, e.g., Tables 5, 12.

CHAPTER III

The Mentally Ill Defendant

The laws of New York State governing hospitalization of mentally ill defendants have made it possible for an uneducated 19-year-old boy to have been accused of committing a burglary in Brooklyn in 1901 and, without ever receiving an opportunity to prove his innocence, to have been confined beyond his 83rd birthday in a maximum-security institution operated and staffed by the New York State Department of Correction. On November 1, 1965, that individual[1] was the patient longest in residence at Matteawan State Hospital. There was no indication that the indictment against him had ever been dismissed, and, in theory, therefore, he was still liable to be put to trial if he should ever recover. This patient is a "forgotten man," but it is not the staff at Matteawan that has forgotten him. He, and hundreds like him, have been forgotten by the laws of New York State. For 64 years the law has denied him not only a speedy trial but even

[1] See Table 8. Information about the patient was supplied by Dr. W. Cecil Johnston, Director of Matteawan State Hospital. See also N.Y. Times, May 1, 1964, p. 71, col. 1, reporting that an individual arrested in Flatbush on April 24, 1905, for "theft of a horse, a buggy and a harness, worth about $125," and committed to Matteawan on June 14, 1905, following a plea of not guilty and a lunacy commission finding of "acute delusional insanity," was released 59 years later at age 89 on a motion to dismiss the indictment because the patient "was no longer 'a menace to society or other patients.'" A staff psychiatrist reportedly noted that "in his younger days . . . he was sometimes violent, but recently he has been docile and cooperative." The patient was reportedly expected to be sent to a civil institution "for further treatment for schizophrenia."

periodic judicial review of his condition, and has confined him decades longer than even proof of his guilt would have supported, in what for many years was an overcrowded and understaffed state correctional institution.

On November 1, 1965, there were 1,062 patients at Matteawan who, like him, were there because they were mentally ill and could not be tried for crimes of which they had merely been accused.[2] Among them were 208 men and women who had been there for periods ranging from 20 to 64 years. Another 252 patients were there 10 to 20 years, and 185 were there 5 to 10 years. Many of them were sent to Matteawan, not because they were too dangerous to be sent to civil hospitals, but only because of procedural, geographical, and financial considerations which had nothing to do with the problems of mental illness.

New York's laws governing pre-trial hospitalization of mentally ill defendants are the fruit of an ancient and respected common-law tradition designed to assure fundamental fairness in criminal proceedings in which life or liberty is at stake, but they need to be revised. In this chapter we analyze those statutes and their administration, and offer recommendations for their revision.

1. LEGISLATIVE HISTORY

New York legislation on the subject of mentally ill defendants can be traced back to 1828 when for the first time a New York statute, based upon ancient common-law principles,[3] provided that "no insane person can be tried, sentenced to any punishment, or punished for any crime or offense while he continues in that state."[4] Sporadic attention over

2 See Table 8.
3 See note 30, *infra*.
4 2 Rev. Stat. 697 (1828).

the following 137 years generated incredible confusion[5] that neither the 1881 Code of Criminal Procedure nor the 1909 Consolidation of the Laws was able to relieve. The long and complex legislative history of the "present insanity" rule in New York has largely been concerned with two basic problems: how to examine the defendant, and what disposition to make of a defendant found unfit to proceed.

Beginning in 1842 (as part of the legislation establishing the first state mental hospital at Utica), the legislation authorized medical examinations of any defendant in custody who appeared to be mentally ill, to be followed by discretionary commitment of mentally ill defendants to the new hospital at Utica.[6] We have previously seen how male and female prisoners who were mentally ill were removed from civil state hospitals in the mid-nineteenth century and were placed in the specially established Auburn Asylum for Insane Convicts.[7] Likewise, in 1869 the legislature first began to experiment with discretionary separate hospitalization, at the Auburn Asylum, of defendants accused but not convicted of arson, murder, and attempted murder.[8]

In the decade between 1871 and 1881 the primary focus of legislation was on the question of the examination of the defendant thought to be mentally ill. It was during this period that the lay lunacy commission type of investigation

[5] Much of the legislation is traced by Parker, The Determination of Insanity in Criminal Cases, 26 Cornell L.Q. 375 (1941). See also People v. Pershaec, 172 Misc. 324 (Gen. Sess. 1939); People v. Whitman, 149 Misc. 159 (Gen. Sess. 1933). We do not deal here with the problem of defendants found incompetent to be tried because of mental defect. (N.Y. Corr. Law §§ 438, 451.)

[6] N.Y. Laws 1842, ch. 135, § 32.

[7] Chapter II, *supra*, at note 11. See also Appendices A and B.

[8] N.Y. Laws 1869, ch. 895, §§ 1–2.

was authorized (as an alternative to the 1842 medical examination procedure), first in limited cases in 1871 [9] and 1874,[10] and then in the case of any indicted defendant by the original section 658 of the 1881 Code of Criminal Procedure.[11]

As noted elsewhere,[12] the 1890 State Care Act brought severe overcrowding to the civil state hospitals, and for a time required the transfer to the Auburn Asylum (as reorganized at Beacon as the Matteawan State Hospital) of all defendants hospitalized as unfit to be tried. Early in the present century the legislature began to require that the examination of certain defendants be conducted at a public hospital instead of in jail. The lingering 1842 statute (which overlapped section 658 as to indicted defendants) was finally brought into the Code of Criminal Procedure in 1909 (as section 836, later renumbered section 870),[13] and was repeatedly amended: first, in 1910 to require public hospital examination in New York City misdemeanor cases, and again in 1924 to require it in all New York City cases.[14] Probably because of the security problem involved in hospital examinations of accused felons,[15] they were largely eliminated in felony cases by a 1933 amendment[16] and the much-abused lunacy commission[17] was granted a brief reprieve. At the

[9] N.Y. Laws 1871, ch. 666, § 1.
[10] N.Y. Laws 1874, ch. 446, tit. 1, art. 2, § 20.
[11] N.Y. Laws 1881, ch. 442, § 658.
[12] Chapter II, *supra*, at note 19.
[13] N.Y. Code Crim. Proc. § 870, as added by N.Y. Laws 1909, ch. 66, § 2, and renumbered by N.Y. Laws 1936, ch. 892, § 2.
[14] N.Y. Laws 1910, ch. 557, § 1; N.Y. Laws 1924, ch. 337.
[15] See, e.g., Appendix A, at note 154.
[16] N.Y. Laws 1933, ch. 564.
[17] See note 20, *infra*.

same time, however, hospital examinations were made applicable to all non-felony cases arising anywhere in the state.

The Law Revision Commission studied [18] the problem during the first year of its existence, and some changes resulted in 1936; thereafter the "three disinterested persons" of the lunacy commissions would include at least one attorney and one psychiatrist.[19] The "Lunacy Commission Racket" was finally smashed in 1939.[20] All the overlapping provisions of the Code of Criminal Procedure were repealed and new procedures were substituted. Thereafter section 658 et seq. would apply to defendants indicted for felonies or misdemeanors, and section 870 et seq. to all others "charged with" crimes or offenses.

After 1939 several of the sections were repeatedly amended, principally in 1953 to make commitment to Matteawan mandatory for all indicted defendants.[21] A full analysis of the 1939 Desmond Act as it existed in 1962 and cur-

[18] 1934 N.Y. Law Rev'n Comm'n Rep. 641, N.Y. Leg. Doc. No. 60(1) (1936).

[19] N.Y. Laws 1936, ch. 460, § 1; see 37 Colum. L. Rev. 151 (1937).

[20] N.Y. Laws 1939, ch. 861; see Desmond, New York Smashes the Lunacy Commission "Racket," 30 J. Crim. L., C. & P.S. 653 (1940); 39 Colum. L. Rev. 1260 (1939). Surveys there cited reported that lunacy commissioners (who did not have to possess any particular qualifications) examining the defendant were likely to be county committeemen, obstetricians, or relatives of the appointing judge. Between 1926 and 1930 there was usually one physician appointed, but in only 6% of the cases was he a psychiatrist. Between 1930 and 1936 New York City paid $1,359,949 in fees to commissioners. During the same period 575 commissioners received 4,799 commissions, one politician receiving 78 (worth $45,750) from his brother who was a county judge.

[21] N.Y. Code Crim. Proc. § 662-b, as amended by N.Y. Laws 1953, ch. 785, § 3, eff. July 1, 1953. See Appendix A, *infra*, at note 220.

rent practice under it was made in the prior report of this committee.[22]

Reduced to its essentials, the Code of Criminal Procedure at present provides[23] that if at any time between arrest and sentencing a court or magistrate having jurisdiction of a defendant charged with a felony, misdemeanor, or offense has reasonable grounds[24] to believe that the defendant "is in such a state of idiocy, imbecility or insanity that he is incapable of understanding the charge, indictment or proceedings or of making his defense," or if an indicted defendant pleads insanity at the time of the crime as a defense, the

[22] Mental Illness and Due Process, 220–38. See also Note, Mental Condition of an Accused: Pre-trial, Trial and Post-trial, 13 Syracuse L. Rev. 287 (1961).

[23] N.Y. Code Crim. Proc. §§ 658–62-f, 870–76. The first group of statutes applies to defendants who have been indicted before the question of fitness arises, and the second group applies to all others. See also N.Y. Family Court Act § 251 (commitment for observation of any person under the court's jurisdiction whenever such examination "will serve the purposes of this act"). Although this provision is outside the scope of our study, the committee believes that the services of the Mental Health Information Service should be made available to persons remanded by the Family Courts. See also N.Y. Mental Hygiene Law § 78 (governing emergency admissions) and its infrequently used provision (subsection 4) authorizing commitments by magistrates in criminal actions.

[24] Grounds relied upon by the court might range from a history of mental illness (cf. People v. Smyth, 3 N.Y. 2d 184, 143 N.E. 2d 922, 164 N.Y.S. 2d 737 [1957]), to attempts at suicide while in custody (e.g., People v. White, 140 Misc. 701, 251 N.Y. Supp. 396 [Gen. Sess. 1931]); see C. E. Smith, Psychiatric Examinations in Federal Mental Competency Proceedings, 37 F.R.D. 171, 173 (1964). In its prior study the committee found that the results of an informal preliminary medical examination were frequently used as a basis for ordering a complete examination and report. Mental Illness and Due Process 223–24 (1962).

court has "discretion"[25] to order a psychiatric examination to determine his present fitness to stand trial (sections 658, 870). The examination must be made by two "qualified psychiatrists"[26] who, in cases outside New York City, are designated by the director of community health services or by the superintendent of a public hospital which has been certified by the Commissioner of Mental Hygiene as having adequate facilities, and who, in New York City cases, are designated by the Director of the Division of Psychiatry in the City's Department of Hospitals from the division's staff (section 659). The examination may be made in the jail in which the defendant is being held, or at another more convenient place of detention, or the court may commit the defendant to a hospital for up to sixty days (section 660). When they complete their examination,[27] the psychiatrists must submit to the court "a full and complete" report (section 662). If the examiners report that the defendant is in-

---

[25] It is also a "duty" if grounds are strong enough, and the court's exercise of discretion may be reviewed upon appeal from a conviction. People v. Brown, 13 N.Y. 2d 201, 205, 195 N.E. 2d 293, 295, 245 N.Y.S. 2d 577, 580 (1963), cert. denied, 376 U.S. 972 (1964); People v. Smyth, 3 N.Y. 2d 184, 187, 143 N.E. 2d 922, 923–24, 164 N.Y.S. 2d 737, 738–39 (1957); accord, Pate v. Robinson, 383 U.S. 375 (1966); note 43, *infra*. On the other hand, a defendant may secure release from an unwarranted commitment for examination by habeas corpus. People ex rel. Schildhaus v. Warden, 37 Misc. 2d 660, 235 N.Y.S. 2d 531 (Sup. Ct. 1962); see People ex rel. Apicella v. Kings County Hosp., 173 Misc. 642, 18 N.Y.S. 2d 523 (Sup. Ct. 1940).

[26] A licensed physician with five years' practice and five years' training and experience in the care and treatment of persons with mental disorders may be certified as a "qualified psychiatrist" under N.Y. Mental Hygiene Law § 27(4).

[27] The statute (N.Y. Code Crim. Proc. § 661) does not prescribe any particular type of examination but does still permit the psychiatrists to conduct formal hearings if they choose.

capable of standing trial, and if the court agrees (after a hearing, if demanded by either side under section 662-a),[28] the criminal proceedings are suspended (or in some cases "terminated")[29] and the defendant is hospitalized (sections 662-b, 872, 873, 875).

2. THE STANDARD

The first area of the committee's concern is the apparent confusion that exists concerning the standards or criteria by which a defendant's fitness to stand trial is determined. In 1828, New York codified the common-law principle that had long forbidden the trial, sentencing, or punishment of an "insane person . . . while he continues in that state." [30] The statute was not interpreted to mean that every mental illness would justify a delay, but only those which prevented the defendant from "understanding the nature and object of the proceedings going on against him," or from rightly comprehending "his own condition in reference to such proceedings," or from conducting "his defense in a rational manner"; if the defendant met these standards he was, "for the purpose of being tried, to be deemed sane, although on some

[28] See note 43, infra.

[29] The distinctions among "suspended," "terminated," and "disposed of" cases are discussed infra, in connection with part 6., Disposition of the Criminal Charge.

[30] 2 Rev. Stat. 697 (1828). See Hale, Pleas of the Crown, 34, 35 (1650). The first English statute was 39 & 40 Geo. 3, ch. 94, § 2 (1800). The various common-law authorities are collected in Youtsey v. United States, 97 Fed. 937 (6th Cir. 1899). Cf. Rubin, Psychiatry and Criminal Law: Illusions, Fictions and Myths 40–52 (1965). See generally Glueck, Mental Disorders and the Criminal Law (1925); Lindman & McIntyre, The Mentally Disabled and the Law (1961); Tompkins, Insanity and the Criminal Law (1960) (bibliography); Weihofen, Mental Disorder as a Criminal Defense (1954).

other subjects his mind may be deranged or unsound." [31] A similar test was thereafter added to the statutes[32] and was continued in the present Penal Law until 1965.[33] At present the required standard of fitness is stated in the Code of Criminal Procedure, and prohibits the conduct of any criminal proceedings against any defendant "in such state of idiocy, imbecility or insanity that he is incapable of understanding the charge, indictment or proceedings or of making his defense. . . ." [34]

The test of mental illness sufficient to deny a defendant, in his own interest, the right to a speedy trial has long consisted, therefore, of two elements: (a) inability to understand the proceedings, or (b) inability to make a defense. In modern practice the second element is commonly expressed in terms of the defendant's ability to cooperate with his counsel or assist in his defense.[35] A survey by the American Bar Foundation found that despite variations in phrasing, the same common law criteria have been retained by most of the United States.[36] They are also applied to defendants in federal criminal prosecutions.[37]

[31] Freeman v. People, 4 Den. (N.Y.) 9, 25 (1847).

[32] N.Y. Laws 1882, ch. 384, § 1.

[33] Former N.Y. Penal Law § 1120, repealed by N.Y. Laws 1965, ch. 593, § 1.

[34] N.Y. Code Crim. Proc. §§ 658, 870.

[35] It has been observed that "the rule arose in a day when defendants were not afforded counsel." Foote, A Comment on Pre-Trial Commitment of Criminal Defendants, 108 U. Pa. L. Rev. 832, 844 (1960).

[36] Lindman and McIntyre, The Mentally Disabled and the Law 357–382 (1961); See also Model Penal Code § 4.04, comment (Tent. Draft No. 4, 1955); Weihofen, Procedure for Determining a Defendant's Mental Condition Under the A.L.I. Model Penal Code, 29 Temp. L.Q. 238 (1956).

[37] 18 U.S.C. § 4244 (1964) ("unable to understand the proceedings against him, or to properly assist in his own defense"). In Dusky

The problem, of course, is to determine how clearly a defendant should and does "understand" the proceedings, and in what manner he should and can "assist" in his defense. For example, a defendant may understand that he is charged with a particular crime and be aware of the possible penalty for it if convicted, but if he is unable "to talk rationally" [38] about the crime or circumstances leading up to it, he may be found unfit to proceed. Such defendant would be ill equipped either to supply his counsel with vital facts, or follow the evidence against him, or testify in his own behalf. On the other hand, if a defendant is willing to work with his counsel and his delusions bear no significant relation to the matters involved, he may be considered fit to proceed even though he is mentally ill. A defendant, of course, need not be able to understand every step or aspect of the proceedings. Few laymen, and not all attorneys, can do so. However, he should be oriented as to time and place, and should be able to appreciate the basic elements of a criminal trial, such

---

v. United States 362 U.S. 402 (1960) (per curiam), the Court paraphrased the test as whether the defendant "has sufficient present ability to consult with his lawyer with a reasonable degree of rational understanding—and whether he has a rational as well as factual understanding of the proceedings against him." Cf. Pate v. Robinson, 383 U.S. 375, 388 (1966) (Harlan, J., dissenting), where it was stated: "I assume no more is asked of state courts [than of federal courts] . . ."; Noble v. Sigler, 351 F. 2d 673, 677 (8th Cir. 1965), cert. denied, 385 U.S. 853 (1966) (Dusky rule applies to state defendants). See also People v. Hudson, 19 N.Y. 2d 137, 278 N.Y.S. 2d 593 (1967), and note 43, *infra*.

[38] See e.g., People ex rel. Fazio v. McNeill, 4 A.D. 2d 686, leave to appeal denied, 4 App. Div. 2d 874, 167 N.Y.S. 2d 422 (2d Dep't 1957), cert. denied, 356 U.S. 943 (1958); People ex rel. Bernstein v. McNeill, 48 N.Y.S. 2d 764 (Sup. Ct. 1944); cf. People v. Skwirsky, 213 N.Y. 151, 153, 107 N.E. 47–48 (1914).

as the roles of the parties, the plea, the jury, the verdict, the right to raise defenses, to testify, etc.[39] It is obvious, therefore, that the test of competence is sufficiently broad to permit the trial of a psychotic defendant when no unfairness will result, and also to forbid the trial of a defendant who is not psychotic because severe depression or emotional stress would prevent his full participation in defending himself.

That there is occasional confusion as to the meaning and application of the criteria, particularly among those psychiatrists not regularly concerned with this issue, is a fact within the individual professional experiences of the committee's members, but that regrettable fact is understandable. In New York, as elsewhere, the statute is couched in familiar but necessarily general legal terminology. It is expected to be applied by psychiatrists who are often themselves without a clear understanding of what the law requires, and who are offered no official guidance either by the form of the examination order signed by the court, or by the examination rules prescribed by the Policy Manual of the Department of Mental Hygiene.[40] It is perhaps to some degree because of an uncertainty as to what they should be looking for that the reports filed by examining psychiatrists have been criticized as failing to meet the statutory require-

[39] What a defendant should "understand" and to what extent he should be able to "assist" are discussed at length in the Report of the Committee on Problems Connected with Mental Examination of the Accused in Criminal Cases Before Trial, Judicial Conference of the District of Columbia Circuit (1965) (privately printed). See also Robey, Criteria for Competency to Stand Trial: A Checklist for Psychiatrists, 122 Am. J. Psychiatry 616 (1965); Slough & Wilson, Mental Capacity to Stand Trial, 21 U. Pitt. L. Rev. 593 (1960).

[40] State of N.Y. Dep't Mental Hygiene, Policy Manual § 409.

ments (N.Y. Code Crim. Proc. § 662) of "a full and complete report." As our prior study revealed, and some members of the committee still find, "often the report contains only a formal statement that the defendant is found to be mentally ill." [41] These difficulties are not peculiar to New York State, however. For example, similar problems have recently been reported in Massachusetts, Michigan, and the District of Columbia.[42] In view of the importance of the issue with respect not only to the defendant's right to a speedy trial, but also to the orderly administration of criminal justice, the committee believes that steps should be taken to assure more accurate and more uniform administration of the standard. Instead of attempting to draft a more particularly phrased statute, we recommend that every psychiatrist designated to conduct a pre-trial examination expressly be required by the court's order to submit his report in a format to be prescribed by agreement between the Commissioner of Mental Hygiene and the State Judicial Conference. The official form should contain instructions to the psychiatrist to give discrete though not necessarily exclusive attention to such particulars as we have discussed. A report in such form would also supply to the court considering whether to accept or reject

[41] Mental Illness and Due Process 227 (1962).

[42] See, e.g., the article by Dr. Robey, Director of the Massachusetts Correctional Institution at Bridgewater, *op. cit. supra* note 39 (Bridgewater, similar in function to Matteawan, is described by Powers, Massachusetts Department of Correction, 27 Am. J. Correc. [July–Aug. 1965] 21–22); Chayet, The Law and the Mentally Ill, Harvard Law School Bulletin 10 (July, 1967); the District of Columbia study mentioned in note 39, *supra;* a study made at Michigan's Ionia State Hospital by Hess & Thomas, Incompetency to Stand Trial: Procedures, Results, and Problems, 119 Am. J. Psychiatry 713 (1963); Vann & Morganroth, Psychiatrists and the Competence to Stand Trial, 42 U. Det. L. J. 75 (1964).

the findings a useful guideline for its own evaluation[43] of the defendant's fitness.

[43] At present either party may demand a hearing to controvert a report of fitness as well as of incapacity, N.Y. Code Crim. Proc. § 662-a. Where the defendant is reported fit and the court itself has no lingering doubts and neither side requests a hearing, it would not appear either necessary or desirable to require the court nonetheless on its own motion to convene a hearing in every case simply because with less information it had earlier been in doubt. But see Pate v. Robinson, 383 U.S. 375, 385–386 (1966), where it was stated: "We believe that the evidence [a "history of pronounced irrational behavior"] introduced on Robinson's behalf entitled him to a hearing on this issue [i.e., competence to stand trial]. The Court's failure to make such inquiry thus deprived Robinson of his constitutional right to a fair trial." See also People v. Hudson, 19 N.Y. 2d 137, 278 N.Y.S. 2d 593 (1967). The defendant in Hudson pleaded not guilty by reason of insanity, was examined as to his fitness to stand trial, and was reported fit. In the Court of Appeals the District Attorney of New York County conceded that Robinson "requires a hearing concerning the defendant's mental competence to stand trial, where—as here—that fact is put in issue during the trial." Respondent's Brief p. 17. "Moreover, while unaccountably failing specifically to controvert the report of the first two qualified examining psychiatrists, which would have called for a hearing under Section 662(a) of the Code, defendant's counsel did, from the outset, alert the court's attention to their inability to communicate with the defendant and his seeming inability to comprehend and participate in the trial. The trial court's response to trial counsel's initial claim—ordering the defendant examined by the Psychiatric Clinic of the court—while perhaps adequate for State purposes, must now be deemed short of the recently enunciated constitutional demand. Moreover, the Supreme Court deemed the issue sufficiently raised in Robinson when the Court heard the defense, notwithstanding the fact that the evidence of incompetence was adduced from lay witnesses. Here the defense consisted of expert testimony which related to the defendant's mental condition immediately preceding trial as well as his state of mind at the time of the trial. Again, if the record in Robinson necessitated a hearing in the interests of a constitutionally fair trial, the unavoidable conclusion is that this one did too." Id. p. 19. The court adopted the

Specifically, the committee makes the following recommendation:

RECOMMENDATION NO. 9 (*Uniform application of the standard of competence to be tried*).

(a) The Commissioner of Mental Hygiene and the Administrator of the State Judicial Conference should jointly develop, establish, and supply to every examining psychiatrist a uniform form of the report of the results of the examination required to be completed by the examiners and filed with the court. It should contain a reasonably detailed explanation of the legal criteria of capacity to be tried.

(b) The examiners' report should specify the nature and extent of the examination, a diagnosis and prognosis, and an opinion as to whether the defendant is dangerously mentally ill. So far as practicable, it should state the reasons for its findings, by making particular reference, for example, to those aspects of the proceedings which the defendant is not able rationally to understand, or by stating in reasonable detail, and in light of the particular circumstances of his own case, why he is believed not sufficiently able rationally to consult with his counsel.

(c) When an order of examination is made, the services of the Mental Health Information Service should be made available to the defendant to inform him of his rights and to report to the court in connection with its consideration of the results of the examination. Before confirming or rejecting the report of the examination the court should hold a hearing if demanded by the defendant or the people, or whenever there is sufficient doubt as to the validity of the report, upon the court's own motion. At any such hearing the defendant should be represented by counsel.

---

district attorney's suggestion that instead of a new trial, relief could appropriately be limited to remanding for "a new proceeding analogous to the so-called 'Huntley hearing' (People v. Huntley, 15 N.Y. 2d 72 [1965])" used for retrospective determination in confession cases. Id. p. 21.

3. PLACE AND DURATION OF EXAMINATION

The observation or examination of a defendant may be made[44] in the jail in which he is being detained, or at another place of detention, or the court may commit the defendant for up to sixty days to a state or county hospital certified by the Commissioner of Mental Hygiene as adequate for the purpose, or in New York City to the prison ward of a city hospital. There is apparently no central source of statistics on the frequency of examinations made in jails and other places of detention. It appears that these examinations (which avoid need for a 60-day commitment under section 660) are performed outside New York City when the nearby state or authorized county hospital has inadequate security facilities.

Outside New York City (and in a few New York City cases) the examination may take place in one of 19 state and county hospitals currently certified by the Commissioner of Mental Hygiene pursuant to section 659 as having adequate

---

[44] N.Y. Code Crim. Proc. §§ 660, 870. It appears that in New York City some post-arraignment defendants who have been remanded to detention are administratively moved to local psychiatric prison wards without court orders when thereafter they apparently become in need of immediate care and treatment for a mental disturbance. The practice does not appear to be expressly authorized by any statute. One statute (N.Y. Corr. Law § 508) authorizes such transfers only for conditions of "bodily health" which require "medical or surgical treatment." The interests of the defendant would better be served by amending section 508 to authorize temporary emergency administrative transfers from jail to prison ward for apparent mental illness requiring immediate attention, and requiring notice of the fact to be given to the court which remanded the prisoner, within 24 hours, for likely exercise of its discretion to order a temporary observation of the defendant as to his fitness to be tried.

facilities.[45] Between April 1, 1959, and March 31, 1964, some 2,178 defendants were examined in state hospitals.[46] Annual admissions for examination have declined over this period from 518 (1960) to 380 (1964).[47]

Representative statistics were supplied to the committee by Bellevue and Elmhurst Hospitals in the New York City Department of Hospitals. At Bellevue, in the six months from January to June 1964, some 648 defendants awaiting trial in the Supreme Court (219) or proceedings in the Criminal Court of the City of New York (429) were examined. Thereafter, 83 patients in the first group were committed to Matteawan, and 188 patients in the second group were committed to civil state hospitals. The average duration of observation at Bellevue is 21 days.

At Elmhurst, which examined only female defendants, 232 women were examined in the same six-month period on order of the Supreme Court (38) or Criminal Court (194). Thereafter, 52 defendants were committed to civil state hospitals and 8 to Matteawan. The Elmhurst ward, according to further information supplied [48] to us, has a capacity of

[45] State of N.Y., Dep't Mental Hygiene, Policy Manual § 450(a) (Feb. 1, 1966).

[46] Information supplied by Dep't of Mental Hygiene. Years ending March 31: 1960 – 518; 1961 – 523; 1962 – 362; 1963 – 395; 1964 – 380. See also Mental Illness and Due Process, App. I, Table 3 (Admissions by county and method for fiscal year ending March 31, 1960) (1962).

[47] See note 46, *supra*. Grasslands Hospital, maintained by Westchester County, but certified by the Commissioner of Mental Hygiene as an appropriate place of examination (see note 45, *supra*), has been examining an increasing number of defendants: 1960 – 179; 1961 – 173; 1962 – 240; 1963 – 251; 1964 – 338. Letter to staff director from Dr. A. Anthony Arce, Assoc. Dir. of Psych., Grasslands Hosp., Sept. 22, 1965.

[48] Letter to staff director from Dr. Harry I. Weinstock, Chief, Dep't Psych., City Hosp. Ctr. at Elmhurst, Oct. 8, 1965.

26 beds, but its average occupancy is 43 patients. The average duration of a patient's residence on the ward is 28 days. Its medical staff includes two attending psychiatrists who average two hours with each patient; a resident psychiatrist who averages 1½ hours per patient; and a psychologist who averages two hours per patient. There is constant supervision by a nursing staff which (a) on the day tour includes three registered nurses, two practical nurses, one nurse's aide, (b) on the evening tour includes one RN, two PNs, and one NA, and (c) on the night tour includes no RNs, two PNs, and one NA. Twenty-four-hour custodial service is provided by 24 men from the City Department of Correction.

These representative statistics appear to indicate that thousands of mental examinations are ordered by courts each year throughout the state. Using as a basis only the limited experience of the six-month period at Bellevue and Elmhurst Hospitals during which 331 out of 880 defendants examined were subsequently judicially determined unfit to proceed and were therefore hospitalized, we find that the criminal proceedings against more than sixty percent were resumed. Percentages on a statewide basis are not available. We do know,[49] however, the total combined admissions to Matteawan and to civil state hospitals of defendants judicially determined incompetent to be tried: 1960 – 549; 1961 – 565; 1962 – 549; 1963 – 599; 1964 – 676. It would appear, therefore, that statewide the number of persons examined far

[49] The following statistics, supplied by the Dep't of Mental Hygiene, indicate the total number of defendants committed to civil hospitals under N.Y. Code Crim. Proc. §§ 872, 873, 875, by fiscal year ending March 31: 1960 – 483; 1961 – 362; 1962 – 349; 1963 – 374; 1964 – 483. To these figures we have added the totals of patients admitted to Matteawan in the same fiscal years under N.Y. Code Crim. Proc. §§ 662-b, 872 (excluding transfers from civil hospitals), 875, appearing in Table 2.

exceeds the number of persons judicially declared unfit to proceed.

The committee is concerned that an unnecessary burden is too frequently being imposed upon the defendants, upon the courts, and upon the hospitals by the requirement of an in-patient examination for up to sixty days in every case. During the month or more that will be required for his examination (either in a jail or in a hospital), a defendant who might otherwise have been released on bail is denied his freedom. Even in a hospital, which may be overcrowded and understaffed,[49a] the defendant will be denied "ground privileges." [50] His family may lose his income. He may even lose his job. All despite the fact that a man accused of a crime is presumed innocent, may ultimately be acquitted, and, even if convicted, may yet be released on probation. He receives a psychiatric examination that even on an in-patient basis will not likely involve more than a few hours or even less. Protection of the defendant against the possibility of an unfair trial, and of the public against unwarranted danger, can be achieved in a less costly manner.

We propose that the statute (N.Y. Code Crim. Proc. § 660) be amended, *first*, to limit the period of remand for observation to thirty days (subject to extension for cause where necessary), and *second*, expressly to authorize the examination in appropriate cases to be conducted on an out-patient basis[51] without mandatory incarceration or hos-

[49a] See e.g., Report of Special Advisory Committee on Psychiatric Services to the Commissioner of Hospitals, New York City (Sept. 21, 1961).

[50] Dep't Mental Hygiene, *supra* note 45, at §450-f (Feb. 1, 1966): "Defendants who are being held for examination pursuant to the Code of Criminal Procedure . . . should not be given ground privileges."

[51] The Judicial Conference of the District of Columbia, *op. cit.* *supra* note 39, has made the following recommendation: "Recom-

pitalization. In questionable cases where the grounds for doubt of the defendant's ability are not truly serious, the statute should authorize the court which orders the examination also to request the official designated to conduct the examination to cause an immediate preliminary medical evaluation to be made either in jail or at the hospital. The court should thereafter be authorized to order the formal examination to be conducted by scheduled out-patient interviews whenever (1) the hospital director (or other appropriate designated official) agrees, based upon the defendant's prior mental history and the results of the preliminary evaluations, (2) the defendant is otherwise entitled to release on bail, and (3) nothing in the defendant's criminal record or in the circumstances of the alleged crime itself suggests the possibility that his release would constitute a danger to himself or to others. If a defendant fails to appear as scheduled for the examination, his bail could be revoked and the examination made, as at present, in a jail or hospital. Adoption of this proposal should help relieve unnecessary overcrowding in hospitals and would avoid placing unnecessary burdens upon defendants and their families without sacrificing the protection of the public.

Accordingly, the committee makes the following recommendation:

RECOMMENDATION NO. 10 (*Out-patient examination*). Psychiatric examinations ordered by courts should expressly be allowed to be conducted on an out-patient basis without mandatory in-

---

mendation 7. The status of an accused who has been enlarged on bail should not be changed because of a pre-trial mental examination being ordered for him and an accused who is otherwise eligible for bail should not be denied bail because a pre-trial mental examination is ordered for him; if, however, the examining psychiatrists report that the accused's confinement is necessary for an effective examination, the court should be empowered to commit to a mental hospital."

carceration or hospitalization in any case in which there is no reason to suspect the defendant to be dangerously mentally ill or in need of immediate hospitalization, providing the director of the examining hospital or clinic or other appropriate official agrees and providing the defendant is otherwise entitled to release on bail. The period of remand for observation at the place of incarceration or in a hospital should be limited to thirty days, subject to extension for cause where necessary.

4. HOSPITALIZATION PROCEDURES

a) The Statutes

In its prior report[52] the committee analyzed the statutes and actual practice relating to the hospitalization of the mentally ill defendant accused of crime. The committee at that time recommended (1) that the statutes be amended to eliminate the unequal treatment involved in hospitalizing some defendants at Matteawan rather than a civil hospital because of geographic or procedural or financial reasons rather than the needs of the patient; (2) that the decision on the kind of hospital be made by the court, with a statutory policy in favor of civil hospitals, in all misdemeanor and felony cases; (3) that defendants charged with simple offenses continue to be hospitalized by civil certification and the charges thus disposed of; (4) that procedures for release of patients from Matteawan in the event of dismissal of the charges against them be clarified, and (5) that the advisability of providing periodic judicial review to patients awaiting trial or those against whom charges had been dismissed be considered by the then newly established Temporary State Commission on Revision of the Penal Law and Criminal Code.

[52] Mental Illness and Due Process 220–38 (1962).

The first recommendation resulted in 1965 amendments[53] eliminating automatic commitment to Matteawan, but the decision on the type of hospital is initially made by the Commissioner of Mental Hygiene, not by a court. Release procedure has been clarified as suggested. No action has been taken with respect to automatic periodic judicial review.

The committee's prior report analyzed the statutes (N.Y. Code Crim. Proc. §§ 658–62-f, 870–76) in terms of three classes of cases.

i) *Cases involving a charge of an offense anywhere, or a nonindictable misdemeanor outside New York City.*

Pursuant to section 873 these defendants were then and are still hospitalized under civil certification procedures, and such hospitalization is still deemed a final disposition of the charge. The committee previously approved this procedure as to "offenses." However, the section still applies to nonindictable misdemeanors *outside* the City of New York[54] and whether or not an information has been filed.

ii) *Cases involving a charge of an indictable crime in which no indictment has been returned, or, in New York City, a charge of a misdemeanor on which no information has been filed.*

At the time of the prior report, section 872 called for civil certification proceedings under section 74 of the Mental Hygiene Law, with the court having discretion to commit

[53] N.Y. Code Crim. Proc. §§ 662-b, 872, 873 (as amended by N.Y. Laws 1965, ch. 540, eff. Sept. 1, 1965).

[54] See Mental Illness and Due Process 228 n.14 (1962); cf. Fifth Interim Rep. Temp. Comm'n on Rev'n Pen. Law and Crim. Code 14–18, N.Y. Leg. Doc. No. 28 (1966) (analysis of structure of lower criminal courts).

either to Matteawan or to a civil hospital. The patient could thereafter be administratively transferred between a civil hospital and Matteawan, or vice versa. The criminal proceedings would "terminate," but an indictment could at any time thereafter be returned or an information filed (and warrant lodged), or the proceedings reopened, unless the district attorney has stated in writing his decision not to do so. The committee found that, except for serious felonies, New York City cases under this section were usually sent to civil hospitals, but that outside New York City the practice was to secure an indictment before certification. The indictment then brought the case under section 662-b (see iii, *infra*) with mandatory commitment to Matteawan. Some district attorneys gave as a reason the fact that the county would not be liable for the expense of hospitalization at Matteawan because of a provision in section 412 of the Correction Law making patients there a charge upon the state.[55]

Effective September 1, 1965, section 872 was amended. The section now requires the court[56] to commit the defendant to the custody of the Commissioner of Mental Hygiene for up to 30 days during which the commissioner may place the defendant either at Matteawan or at a civil hospital, whichever he deems "*appropriate*."

If within the 30-day period the director of a *civil hospital* into which the defendant has been placed believes retention for "continued care and treatment" is necessary, he must

[55] Former N.Y. Correc. Law. § 412, repealed by N.Y. Laws 1965, ch. 254.

[56] On its face the statute now authorizes the lower criminal court in which the defendant has been arraigned (after arrest, by a committing magistrate) to entertain the hospitalization proceedings. See, e.g., People v. Dumas, 51 Misc. 2d 929, 274 N.Y.S. 2d 764 (Sup. Ct. 1966) (committed under section 872 by a "police justice").

obtain a further court order by applying under section 73 of the Mental Hygiene Law for an order of involuntary[57] retention.

However, if the defendant was administratively placed at *Matteawan* and the superintendent believes the defendant "is so dangerously mentally ill" as to require continued treatment and confinement there, he may request permission of the Commissioner of Mental Hygiene to apply for a new court order of certification to Matteawan under section 85 of the Mental Hygiene Law.

Section 872 continues to provide that the proceedings "terminate," but may be reopened.[58] It also continues to provide for administrative inter-departmental transfers of such patients.[59] District attorneys who would formerly have

[57] After hospitalization under section 872, and prior to the lodging of a warrant (if any) against the patient by the district attorney, the former defendant becomes "a civil patient in all respects and . . . all the therapies and privileges accorded other civil patients in our institutions must be accorded these patients. . . ." Dep't of Mental Hygiene, Office of Legal Affairs, Memorandum No. 66 (Nov. 23, 1965). Moreover, "the department has also made the administrative determination that if such patient [i.e., one committed under section 872] improves sufficiently within the thirty-day period to be suitable and is willing, he may be converted to voluntary status rather than a court-authorized retention order being obtained." Memorandum No. 67 (Dec. 28, 1965).

[58] The district attorney is free to "reopen" the proceedings by causing an indictment to be filed with the trial court and a warrant thereon lodged against the patient at the hospital. Section 872 then provides that "all further proceedings" are governed by section 662-b (as though he had been indicted before the issue arose).

[59] Prior to amendment in 1965, section 872 required the court to use the civil certification procedures of the Mental Hygiene Law § 74, but with the added option of committing to Matteawan. Although treated as a "civil patient" for some purposes, the patient whom the court placed in a civil hospital and who was thereafter indicted, was held properly subject to administrative transfer to Matteawan

averted the possibility of a civil certification under old section 872 will now profit nothing from securing an indictment prior to commitment, for section 662-b, discussed next, has

because "her confinement under a civil commitment arising out of a criminal charge is sufficiently close to the status of a sentenced and incarcerated person so as to render the cases dealing with administrative transfers of prisoners to be pertinent and applicable herein by analogy. As to sentenced prisoners, the New York courts have held that the question of the place of confinement is not an open question once a valid commitment has been made. [Citing cases.] . . . New York State could well consider that a person under a criminal charge, and in particular a charge of a crime of violence, need not be given the opportunity to rebut an administrative determination that he or she requires transfer to a security institution. Under the instant facts, this court holds that New York's decision to treat the problem of transferring an insane criminal defendant *who has committed a crime of violence* differently from the transfer of a non-criminal insane inmate is not arbitrary or capricious." United States ex rel. Morgan v. Wolfe, 232 F.Supp. 85, 99–101 (S.D.N.Y. 1964) (Edelstein, J.). (Emphasis added.)

As to prisoners, the court misconstrued the significance of People ex rel. Brown v. Johnston, 9 N.Y. 2d 482, 174 N.E. 2d 725, 215 N.Y.S. 2d 44 (1961), since the "valid commitment" there referred to would be to the correctional hospital itself (Dannemora), and not, as here, to a civil hospital. (See Chapter I *supra,* at note 11.) The court presumed that the patient had in fact committed the crime and could therefore be treated as a prisoner serving a sentence. An earlier decision, U.S. ex rel. Carroll v. McNeill, 294 F. 2d 117 (2d Cir. 1961) (discussed in Chapter II *supra,* at note 39), holding it unconstitutional to make an administrative transfer (under N.Y. Correc. Law § 412) to Matteawan of a patient admitted to a civil hospital on civil process simply because of a past criminal conviction, was held to be "distinguishable" apparently because an indicted defendant is more nearly analogous to a time-serving prisoner than a time-expired prisoner.

However, section 872 then and now also permits transfers of defendants whose hospitalization (and "termination" of the proceedings) has not been followed by an indictment or who were indicted, but against whom the indictments have since been dismissed. Such patients are no longer even accused of crime and under Baxstrom v.

also been amended to eliminate automatic commitment to Matteawan.

iii) *Cases involving a crime for which an indictment has been returned, or, in New York City, a misdemeanor for which an information has been filed.*

Since 1953 these defendants have been subject to mandatory hospitalization at Matteawan under section 662-b which applies to all indicted defendants, and section 875 applying to New York City misdemeanants[60] against whom informations are filed. The committee was critical of this inflexible rule.

Effective September 1, 1965, section 662-b was amended to require the court to commit the defendant to the custody of the Commissioner of Mental Hygiene who may administratively decide to place the defendant in a civil hospital or Matteawan, whichever he deems "appropriate." The

---

Herold, 383 U.S. 107 (1966), they should not be subject to administrative transfer since all other civil patients are entitled to judicial proceedings under N.Y. Mental Hygiene Law § 85. Placements of section 872 patients at Matteawan were stopped for a time (see note 70, *infra*) and those previously placed at Matteawan had almost all been removed (compare Tables 3, 8, 9).

[60] A minor fact that seems to have escaped notice is that section 875 (which governs post-information misdemeanor cases in New York City and incorporates by reference the rules of section 662-b) was amended in 1962 (N.Y. Laws 1962, ch. 698, § 27) to reflect the merging of N.Y.C. Magistrates' Court and Special Sessions. New York City Criminal Court Act, N.Y. Laws 1962, ch. 697, eff. Sept. 1, 1962. Section 875 now refers to cases in "the Criminal Court of the City of New York," rather than "in the Court of Special Sessions." Since all offenses, and misdemeanors at any stage, come before some term of the Criminal Court, a needless possibility has been created that argument can be made to apply section 662-b to offenses or section 872 to misdemeanors after information, or section 875 to misdemeanors before information.

defendant may be administratively transferred thereafter (as formerly) between departments. On hospitalization, the proceedings in such cases are neither finally disposed of nor terminated, but are simply suspended until the hospital returns the defendant as ready to be tried. The commitment will last as long as the defendant is still unfit.[61] If years or decades later the indictment or information is dismissed, the defendant may be retained in the hospital for an additional 30 days after service of notice of the dismissal upon the Commissioner. Within those 30 days the hospital director may apply for a court order to retain the defendant (*a*) under section 73 of the Mental Hygiene Law if it is a civil hospital and the defendant is in need of continued care and

[61] Patients placed at Matteawan under section 872 must receive immediate attention and either be discharged or recommitted within 30 days. There is no urgency or deadline for section 662-b patients. This perhaps explains why (according to statistics supplied by Dr. W. C. Johnston, Director of Matteawan), out of the first 41 patients admitted under section 662-b between September 1 and December 31, 1965, only one had been discharged as of December 31, 1965. However, out of the first 34 patients admitted under section 872 between October 11 and December 31, 1965, by the latter date 15 had been discharged to a jail (ready to be tried), or to home (recovered and district attorney not interested in prosecuting, or charge dismissed), or to a civil hospital (still unfit to be tried but not eligible for recommitment under N.Y. Mental Hygiene Law § 85 as dangerously mentally ill), and four had been recommitted under N.Y. Mental Hygiene Law § 85.

The statute seems to guarantee a difference in the promptness with which the first class of patients can be processed. The figures also indicate that in only 20% of the section 872 cases did a court agree with the Commissioner of Mental Hygiene that a defendant was dangerously mentally ill. Finally, it was suggested that in some cases a 30-day period of observation may be inadequate to determine whether to testify that a patient is dangerously mentally ill.

For a significant post-Baxstrom development see note 70, *infra* (administrative placements at Matteawan terminated and then resumed).

treatment, or (*b*) under section 85 of the Mental Hygiene Law if it is Matteawan and the defendant is dangerously mentally ill.

These provisions are basically similar to those added to section 872 dealing with the same accused felons and misdemeanants *before* indictment or information. The major distinction is that administrative placement[62] at Matteawan is limited to 30 days under section 872 whereas under section 662-b the administrative placement may last a lifetime if the indictment is never dismissed. It is impossible rationally to justify this distinction since so far as the statutes are concerned the only difference between the two classes is purely mechanical—one is indicted sooner than the other.

b) The Need for Revision

The 1965 amendments made a significant advance by eliminating mandatory hospitalization at Matteawan. At the same time, however, the decision as to where to send the defendant was completely taken out of the courts' hands. The purpose was to allow the place of an individual's hospitalization to be determined by his medical needs. What might be called the conclusive presumption of dangerousness based on the mere fact of an early indictment for any crime was rejected. Presumably, fewer defendants would thereafter be sent to Matteawan. However, at least in the early months of their application, the statutes entrusting the choice of hospital to administrative decision based upon clinical judgment caused a perceptible increase in the volume of patients going to Matteawan. In other words, experience here appears to agree with that reported above

---

[62] See note 70, *infra.*

concerning hospital placements of time-expired prisoners. The amended procedures took effect on September 1, 1965. In the entire prior fiscal year (ending March 31, 1965), 135 indicted patients had been sent to Matteawan under the mandatory provisions of former section 662-b.[63] In the first four months[64] (September 1 to December 31, 1965) under the amended section, 41 indicted patients were administratively assigned to Matteawan and the total for the fiscal year ending March 31, 1966, actually increased from 135 (1965) to 149.[65] During October and November of 1965 only five indicted patients were administratively placed in civil hospitals.

Under amended section 872, again during its first four months, the number of pre-indictment patients sent to Matteawan ratably increased. During the entire prior fiscal year (ending March 31, 1965) *courts* decided to send only 47 defendants[66] to Matteawan under section 872. In the first four months after the decision was left to clinical judgment, however, there were 34 assignments to Matteawan, and by March 31, 1966, the total number of section 872 admissions for the fiscal year rose to 85 or almost double the volume (47) of the prior fiscal year.[67] These placements were made by the Commissioner of Mental Hygiene on the basis of a copy of the report of the examination filed with the court. The commissioner required those reports to include any indications that the defendant may be "dangerous to him-

[63] See Table 2.
[64] These statistics on early use of sections 662-b and 872 were supplied by Dr. W. Cecil Johnston, Director of Matteawan, and by the Department of Mental Hygiene.
[65] See Table 2.
[66] See note 64, *supra*.
[67] See Table 2.

self or others," his "criminal history, if known," and any other "information which may be useful to the commissioner in designating the appropriate institution to which to assign the defendant." [68]

We agree with the basic but unarticulated premise of the new procedures—that a defendant who is to be hospitalized should be cared for in an ordinary civil state hospital unless the nature of his illness requires care and custody under high-security conditions. We also believe, however (as discussed in connection with our recommendation no. 6),[69] that, so long as a central high-security facility is used for these patients, the decision as to their need for such custody should be made by a court[70] (at the time of commitment or, as with other patients, at any appropriate time thereafter). The available statistics appear to indicate that when the decision is left to clinical judgment, placement at Matteawan occurs in a far greater number of cases than when a court decides, and that very few defendants sent by courts to civil

[68] Dep't Mental Hygiene, *supra* note 45, at § 450 (Feb. 1, 1966). It is worthy of note that a patient's being "dangerous to himself" has never been a basis for commitment (under N.Y. Corr. Law § 412 or N.Y. Mental Hygiene Law § 85) of a civil patient to Matteawan, and that danger "to others" is rarely shown to a court's satisfaction (Chapter II, *supra*); and that so far as a "criminal history" is concerned, the Baxstrom decision and repeal of section 412 prohibit reliance upon former convictions as reason to dispense with judicial determination of dangerous mental illness.

[69] See Chapter II, *supra*.

[70] The committee was advised in April, 1966 by E. David Wiley, Counsel to the Department of Mental Hygiene, that in light of the Baxstrom decision the department would send all section 872 patients to civil hospitals, and as many section 662-b patients as possible. However, it appears that in May, 1967, the department resumed administrative placement of some section 872 patients at Matteawan. Our recommendation therefore states to some extent the existing practice.

hospitals under the former procedures had to be transferred to Matteawan at a later date.[71]

Defendants accused but not yet convicted of crime should be treated as civil patients. Apart from the interference with personal liberty occasioned by a denial or requirement of bail and his obligation to appear for trial, a citizen loses none of his rights simply because he has been accused, even when the accusation is made by a busy grand jury. The defendant has forfeited none of the rights to vote, to pursue a profession, etc., that a convicted former prisoner may have forever surrendered, but he is treated far less generously when it comes to his need for hospitalization. In our view the state should not continue to view the mere pendency of a criminal charge or indictment as a rational basis for denying these patients the same protection against unnecessary confinement in a central maximum-security correctional institution which is given to every other patient not actually serving a penal sentence—a judicial determination of dangerous mental illness.

We have already indicated [72] why in our view it is eminently unwise for the state to maintain a maximum-security mental hospital outside the Department of Mental Hygiene. We would propose, therefore, that such pre-conviction defendants as are determined by a court to require care and treatment under high-security conditions should be hospitalized under appropriate security within that department. All other defendants should be hospitalized in ordinary civil institutions, subject, of course, to such routine security as

[71] As indicated by Table 2, between April 1, 1959, and March 31, 1966, only 20 patients were transferred from civil state hospitals to Matteawan under section 872. As reported above, however (note 49, *supra*), in only the first five years of the same seven-year period, over 2000 defendants were admitted to civil hospitals (under all sections).

[72] See discussion of recommendation no. 6, Chapter II, *supra*.

will assure their continued amenability to prosecution. We would add, however, that a defendant who is found currently unfit to proceed but who, in medical judgment, is suitable for participation in such therapeutic programs as home visits, open-ward hospitalization, etc., should not *automatically* be denied an opportunity to benefit from such programs simply because he is accused of crime. A defendant whom a court has authority to release on bail, or parole on his own recognizance, should continue to be eligible for consideration for such release pursuant to an order of the court despite a finding of incapacity to be tried.

Specifically, we make the following recommendation:

RECOMMENDATION NO. 11 (*Civil hospitalization*). Any defendant accused of a misdemeanor or a felony, who is judicially determined to be incompetent to be tried, whether or not indicted, should be hospitalized for treatment, under such security as is necessary to assure his continued availability to prosecution, in an appropriate institution under the jurisdiction of the Department of Mental Hygiene, to be returned to court when he is again fit to proceed unless otherwise lawfully discharged.

The order of hospitalization shall authorize the hospital director, under such conditions of bail or parole as the court deems necessary, to permit the defendant to participate in such therapeutic programs (including open-ward and home visits) as the director in his discretion deems appropriate, unless for good cause the court decides to withhold such permission until further order of the court. Such an order may be made at any time thereafter upon the application of the hospital director, the defendant, or the Mental Health Information Service.

5. AUTOMATIC PERIODIC JUDICIAL REVIEW

There has never been any provision of law requiring a court periodically to review the condition of an *indicted* defendant hospitalized under section 662-b as unfit to stand trial. The law is unclear as to defendants who are *charged with* a crime(but not yet indicted) and who are hospitalized under section 872 as civil patients: those placed in civil hospitals are regarded [73] as entitled to the same periodic review procedures (N.Y. Mental Hygiene Law §§ 73, 74) as have been available to other civil patients since 1965, but the status of those placed at Matteawan and retained after the first 30 days by a section-85-like proceeding is uncertain.[74]

As a result, at least under section 662-b of the Code of Criminal Procedure, the decision whether to return a patient to court for a resumption of the criminal proceedings is left to the discretion of the director of Matteawan or of the civil hospital, guided by the opinions of his staff. With the right to trial dependent upon staff review and evaluation, and with the chronic staff shortages which characterized its early decades,[75] it is no wonder that by 1930 Matteawan

[73] See note 57, *supra.* Since by direction of section 872 the defendant in such a case is originally admitted as a civil patient against whom no criminal proceedings are pending, he is entitled to periodic review, etc., under N.Y. Mental Hygiene Law §§ 73–74 as an ordinary civil patient. After indictment, however, the criteria governing his eligibility for release must automatically shift (under section 872) to include consideration of his fitness to stand trial. The statutes do not expressly indicate whether he thereupon forfeits the rights to review, etc., which he enjoyed upon admission, or whether the right to review survives and is broadened to include fitness to be tried.

[74] See text accompanying note 57, *supra.* The section 872 patient retained at Matteawan by a section 85 proceeding after 30 days would at least receive the periodic review of the issue of need for secure hospitalization as dangerously mentally ill as added to section 85 in 1966 (see Chapter II, *supra,* at note 74).

[75] See Appendix A.

reported [76] that unconvicted defendants had "accumulated" to over 60% of its population. The conservative release policy evidenced in 1897 by the "fact that the average length of confinement [of defendants] . . . considerably exceeds, excluding life sentences, the average length of time served by convicts in the three great state prisons," [77] was apparently still in effect as recently as 1940 and 1950 when, respectively (and still with severe staff shortages), only 11 and 15 defendants were returned to courts for trial.[78] In current years, however, the annual volume[79] of returns to court has ranged from 97 (1960) to 254 (1966). We are informed that during 1965 there were 900 appearances by patients (of all classes) at staff release conferences. Increased admissions, staff expansion, and the availability of tranquilizers[80] have all doubtless contributed to these recent and tremendous increases. It is also obvious, however, that staff attitudes toward eligibility for return have changed.

Nevertheless, the historical and essential fault of the present system is that it permits the right to a speedy trial to depend too much upon the irrelevant circumstance of the size of an institutional budget. The system should, so far as possible, assure both the defendant and society that charges will promptly be disposed of by dismissal, plea, acquittal, or

[76] 1930 Ann. Rep. Comm'n'r Correc. 20 N.Y. Leg. Docs. 311, 313 (No. 85, 1931).

[77] N.Y. Times, Aug. 28, 1897, p. 2, col. 1. See Appendix A.

[78] See Table 6.

[79] See Table 5.

[80] The committee was advised that Matteawan does not return to court any patient who is receiving tranquilizing medication. (See recommendation no. 16.) In another context we were also advised that the hospital will "on occasion" return a patient to court even though he denies the crime he is alleged to have committed. See generally Scrignar, Tranquilizers and the Psychotic Defendant, 53 A.B.A.J. 43 (1967).

conviction. At present, and putting aside vain recourse to habeas corpus[81] and the uncertain scope of civil review procedures,[82] that assurance against unnecessary delay depends solely upon the number, quality, and attitude of a hospital's medical staff. Despite present circumstances, in our view that assurance must be bolstered by an express statutory requirement of automatic periodic review of the defendant's condition by a court. All other civil patients receive this protection, and there is no reason to justify withholding it from this class of patient.

After hospitalization of a defendant the courts should not, as they now do, assume a purely passive role, merely waiting for a medical judgment of recovery and then, perhaps, ordering a new local examination[83] and hearing to verify that judgment. Instead, at essentially[84] the same intervals as in the case of involuntary civil patients (six months, one year, then every two years) the unrecovered defendant's condition should automatically be reported to a court with a request for authority to retain him. The same procedures (N.Y. Mental Hygiene Law §§ 73, 74) respecting notice, the right to demand a hearing, and the assistance of the Mental Health Information Service should apply to

[81] Out of 292 "appearances by patients on writs of habeas corpus" during the entire 1965–1966 fiscal year only 5 patients (of all classes) obtained discharge from Matteawan via this route. Ann. Rep. Matteawan State Hosp. (March 31, 1966). See also Table 5 (discharges by court order).

[82] See text accompanying notes 73–74, supra.

[83] See text following note 99, infra.

[84] Initial involuntary admission (on two physicians' certificates) of a civil patient is valid for only 60 days (N.Y. Mental Hygiene Law § 72). Here, however, the initial admission is made by a court after an opportunity for a hearing and, therefore, we do not believe it necessary or desirable to provide for court review with exactly the same frequency as in civil cases.

defendants, except that the issue to be decided would include the defendant's fitness to be returned to court. To facilitate such hearings, a copy of the papers filed in the criminal proceedings should accompany the defendant upon hospitalization. If the defendant has been judicially ordered hospitalized in a central high-security facility (see recommendation no. 6, *supra*), then, of course, the court should also consider the question of continued dangerous mental illness. We would make one qualification, however. Since in New York the complex issue of competence to be tried is at present[85]—and, in our opinion, properly—decided by a court, we would not recommend that an order authorizing continued retention of a defendant be made subject to a jury trial review. In terms of the issue to be decided the proceeding is sufficiently distinct from the review in ordinary civil cases to support the difference in treatment as a rational limitation with a legitimate purpose.[86]

Accordingly, we make the following recommendation:

RECOMMENDATION NO. 12 (*Automatic periodic judicial review*). The procedure for the involuntary retention and periodic judicial review of ordinary civil patients, including the assistance of the Mental Health Information Service, should apply to defendants hospitalized as at present unfit to stand trial (*a*) except that the issues considered upon review should be whether the defendant

[85] See generally Parker, The Determination of Insanity in Criminal Cases, 26 Cornell L. Q. 375 (1941).

[86] The same would not be true of the question of continued dangerous mental illness, however, since on that issue there is no distinction between defendants and other patients to warrant or support less favorable treatment.

In the event a jury trial review of need for hospitalization resulted in favor of defendant's release while in medical opinion he is still unfit to be tried, an appropriate case might be made for court supervised out-patient treatment as discussed in our recommendation no. 16, *infra*.

is currently fit to proceed as well as whether he is in need of continued hospitalization, and (b) except that a determination that a defendant is unfit to be tried should not be subject to a jury trial review, and a determination of need for continued hospitalization should be subject to a jury trial review.

6. DISPOSITION OF THE CRIMINAL CHARGE

a) Present Procedures

The criminal proceedings against a defendant who has been indicted before he was ordered hospitalized are "suspended" for the period of his disability under section 662-b of the Code of Criminal Procedure. If he is hospitalized after a post-arrest arraignment, but before the formal charge (e.g., indictment) is made, then, under section 872, the proceedings are "terminated." [87] However, unless after at least six months of inactivity he indicates in writing his intention not to prosecute, the district attorney may at any time reopen the "terminated" proceedings by causing an indictment (or in New York City misdemeanor cases, an information) to be filed and a warrant thereon lodged at the hospital. In the latter case the proceedings on the indictment (or information) then are transferred to the "suspended" category, just as though the indictment preceded hospitalization.

There is no statutory limit upon how long prosecution may be "suspended," and no effective limit upon the length of time a prosecutor may wait before deciding whether to reopen a "terminated" prosecution. Thus, a prosecution might be "suspended" for as long as 64 years,[88] or, as is reported

[87] As indicated at note 52, supra, proceedings involving non-criminal offenses (e.g., disorderly conduct, N.Y. Penal Law § 722, and vagrancy, N.Y. Code Crim. Proc. § 887) are deemed finally disposed of under N.Y. Code Crim. Proc. § 873. The section also applies to nonindictable misdemeanors outside New York City.

[88] See note 1, supra, and accompanying text, and Tables 8, 9.

to have recently occurred in Nassau County,[89] a "terminated" case might be reopened by securing an indictment, 20 years after the defendant was first arraigned and ordered hospitalized.

i) Pre-trial motions

A blanket[90] suspension of all further proceedings against the indicted defendant is more a burden than a blessing in this age of universal representation by counsel.[91] There is no

[89] See People v. Delfs, 31 Misc. 2d 655, 220 N.Y.S. 2d 535 (Dist. Ct. 1961). We are advised that in 1965 the defendant was finally indicted for the homicide of his wife in 1940. The defendant had been continuously confined at Matteawan since March 1941. The 1961 proceeding cited was a successful motion to dismiss the original post-arrest information, etc., in the court of first arraignment, designed to achieve complete civil-patient status for defendant (including possibility of transfer out of Matteawan). When efforts to secure transfer were made the defendant was then indicted.

[90] Under section 662-b(3), the suspension is lifted only to the extent of allowing motions to dismiss the indictment (a) at any time to facilitate removal of a non-resident to another state or federal institution, and (b) after two years of hospitalization in any other case. See note 93, infra. In both cases, however, the consent of the district attorney is an express requirement, and the court may not act without it. See e.g., Negro v. Dickens, 22 App. Div. 2d 406, 255 N.Y.S. 2d 804 (1st Dep't 1965). See also, Proceedings of the American Law Institute 319 (1961). But see People v. Dumas, 51 Misc. 2d 929, 274 N.Y.S. 2d 764 (Sup. Ct. 1966) (motion by counsel to inspect grand jury minutes preliminary to motion to dismiss indictment filed against patient after admission to Matteawan under section 872 was granted even though defendant was still hospitalized; no discussion of the "suspension" rule).

[91] See e.g., N.Y. County Law § 722, as added by N.Y. Laws 1965, ch. 878 (assigned counsel systems); People v. Witenski, 15 N.Y. 2d 392, 207 N.E. 2d 358, 259 N.Y.S. 2d 413 (1965). See also Chapter I at note 15.

provision[92] authorizing the court to entertain a well-founded motion by counsel challenging the sufficiency of the indictment. No authority is provided to move to suppress illegally seized evidence or to exclude statements and confessions. No method is provided, while memories are fresh and documentary evidence still available, to establish and preserve a defense, such as an alibi. The statute appears even to deny counsel for the hospitalized defendant the opportunity to show that the statute of limitations had lapsed prior to his indictment. In short, suspension of the proceedings is a positive handicap to the defense, and when it lasts for years or decades, it is for all practical purposes an insurmountable bar to effective assertion of the defendant's constitutional rights.

The only actions expressly permitted are motions (under section 662-b [3]) to dismiss the indictment (*a*) at any time to facilitate removal of a non-resident mentally ill defendant to another state or country or (*b*) after two years of hospitalization in any other case.[93] The motions require the express consent of the district attorney, however, and the court cannot act without that consent. The statistics avail-

[92] That there should be, see Foote, A Comment on Pre-Trial Commitment of Criminal Defendants, 108 U. Pa. L. Rev. 832 (1960); Report of the Committee on Problems Connected with Mental Examination of the Accused in Criminal Cases Before Trial, Judicial Conference of the District of Columbia Circuit 143 (1965) (privately printed); Model Penal Code § 4.06(3) (1962). New York procedures for "conditional examination" and "depositions" are not geared to assist mentally ill defendants. N.Y. Code Crim. Proc. §§ 620–657.

[93] These provisions were added to section 662-b in 1958 (N.Y. Laws 1958, ch. 705). According to the Commissioner of Mental Hygiene, as to non-residents the change was expected to "help to relieve overcrowding in our mental institutions . . . and save the taxpayers of this state the cost of their care." As to residents confined at least two years: "under the present law these mentally deranged defendants must be held in our civil mental institutions in close confinement in

able to us would indicate either that few such motions are made,[94] or that few prosecutors will consent to them. Whatever the reason, our survey of the 1965 resident population at Matteawan indicated that there were at least 820 indicted patients[95] in residence and that indictments had been dismissed against only 79. Of the 79 dismissals, 68 were from New York City's five counties including 43 from Kings County. There were four homicide cases[96] among the 79

a manner approximating a jail. The most effective treatment procedures must be denied to them because of the restrictive nature of their custody. This results in delay and in most cases obviates any possibility of recovery, amounting to virtual life imprisonment of many. In the interest of humanity, justice, and plain common-sense economy, the rigid provisions of this law need modification with proper safeguards that are provided in this bill. . . . These are enabling and permissive amendments which vest in the prosecuting authorities and the courts the ultimate judgment as to the wisdom in the public interest of dismissal of an indictment in any case; a power which they do not have under present law." N.Y. Legislative Annual 468 (1958). As to the anticipated assumption of decisional responsibility by prosecutors see Negro v. Dickens, 22 App. Div. 2d 406, 255 N.Y.S. 2d 804 (1st Dep't 1965).

[94] The director of Matteawan is authorized by the statute to make the motion on defendant's behalf and in many cases contacts the district attorney for his consent. We are advised that in one such case, a 1965 request for consent to dismissal of murder charges against a patient admitted on March 26, 1918, it was revealed that the district attorney's files went back only to 1921 and no record or indictment relating to the case could be found.

[95] To this figure, based on admissions under section 662 (see Table 8), would have to be added the number (not known to us) of preindictment (section 872) patients who were indicted after arrival at the hospital. After the Baxstrom decision (see Chapter II, *supra*), and because of the hospital's diligent efforts to obtain dismissals of old indictments (see note 94, *supra*), the number of section 662-b patients at Matteawan against whom there were indictments outstanding as of December 20, 1966, was reduced to 500 (of which, we are informed, 243 were "murder and homicides"). See Tables 8 and 9. Upon dismissal the patients were transferred to civil state hospitals.

[96] Crimes charged in the 79 cases included assault (28), sodomy

110

indictments, and only 24 dated from years prior to 1945 [97] (although there were at least 172 indicted patients at Matteawan since 1945 or longer[98]).

ii) *Disposition of defendants returned to court*

An effort was made to ascertain the final disposition of all defendants returned to courts from Matteawan as ready to be tried (or sentenced) in the period April 1, 1963, to March 31, 1964. Questionnaires were sent to 41 district attorneys for information on 261 cases against 259 defendants. Replies were received on 235 cases in 30 counties. In some cases of incomplete answers, it was possible to interpret the information provided, but where the response was too vague to permit reasonable interpretation it was counted as "Not Clear."

Crime charged

The 261 cases included the following alleged crimes.[99]

Murder	39	Carnal abuse	4
Manslaughter	6	Endangering health	4
Homicide	4	Incest	1
Robbery	49	Dangerous weapon	11
Assault	40	Arson	9
Burglary	38	Narcotics	4
Larceny	28	Malicious mischief	3
Rape	7	Kidnapping	2
Sodomy	11	Libel	1

---

(8), larceny (8), robbery (6), burglary (6), arson (5), rape (4), dangerous weapon (4), murder (2), manslaughter (2), carnal abuse (2), forgery (1), extortion (1), obstructing a railroad (1), not clear (1).

[97] Dismissals by year admitted to Matteawan: 1960–1965 (6); 1955–1959 (23); 1950–1954 (14); 1945–1949 (12); 1940–1944 (1); 1935–1939 (12); 1930–1934 (4); 1925–1929 (4); 1920–1924 (3).

[98] As of September 16, 1966, this figure was reduced to 93. See Table 9.

[99] In 49 out of 261 cases the charge was a type of homicide. It is

Period of hospitalization and new mental examinations

New mental examinations were ordered in 77 or approximately one-third of the cases, but most (69) were in New York City (52) and Erie County (17). In 21 cases the charge was homicide, in 17 robbery, in 11 burglary, in 9 assault, and in 7 larceny. Twelve of the re-examined defendants were subsequently re-hospitalized.

	Total	Erie County	New York City Total	Bronx	Kings	New York	Queens
Selected Geographical Analysis							
Cases studied	235	18	145	9	45	68	23
Re-examined	77	17	52	8	8	23	13
At a hospital	56	–	52	8	8	23	13
In jail	20	17	–	–	–	–	–
Not clear where	1						
District attorney's motion	25	17	8	4	–	1	3
Court's motion	18	–	15	4	1	1	9
Defendant's motion	4	–	2	–	1	–	1
Not clear	30						
Result: Fit	59	16	37	8	4	13	12
Result: Unfit	12	1	10	–	4	5	1

We might note that in 23 out of 25 cases there was no opposition to the district attorney's motion, and in 15 out of 18 cases no opposition to the court's motion. The re-examined defendants had been awaiting trial up to 32 years, but 55 out of 77 had been hospitalized no more than 3 years:

not correct to assume, therefore, that the alleged murderer committed to Matteawan currently faces a release policy as conservative as once it might have been. We should note, however, that a 1965 population

Year Committed	Total Returns	Patients Re-examined
1963	63	22
1962	58	19
1961	30	14
1960	19	4
1959	14	5
1958	7	1
1957	6	2
1956	2	–
1955	1	–
1954	6	4
1953	7	2
1951	4	1
1950	1	–
1949	3	1
1948	4	1
1947	1	–
1946	1	–
1943	1	–
1931	1	1
Not clear	6	–
Total	235	77

study (see Table 8, note 1) indicated that 365 patients then hospitalized at Matteawan were accused of manslaughter, murder, homicide or attempted murder. Most of them (240 cases) were from New York City: Bronx – 35; Kings – 72; New York – 110; Queens – 19; Richmond – 4. Although classified according to 22 different diagnoses, more than half (217) were schizophrenic, and the second largest group (33) were diagnosed as suffering from psychosis with psychopathic personality. They had been hospitalized at Matteawan as long as 55 years. After old indictments were dismissed in 1966 (see note 95, *supra*) the number was reduced to 243. We might note that upon return to court in New York County, 8 homicides were reexamined, 3 in Queens, 3 in Kings, 3 in Erie, 2 in Suffolk, and 1 in Ulster for a total of 20 out of 49. An analysis of 150 consecutive case records of patients accused of murder and committed to Matteawan over five years (1956–1961) has been published. See Lanzkron, Murder and Insanity: a Survey, 1963 J. Am. Psych. Ass'n 754–758.

Final disposition of defendant

So far as we can determine only 11 defendants were actually tried, and of those only two were acquitted (both as having been insane at the time of the crime—one of first-degree murder after two years at Matteawan, and the other of robbery after six months at Matteawan). By far the largest number chose to plead guilty to a reduced charge which in many of the older cases may have led to a sentence of "time served." [100]

Disposition	Total	Among Cases Re-examined
1. Tried and acquitted as insane	2	–
2. Tried and convicted	9	3
3. Pleas of guilty		
a) As charged	17	–
b) As reduced	137	43
c) Not clear	4	–
4. Youthful offender	11	3
5. Charge dismissed [101]	21	7
6. Discharged on own recognizance[102]	1	1
7. Recommitted as unfit	12	12
8. Sentenced on return[103]	5	–
9. Not clear	16	8
	235	77

[100] Time spent in custody is credited toward satisfaction of sentence. N.Y. Penal Law § 2193. Cf. N.Y. Times, Sept. 2, 1966, p. 13, col. 4 (defendant indicted for murder and committed to Matteawan in 1940 allowed to plead guilty to assault upon return to court in 1966 and was ordered "discharged").

[101] For possible significance of this figure on actual rate of "insanity acquittals" see Chapter IV, *infra*.

[102] See N.Y. Code Crim. Proc. § 669; Mental Illness and Due Process 233 (1962).

[103] See N.Y. Code Crim. Proc. § 481.

b) Proposed Revisions

i) Partial suspension of proceedings

In our view only those aspects of the proceedings absolutely requiring the participation of the defendant should be postponed, and principally that means trial on the question of guilt.[104] Counsel should not be barred from making pre-trial motions otherwise available to the defendant and, in the circumstances, not requiring his assistance or dependent upon his testimony. To protect the defendant who upon recovery can supply further grounds for any such relief as counsel may have previously sought unsuccessfully, denial of relief should be without prejudice to renewal after defendant's recovery.

RECOMMENDATION NO. 13 (*Partial suspension of proceedings*). The proceedings against a defendant judicially found to be unfit to be tried should, as at present, be suspended during the period of his disability, but the suspension should not operate to disadvantage the defendant unnecessarily. Only those aspects of the proceedings requiring the participation of the defendant should be postponed. Counsel should be permitted to make pre-trial motions otherwise available to the defendant and, in the circumstances, not requiring his assistance. Denial of relief should be without prejudice to renewal after defendant's recovery. There should also be provision to take and preserve essential evidence that might otherwise be unavailable at trial.

[104] We do not believe the defendant should have a right to insist upon an immediate "trial" at which the prosecution must establish a prima facie case and, if it does, a right to a second trial upon recovery (or immediate dismissal if it cannot). See 1961 Proceedings of The American Law Institute 318–22; Model Penal Code § 4.06 (3), (4) (1962) (alternative sections), and 1962 Proceedings 116 (such "post-commitment hearing" included in Model Penal Code only as an "alternative").

Adoption of this proposal would make possible and encourage earlier disposition of pending charges and would avoid forfeiture of valuable evidence. The mechanics for implementing the criminal law's ancient concern for the mentally ill defendant would no longer be more likely to cause than to avoid prejudicing the defendant who is now aided by counsel.

ii) *Prompt and uniform prosecution in felony and misdemeanor cases*

Felony cases

Under Section 872 the proceedings against defendants hospitalized prior to indictment are terminated, but the defendant may at any time thereafter be indicted (or, in New York City misdemeanor cases, be informed against) unless the district attorney states in writing his intention not to prosecute.[105] We believe that the period within which a decision to prosecute may be made should be reasonably limited. To protect defendants against unnecessarily prolonged uncertainty as to their need to anticipate and prepare a defense, and at the same time to afford the prosecution a reasonable opportunity to make an informed decision, we propose that, in the case of a felony, the period be fixed at one year. If the prosecution is re-opened within that year, then of course the defendant or his counsel may begin immediately to take such steps as are appropriate within our prior recommendation.

During the period between hospitalization and the indictment the patient should be treated as a civil patient so far as eligibility for treatment, privileges and discharge is con-

---

[105] Thus, a defendant who is a veteran was made eligible for transfer to a veteran's hospital. See N.Y. Legislative Annual 255 (1960).

cerned. However, we would recommend that as a precaution against the possibility of a hospitalized defendant's being discharged so soon that through administrative problems, or despite his best efforts, the district attorney may not have had time to secure an indictment and lodge a warrant,[106] the statutes should require the hospital directors to notify the district attorney at least two weeks in advance of their expectation to discharge a defendant who will have been hospitalized less than one year. In anticipation of the possibility of exceptional cases in which the one-year limitation might prove to be an unjustified imposition upon the prosecution, provision might be included to authorize the court in its discretion to permit, prior to the expiration of one year, an additional extension of time upon an application by the district attorney.

Misdemeanor cases

The "terminated" prosecution of a misdemeanor may also be reopened under section 872 "at any time" by the district attorney's filing an information (or where appropriate in cases outside New York City obtaining an indictment), unless after six months he indicates in writing "his determination not to reopen the matter." As in the case of a "terminated" felony case, we recommend that the period within which the case may be reopened should be reasonably limited. Six months would appear to us to be a sufficient time within which to require the decision to reopen to be made and an information (or an indictment) to be filed. The

---

[106] In its present form (as amended in 1965) section 872 requires the hospitals to recommit or to discharge (as recovered) a patient within 30 days of his arrival. If no indictment (and warrant) has been filed by that time there is no basis for returning a recovered patient to the court instead of to the community. See note 61, *supra.*

same precautions as to notice by the hospital director and discretionary extensions suggested above in connection with felony cases should also apply to misdemeanors except that instead of one year the basic period for these matters should be six months.

We also note that, under section 873, an order hospitalizing a defendant informed against or charged outside New York City with certain misdemeanors is deemed to be a final disposition of the crime charged.[107] No similar provision is made with respect to similarly charged defendants in New York City. The two classes of defendants may be distinguished only by geography, and therefore both should be treated alike. We recommend that in *every* misdemeanor case in the state the prosecution be terminated subject to reopening, as discussed above, if the order of hospitalization precedes filing of the information (or indictment).

If hospitalization occurs after filing of the information (or indictment) in any misdemeanor case, the proceedings should uniformly be "suspended" subject to resumption upon defendant's return to court. This is at present the rule as to indicted misdemeanors outside New York City (under section 871) and those misdemeanor cases in New York City for which an information has been filed in the Criminal Court (under section 875). It should also apply (under section 873) to non-indictable misdemeanors[108] outside New York City for which an information has been filed.

RECOMMENDATION NO. 14 (*Prompt and uniform prosecution*).

107 Under section 873 a charge of a non-criminal "offense" (e.g. N.Y. Penal Law § 722, disorderly conduct) against a defendant in any part of the state is also deemed finally disposed of by hospitalization (but see note 60, *supra*). The committee previously approved this procedure, Mental Illness and Due Process 221 (1962).

108 See Mental Illness and Due Process, ch. 7 n. 14; note 54, *supra*, and accompanying text.

(a) Felony cases. If a defendant charged with a felony is examined and hospitalized before an indictment is filed, the district attorney should be required to secure an indictment within 12 months or during such additional period as the court may grant. If an indictment is filed before or during such period, a warrant should be lodged at the institution in which the defendant is hospitalized, and when sufficiently recovered to proceed, he should be returned to court. If the formal charge is not timely filed, the proceedings should be dismissed and further prosecution permanently barred, and the defendant should be discharged by the hospital unless within 30 days a new order is obtained authorizing his retention as an ordinary civil patient until he is no longer in need of hospitalization.

(b) Misdemeanor cases. Similar provisions should be applied to defendants charged with any misdemeanor anywhere in the state who are hospitalized prior to the filing of an information or indictment in the trial court, except that the period within which the district attorney must act should be six months.

(c) The proceedings against any defendant accused of any misdemeanor, and against whom an information or indictment has been filed prior to (or timely, after) the order of hospitalization, should be "suspended" as in all felony cases.

iii) *Dismissal of prosecution*

Our previous recommendation proposed setting one-year and six-month limitations respectively upon the right to reopen "terminated" felony and misdemeanor prosecutions against defendants hospitalized *before* the filing of formal charges. Further protections are required for those who are hospitalized *after* (or when) the indictment or information is filed. Thus far, we have proposed (recommendation no. 13) merely that such defendants, against whom proceedings are "suspended," not be denied access to the court to assert or preserve defenses that might elicit early and favorable disposition of the charge. More is needed.

119

Our study indicated that a defendant may be hospitalized, and the opportunity for trial delayed, for months, years, decades, or even a lifetime. There obviously are cases of such great delay that it is manifestly unfair to require the defendant to anticipate even the possibility of a prosecution. A defendant who has been hospitalized longer than the maximum period for which a conviction could have (or probably would have) sent him to prison receives credit for that time[109] and is unlikely to demand a trial. A plea of guilty and sentence costs him nothing—except the innumerable social and economic impediments that follow automatically upon the fact of a conviction.[110] It is not unreasonable to suppose that an innocent defendant returned to court as recovered may elect to plead guilty simply to achieve immediate and complete release from custody.

The statutes should be amended to permit the court, during the period of hospitalization and suspension, and without awaiting the defendant's recovery and return, to dismiss the prosecution in any felony or misdemeanor case, without requiring as they now do (section 662-b[3]) that two years elapse and that the district attorney consent. Upon application made by or on behalf of the defendant hospitalized, the court should be expressly authorized to dismiss the information or indictment whenever the nature of the charge, the maximum or probable sentence that would be imposed if he were convicted, and the length of actual [111] delay would, in its opinion, make it unfair to further postpone the case.

---

[109] N.Y. Penal Law § 2193.

[110] See, e.g., Amnesty Rules, N.Y.L.J., Oct. 3, 1966, p. 1. See also N.Y. Correc. Law §§ 700–06 (as added by N.Y. Laws 1966, ch. 654, eff. Oct. 1, 1966) (discretionary relief of first offenders from forfeitures and disabilities automatically imposed by law).

[111] As to prospective delay see Greenwood v. United States, 350 U.S. 366 (1956); Foote, *op. cit. supra* note 92, at 838.

After dismissal the defendant's release from hospitalization should in all respects be governed by the procedures applicable to ordinary civil patients.

Accordingly, we make the following recommendation:

RECOMMENDATION NO. 15 (*Dismissal of prosecution*). If a defendant charged with a felony or misdemeanor against whom proceedings are left "suspended" is hospitalized for so long a period as to render it unjust in the court's opinion thereafter to resume the proceedings, the court should expressly be allowed to dismiss the prosecution in the interest of justice, and the defendant should thereafter be hospitalized as an ordinary civil patient under a new court order.

iv) *Discretionary alternatives to hospitalization*

The committee is of the opinion that in some rare cases a defendant who is not mentally fit to be tried may not require actual hospitalization. Only in cases of non-criminal offenses (such as vagrancy and disorderly conduct) and lesser misdemeanors outside New York City does the existing statutory system (N.Y. Code Crim. Proc. § 873) permit release of a defendant to out-patient treatment. If a defendant does not require and would not benefit from actual hospitalization, the court should be authorized in its discretion to release him, whether charged with a felony, misdemeanor, or offense, if he is otherwise entitled to release on bail. The court in such a case should be authorized to condition the release and postponement upon such terms as it deems appropriate, including out-patient treatment and periodic examination as to fitness as well as to need for hospitalization. The court, of course, should base its decision upon all the information available to it, including the defendant's past criminal record, prior mental history, the nature of the alleged crime, the nature of his incapacity, and the recommendations of the examining psychiatrists.

Granting courts this discretion would avoid mandatory hospitalization of those patients, however few, who can adequately and safely be treated on an out-patient basis or cared for in some other suitable manner, with revocation of bail and remand or hospitalization as assurance of co-operation. It might also avoid mandatory hospitalization of those persons who, for example, through great age, are found technically unfit to be tried but who are not dangerous to themselves or to others, are not likely to be improved by hospitalization, and will be adequately cared for in some other suitable manner subject to the right of the prosecution to request periodic re-examination.

Where no sacrifice of public protection or of the interests of justice is involved, to insist upon hospitalization in every case may, in some cases, be to demand surrender of an accused's liberty as the price of what is justified as a protection of his rights.[112] Protection against abuse through malingering can be provided by (*a*) frequent re-examination, (*b*) discretionary hospitalization, especially if the apparently affected symptoms indicate either a treatable or potentially dangerous condition, (*c*) exclusion of the pre-trial medical release period from computation of satisfaction of the sentence ultimately imposed, and (*d*) revocation and remand or hospitalization for non-cooperation in treatment.

The limited period recommended for formal presentation of charges against a defendant (recommendation no. 14, *supra*) should be counted, in this case, from the date of release to out-patient treatment, and should be applied in the same way as it is recommended to be applied to hospitalized defendants.

---

[112] Federal practice permits such release. See, e.g., United States v. Gorobetz, 156 F. Supp. 808 (D.N.J. 1957).

If a defendant who was initially hospitalized is, in the opinion of the hospital director,[113] no longer in need of hospitalization but is not yet competent to be tried, a report to that effect should be made to the court for possible exercise of its discretion to order a suitable alternative to hospitalization if the defendant would be entitled to bail.

In summary, we make the following recommendation:

RECOMMENDATION NO. 16 (*Discretionary alternatives to hospitalization*). Courts should be granted discretion, where appropriate, to order suitable alternatives to hospitalization of defendants mentally unfit to be tried. The decision should be based upon a complete evaluation of the defendant's circumstances and the public interest, and should contain such terms and conditions as are necessary to protect against malingering.

v) *Old-law patients*

All defendants admitted to Matteawan or to a civil state hospital as incompetent to be tried under the Code of Criminal Procedure should expressly be granted the benefits of the proposed statutory revisions. They or their counsel should be permitted to make motions and to preserve defenses, etc. Patients charged with felonies or misdemeanors who have been hospitalized longer than one year or six months, respectively, should enjoy the benefit of the proposed limitation upon the right of the prosecution to reopen "terminated" cases unless the prosecution is reopened one year or six months (respectively) from the effective date of the statutory revision. The hospital directors should be required to notify the appropriate district attorneys of the name and status of every "charged-with" patient in residence who will have been hospitalized prior to that effec-

---

[113] See also note 86, *supra.*

tive date, so that deliberate decision whether to reopen may be made as to every old-law patient who has not yet been indicted, and to avoid oversights.

Every defendant-patient should be granted access to the Mental Health Information Service and automatic periodic judicial review beginning within six months of the effective date of such revision.

No defendant should be retained at Matteawan State Hospital longer than six months after the effective date of the proposed revisions. Any defendant-patient at Matteawan for whom continued hospitalization is judicially determined to be required (as, e.g., upon the first occasion for periodic review) should thereupon be ordered hospitalized in a civil state hospital. Thereafter such patient[114] should in all respects be governed by the procedures we have recommended to be adopted for all future cases.

In summary, as to old-law patients we recommend the following:

RECOMMENDATION NO. 17 (*Old-law patients*). The benefits of each of our proposed revisions (recommendations nos. 11–16) should be expressly extended to apply to all patients previously admitted to state mental hospitals under these procedures.

[114] We are informed that as of December 20, 1966 with no new admissions then expected under section 872 (but see note 70, *supra*) and with a reduced volume of admissions under section 662-b, the total number of defendants hospitalized at Matteawan was only 508. (See Table 3.)

CHAPTER IV

Persons Acquitted of Crime by Reason of Insanity

We turn finally to the statutes governing commitment to a mental hospital of defendants who have been tried for crimes, but who have been acquitted on the ground that they were "insane" at the time of the commission of the act. As in our 1962 study, we do not deal with the insanity defense itself.[1] Our concern is limited to the procedure governing disposition of the defendant who has successfully raised the defense.

1. THE STATUTES

At Governor Seward's suggestion,[2] the landmark 1842 legislation establishing New York's first state mental hospital at Utica also contained the state's first statute dealing specifically with the disposition of persons acquitted of crime

[1] Mental Illness and Due Process 238–44 (1962). See N.Y. Penal Law § 1120 (as added by N.Y. Laws 1965, ch. 593, § 1, eff. July 1, 1965).

[2] 3 Messages from the Governors 935 (Lincoln ed. 1909) ("prudence, justice and humanity recommend that persons acquitted of crimes on the ground of mental aberration should be brought under sanity discipline"). According to Deutsch, The Mentally Ill in America 401 (2d rev. ed. 1949), a defendant so acquitted in New York in 1674 was banished from Flushing to Staten Island where he was to be put to work by order of the local magistrate who was also empowered "to *punish* him according as he may deserve" if he should "*behave badly.*"

by reason of insanity. If the court found the defendant's insanity continued in any degree, it was obliged to commit him to the Utica Asylum where he would remain until a court believed it "safe, legal and right" to order his release.[3] After 1869 the court had discretion to commit the defendant to the 10-year-old "State lunatic asylum for insane criminals, at Auburn," if the crime of which he was acquitted was arson, murder, or attempted murder.[4] After further amendments in 1874,[5] a provision was included in the 1881 Code of Criminal Procedure[6] and survived, without further legislative attention, until 1960.

Between 1881 and 1960, section 454 of the Code of Criminal Procedure required the criminal court to commit the defendant "to the State lunatic asylum" if it deemed "his discharge dangerous to the public peace or safety." Thereafter the patient might be released only upon the criminal court's approval of the hospital director's certificate of recovery.[7] In 1960 New York enacted new procedures for commitment and discharge of this class of patient.[8] Section 454

[3] N.Y. Laws 1842, ch. 135, §§ 31, 34; see People v. Griffen, 1 Edm. Sel. Cas. 126 (Chenango O.&T. 1845), and People v. Kleim, 1 Edm. Sel. Cas. 13 (N.Y. O.&T. 1845) for early applications of the new provision.

[4] N.Y. Laws 1869, ch. 895, § 1.

[5] N.Y. Laws 1874, ch. 446, §§ 2, 28, 30–33.

[6] N.Y. Laws 1881, ch. 442, § 454 ("When the defense is insanity of the defendant the jury must be instructed, if they acquit him on that ground, to state the fact with their verdict. The court must, thereupon, if the defendant be in custody, and they deem his discharge dangerous to the public peace or safety, order him to be committed to the state lunatic asylum, until he becomes sane.").

[7] Note 6, supra; see N.Y. Mental Hygiene Law § 87(3) (prior to amendment by N.Y. Laws 1960, ch. 550, § 2); 1942 Ops. Att'y Gen. 285.

[8] N.Y. Code Crim. Proc. § 454, as amended by N.Y. Laws 1960, ch. 550, § 1. See N.Y. Legislative Annual 513–17 (1960).

now provides for *mandatory* commitment of the acquitted defendant to the custody of the Commissioner of Mental Hygiene for hospitalization either at Matteawan or at a civil institution.[9] Discharge from hospitalization can be had only by a court order granted upon an application either by the commissioner[10] or the defendant himself,[11] which satisfies the committing court that the patient "may be discharged or released on condition without danger to himself or to others."[12] To aid in its decision, the court may order

[9] N.Y. Code Crim. Proc. § 454(1).

[10] N.Y. Code Crim. Proc. § 454(2), (3).

[11] N.Y. Code Crim. Proc. § 454(5).

[12] This standard for release is derived from Model Penal Code § 4.08(3) (1962) and also reflects the pre-1960 standard for discretionary commitment under old section 454 (note 6, *supra*). The discussion in People v. Lally, 19 N.Y. 2d 27, 33 (1966) (note 35, *infra*) appears to proceed on the assumption that despite its new phrasing the standard still involves consideration of "sanity" and need for hospitalization as it did prior to the 1960 revision (note 6, *supra*), and as distinguished from a broader test of dangerousness from any cause including mental illness (see generally Hamann, The Confinement and Release of Persons Acquitted by Reason of Insanity, 3 Harv. J. Leg. 55, 81–91 (1966). Thus, in Lally the Court noted: "As the Appellate Division said . . . long ago, the Legislature could and did limit the effect of such a 'not guilty because insane' verdict so that it would not be an absolute discharge but would result in the detention for such period as was necessary to determine whether insanity continued and, if so, whether defendant would be dangerous to himself or others if liberated. . . . We will remember that all we are passing on here is the constitutionality of this old law." 19 N.Y. 2d at 33. The Court of Appeals appears, therefore, to understand the section 454 standard of dangerousness as meaning the need or not for hospitalization for mental illness and as distinct from the section 85 test of dangerous mental illness requiring *high-security* hospitalization. Thus, it remanded the Lally case with instructions that the issues "to be tried are whether appellant may be discharged or released without danger to himself or to others [*i.e.*, is he in need of hospitalization for mental illness], and, if that question be answered in the negative

an examination by two qualified psychiatrists. If thereafter the court is satisfied that no "danger" is involved, it may order discharge or release on such conditions as it deems necessary. If not so satisfied, the court must hold a hearing (which "shall be deemed a civil proceeding") and thereafter may order discharge or conditional release (revocable for five years), or recommit the patient to the commissioner's custody. The patient may at any time be administratively transferred between Matteawan and civil state hospitals.[13]

2. ADMINISTRATION

The revised procedures which required mandatory commitment to the Commissioner of Mental Hygiene became effective on September 1, 1960. According to information supplied [14] to us on behalf of the Department of Mental Hygiene, in the following five years only 11 defendants were hospitalized under section 454. The group included 9 men and 2 women. Five of the patients (including both women) were administratively placed in civil hospitals and 6 were assigned to Matteawan. Information available as to 9 of the 11 defendants indicates that they had been acquitted either of first degree murder (4), or attempted first degree murder

[i.e., because he is in need of hospitalization], whether he is so dangerously mentally ill as to require hospitalization in Matteawan State Hospital [i.e., under N.Y. Mental Hygiene Law § 85]." Id. at 34–35.

[13] Code Crim. Proc. § 454(6).

[14] Letter to staff director, Jan. 7, 1966, from Grant H. Morris, Recodification Attorney, Dep't of Mental Hygiene. See also 1966 Rep. Jud. Conf. 129, N.Y. Leg. Doc. No. 90 (1967) (a trial judge noting that in over 2,000 trials he had had to deal with the insanity defense only three times). Compare Rep. Pres. Comm'n on Crime in the Dist. of Col. 536 (1966) (between 1954 and 1965, 591 persons in the District were committed to St. Elizabeth's Hospital following acquittal by reason of insanity).

(1), or rape, sodomy and kidnapping (1), or second degree assault (2), or first degree robbery (1). The five patients assigned to civil hospitals included three of the murder acquittals, the one attempted-murder acquittal, and the robbery acquittal. Six of the 11 defendants previously had been committed to Matteawan as unfit to stand trial. As of January 1966, five of the 11 patients had been released: assault after 22 months; rape after five months; murder after three weeks[15]; attempted murder (on convalescent status) after 10 months, and robbery after 27 months. Following is a brief description of the 11 cases in chronological order (by commitment upon acquittal under section 454) indicating (a) sex; (b) county; (c) crime; (d) where placed for hospitalization; in appropriate cases, (e) date discharged, and (f) whether hospitalized prior to trial:

1. November 22, 1960. (a) Male; (b) Nassau; (c) kidnapping, assault second degree (4 counts), rape first degree (2 counts), sodomy first degree (4 counts); (d) Matteawan, but transferred April 18, 1961 to Pilgrim State Hospital; (e) discharged May 2, 1961; (f) had been examined under section 870 at Pilgrim State Hospital from January 30, 1960 to March 2, 1960 (found competent).

2. December 15, 1960. (a) Male; (b) Erie; (c) first degree murder (two counts); (d) Buffalo State Hospital.

3. December 30, 1960. (a) Male; (b) Nassau; (c) robbery first degree; (d) Kings Park State Hospital; (e) discharged April 15, 1963; (f) had been committed to Matteawan under section 662-b on March 10, 1959, transferred to Kings Park August 31, 1960, discharged for trial December 15, 1960.

4. May 2, 1962. (a) Female; (b) Kings; (c) not clear; (d) Kings Park State Hospital (transferred to Brooklyn State Hospital May 14, 1963).

5. September 26, 1962. (a) Male; (b) Erie; (c) second degree

[15] The defendant had been hospitalized at Matteawan for more than 12 years prior to trial and acquittal. See Case No. 7, *infra*.

assault; (d) Matteawan (transferred to Buffalo State Hospital June 4, 1964); (e) discharged July 7, 1964.

6. January 18, 1963. (a) Male; (b) Queens; (c) second degree assault (five counts) and dangerous weapon; (d) Matteawan; (e) not applicable; (f) had been hospitalized at Matteawan from November 28, 1960 to July 17, 1962 under section 872 as unfit to stand trial.

7. May 8, 1963. (a) Male; (b) Suffolk; (c) first degree murder; (d) Central Islip State Hospital; (e) discharged May 29, 1963; (f) had been hospitalized at Matteawan from April 5, 1950 to November 20, 1962 under section 662-b as unfit to stand trial.

8. June 29, 1964. (a) Male; (b) Kings; (c) attempted murder first degree, first and second degree assault, dangerous weapon; (d) Kings Park State Hospital (transferred to Brooklyn State Hospital on April 22, 1965); (e) on convalescent status; (f) had been hospitalized at Matteawan from November 6, 1961 to August 5, 1963 under section 662-b as unfit to stand trial.

9. July 20, 1964. (a) Male; (b) Queens; (c) not clear; (d) Matteawan; (e) not applicable; (f) had been hospitalized at Matteawan from July 30, 1963 to February 7, 1964 under section 872 as unfit to stand trial.

10. October 20, 1965. (a) Male; (b) Broome; (c) first degree murder; (d) Matteawan; (e) not applicable; (f) had been examined under section 870 at Binghamton State Hospital from March 21 to May 18, 1963; thereafter hospitalized at Matteawan from May 24, 1963 to April 14, 1965 under section 662-b as unfit to stand trial.

11. December 17, 1965. (a) Female; (b) Erie; (c) first degree murder; (d) Buffalo State Hospital.

We do not believe that the true frequency of acquittals by reason of insanity is accurately reflected by these eleven cases in five years. As we noted in Chapter III, charges were dismissed against 21 out of 235 defendants returned to courts from Matteawan (as ready to be tried) between April 1, 1963 and March 31, 1964.[16] Additional details were

[16] *Supra*, p. 114.

supplied to us on three of those cases from two counties indicating that the insanity defense may be raised by a simple motion to dismiss (which avoids the automatic commitment following a jury acquittal), and that some prosecutors may regard a pre-trial commitment almost as an assurance of a successful insanity defense. The district attorney's replies to our questionnaires on the three cases included the following unsolicited information:

1. Carnal abuse of a child: "The nature and circumstances of this case indicated that a psychiatric evaluation of the defendant was necessary. The psychiatric report revealed the incompetence of the accused who could then neither plead nor stand trial. Since an incompetent person is incapable of committing a crime and since he was confined for more than 2 1/2 years [at Matteawan] it was felt that justice could be best served by dismissing the indictment since no jury could reasonably be expected to find him guilty under the circumstances."

2. Robbery first degree: On return to county jail from Matteawan (after 15 months) for trial on a robbery charge, the defendant "assaulted a fellow prisoner." He was sentenced to one year for the assault. "He was not prosecuted on the original charge . . . on the theory that if he were insane or incompetent he could not be held answerable for commission of the crime of robbery, etc. and that furthermore consideration should be given to the fact that he had been confined to Matteawan State Hospital for more than a year and was to be further confined . . . [in jail for a year on the assault] and it would serve no useful purpose to try him on the original robbery charges when it was reasonable to expect only a verdict of not guilty because of his incompetency."

3. Murder, second degree: This woman "killed her infant daughter by suffocating her with a pillow." She was hospitalized at Matteawan under section 662-b for 4 1/2 years. Upon defendant's return and plea of not guilty by reason of insanity, the district attorney moved (pursuant to Code Crim. Proc. § 671 [17])

[17] N.Y. Code Crim. Proc. § 671: "The court may, either of its own motion, or upon the application of the district attorney, and in

"to dismiss the indictment on the ground of the insanity of the defendant at the time of the commission of the act" and the defendant's attorney "joined in this motion." The court held "a hearing on the motion . . . and the testimony of two psychiatrists has been received. The effect of the testimony is that the defendant was actually in such a state of insanity at the time of the commission of the crime that she would not be legally responsible for her act. Accordingly . . . and in the interests of justice, the motion of the district attorney is granted and the indictment is dismissed."

Our analysis of the 235 defendants returned to courts for trial indicated that only 11 defendants chose to stand trial and that of these only two defendants were "acquitted by reason of insanity." [18] We do not know, beyond the three cases just discussed, how many of the 21 dismissals were, in effect, insanity acquittals, nor for that matter in how many of them the court held a hearing and received psychiatric testimony before ordering dismissal. Finally, neither do we know the role played by anticipation of a successful insanity defense in prosecutive decisions to offer or accept the pleas of guilty to reduced charges in another 137 of the 235 cases.[19] What does seem reasonably clear, however, is that there either is occasional confusion between the test of competence and that of responsibility,[20] or that there is some measure of doubt that a jury will recognize the distinction. It is also clear that more than 11 defendants suc-

---

furtherance of justice, order an action, after indictment, to be dismissed. In such case a written statement of the reasons therefor shall be made by the court and filed as a public record."

[18] *Supra,* p. 114.

[19] *Supra,* p. 114. Cf. Newman, Conviction: the Determination of Guilt or Innocence Without Trial 162 (1966) (dismissals upon promise to secure private psychiatric treatment are "one of the most widely used alternatives to conviction and sentencing").

[20] See the district attorney's comments in case 2., *supra.*

cessfully interposed the insanity defense between 1960 and 1965, but because they did so by motion or perhaps even through a "bargain plea," they avoided the automatic commitment of section 454 and therefore are not reflected in the Department of Mental Hygiene's statistics. Thus, while it is interesting to note that between 1940 and 1965 only 19 patients were committed to Matteawan[21] pursuant to section 454, we cannot conclude that the true volume of "acquittals" was not significantly larger.

3. PROPOSED REVISIONS

In its prior report[22] the committee suggested that the 1960 revisions of section 454 were "sound and flexible." Although not overlooking a possible constitutional objection to automatic commitment,[23] the committee at that time stated that any "vice" in the statutory system

probably lies less in the automatic commitment as such than in a possibly insufficient guaranty that the patient will receive good medical treatment, will be followed up with continuing solicitude for his freedom, and will be released as soon as his welfare and that of the community allow.[24]

The committee suggested however that the patient's rights (1) to a hearing on his request for discharge, and (2) to

[21] See Table 2. We do not know the number of other such patients who may have been committed to civil state hospitals over the years 1940–1960. However, since commitment prior to 1960 occurred where a court believed discharge would be "dangerous," it is not unreasonable to suppose that most patients were committed to Matteawan. Cf. 1935 Law Revision Comm'n Rep. 669, N.Y. Leg. Doc. No. 60 (1935).

[22] Mental Illness and Due Process 238–44 (1962).

[23] See People v. Lally, 19 N.Y. 2d 27 (1966); notes 25–28 and accompanying text.

[24] Mental Illness and Due Process 243 (1962).

seek release on a writ of habeas corpus, might be more fully protected by extending to this class of patient its recommendations (since enacted as to civil patients in N.Y. Mental Hygiene Law §§ 73, 74) concerning (3) retention orders of limited duration, and (4) automatic periodic judicial review of the need for hospitalization.

On December 30, 1966, during the final months of the present committee's work, the New York Court of Appeals in *People v. Lally*[25] upheld the constitutionality of section 454 as amended in 1960. It did so, however, by reading into the statute "all the protections of sections 74 and 85 of the Mental Hygiene Law" which are available to civil mental patients and which, under the *Baxstrom* decision, could not constitutionally be denied to patients committed under section 454.[26] At present therefore the acquitted defendant must still be committed to the custody of the Commissioner of Mental Hygiene, but he may not be "placed" at Matteawan State Hospital except upon a judicial determination of dangerous mental illness under section 85. Moreover, any such determination under section 85, as well as a denial of any subsequent application for release under section 454,[27] may be reviewed [28] by a jury trial under section 74. In addition, section 85 itself at present includes the right to auto-

[25] 19 N.Y. 2d 27 (1966).

[26] Id. at p. 35. "To comply with the spirit if not the express language of the Baxstrom decision . . . we hold that, before there can be any commitment to Matteawan State Hospital for the insane under section 454 procedures, a person must be accorded all the protections of sections 74 and 85 of the Mental Hygiene Law including a jury trial, if requested." Ibid.

[27] N.Y. Code Crim. Proc. § 454(2), (3), (5).

[28] The court's language (19 N.Y. 2d at 35) is open to interpretation as granting the jury trial either as an optional *substitute* for judicial determination of the section 454 application, or as an optional subsequent *review* of that determination.

matic periodic review of the question of dangerous mental illness. Taken together, therefore, section 454 (as construed by the Court of Appeals) and section 85 (as amended in 1966) appear to establish the following procedures:

(*a*) The acquitted defendant is still automatically committed to the custody of the Commissioner of Mental Hygiene for an indefinite period.[29]

(*b*) If the Commissioner wishes to hospitalize the patient at Matteawan, (i) he must first initiate a proceeding under section 85, and (ii) the patient is entitled to challenge the result[30] of that proceeding at a jury trial under section 74, and (iii) if he again is unsuccessful, the patient, while at Matteawan, is entitled to automatic periodic judicial review of his condition (and subsequent jury trial review on each occasion) under sections 73 and 74 (as is expressly provided in section 85), and (iv) is also entitled at any time to seek release by a section 454 application (which may also be subject to jury trial review).

(*c*) If the commissioner initially chooses to place the patient in a civil state hospital, (i) the patient may apply for his release under the procedures set forth in section 454, and (ii) he is entitled to a jury trial review[31] of an adverse decision under section 74 (as read into section 454), but (iii) neither on its face nor as construed by the Court of Appeals does section 454 grant automatic periodic judicial review (under section 73) to the acquitted defendant who is not processed under section 85.

In addition to the apparent inequity of granting (even if only indirectly or inadvertently) the right to automatic review to some acquitted defendants but not to all, there is

---

[29] As to release see note 12, *supra*.
[30] But see note 28, *supra*.
[31] Ibid.

another aspect of these procedures which requires attention. We recommend that the system of automatic, mandatory commitment be amended to require hospitalization only in those cases in which the present need therefor is demonstrated to the court at a separate hearing following a new mental examination upon acquittal.[32]

The procedure we recommend lies midway between the pre-1960 discretionary hospitalization and the present system of mandatory hospitalization. We believe that for the protection of society and of the defendant himself there should be a psychiatric examination and a judicial hearing concerning the present[33] mental health of the acquitted defendant *in every case*. However, we would recommend for that purpose that there be only a temporary commitment instead of for an indefinite period as at present. If the court finds the defendant to be in need of hospitalization,[34] it should order his hospitalization according to the same procedures as govern other patients (including periodic retention orders, judicial review, transfer and discharge, assistance of the M.H.I.S., and possibility of hospitalization as dangerously mentally ill). However, if the court finds no present need for hospitalization, the defendant should be released.

[32] Two bills were introduced in the United States Senate (S. 3689 and S. 3573, 89th Cong., 2d Sess.) in August 1966 by Senators Robert F. Kennedy and Joseph D. Tydings to provide for hospitalization, only where necessary, following acquittal by reason of insanity in federal courts outside the District of Columbia. See 112 Cong. Rec. (Nos. 127, 140) (daily ed. Aug. 4, Aug. 23, 1966).

[33] The defendant will already have been examined pursuant to N.Y. Code Crim. Proc. § 658 upon entry of the insanity plea, and, if he had thereupon been hospitalized, will have been certified as recovered. However, such examination and recovery involve the specific and narrow question of competence to stand trial.

[34] See note 12, *supra*.

The only essential distinction between our proposals and the existing procedures is that the court decision to commit or release is made (on the basis of an examination, notice, and hearing) reasonably promptly following acquittal rather than at some indefinitely postponed date on which the Commissioner of Mental Hygiene (or the defendant himself) may decide to apply to the court for permission to discharge. In our view there will be a more efficient implementation of the protective policy adopted in 1960,[35] and at the same time a more equitable accommodation of the perhaps conflicting interests of an individual defendant not actually in need of further hospitalization, and of society at large. Finally, the revised procedures concerning periodic review, retention orders, assistance of the M.H.I.S. and discharge should be made applicable to all patients at present hospitalized pursuant to section 454 in its prior or existing forms.

Accordingly, we make the following recommendations:

RECOMMENDATION NO. 18 (*Persons acquitted of crime by reason of insanity*). Any person acquitted of crime by reason of insanity must automatically and immediately be ordered examined as to his present mental health and possible need for hospitalization. The procedures governing observation and examination of mentally ill defendants should apply. Incarceration or hospitalization

[35] Upholding the constitutionality of section 454 in People v. Lally, 19 N.Y. 2d 27 (1966), the New York Court of Appeals twice characterized the automatic commitment as calling principally for an examination and report: "We see no reason why a man who has himself asserted that he was insane at the time the crime was committed and has convinced the jury thereof should not in his own interest and for the protection of the public be forthwith *committed for detention, examination and report as to his sanity*." Id. at 33. (Emphasis added.) "The Legislatures of this and other States have felt that such a jury verdict creates a situation where public safety as well as the defendant's safety require that he be *committed and examined before returning to society*." Id. at 34. (Emphasis added.)

for such purpose should not exceed thirty days, except that the court may extend the period to a maximum of sixty days.

If, following a hearing upon the results of such examination, the acquitted defendant is determined to be in need of hospitalization for mental illness, the court should commit him to the custody of the Commissioner of Mental Hygiene for care and treatment at an institution within the Department of Mental Hygiene under the procedures regulating other civil patients, including periodic review, notice of applications to retain the patient, jury trial review of orders authorizing retention, assistance of the Mental Health Information Service, and eligibility for transfer and release.

RECOMMENDATION NO. 19 (*Old-law patients*). Defendants who have been hospitalized automatically upon acquittal should receive the benefits of the proposed new law within six months of its effective date.

APPENDIX A

A HISTORY OF MATTEAWAN
STATE HOSPITAL

1. Antecedents: 1788–1858

As colonial New York grew in size and complexity, for it as for the other colonies, "the need for institutional provision for the criminal and dependent classes became more and more imperative." [1] Stocks and pillories, tools of summary corporal punishment, were replaced by jails, bridewells, houses of correction and prisons. Although antedated by city jails, the first major place of penal confinement in New York was the 1736 combined "Poor-House, Work-House and House of correction of New York City." [2] New York's state prisons began with Newgate, built in New York City in 1796–1797, Auburn prison built in 1816–1821, and Mount Pleasant (now Sing Sing) built in 1825–1828. [3]

In 1788 the New York legislature's "Act for apprehending and

[1] Deutsch, The Mentally Ill in America 51 (2d rev. ed. 1949).

[2] The first poorhouse in New York opened in 1736, as "a combined 'House of correction, workhouse and poorhouse,' " to receive " 'all disorderly persons' " and a variety of other unfortunates. 8 History of the State of New York 302 (Flick ed. 1935) (herinafter cited as "History"); there was a "Madman in Prison" in 1726, Select Cases of the Mayor's Court of New York City: 1674–1784 69 (Morris ed. 1935). See also the "few orders respecting lunatics" in the colonial Sessions courts, including a 1726 commitment to " 'the Common gaol,' " Goebel & Naughton, Law Enforcement in Colonial New York 109 n. 217 (1944). See Harms, I Institutional Care of the Insane in the United States and Canada 86 (1916), and the many entries in the Minutes of the Common Council of the City of New York: 1784–1831 (1930).

[3] Lawes, Life and Death in Sing Sing 30 (1929); see generally W. D. Lewis, From Newgate to Dannemora: the Rise of the Penitentiary in New York, 1796–1848 (1965).

punishing disorderly persons" included provisions for seizing, on the order of "any two or more justices of the peace," any "furiously mad" person who would then be "kept safely locked up in some secure place," and, if necessary, "be there chained."[4] The most obviously secure places were, of course, the jail and the poorhouse. Hospital care in the basement of New York Hospital became available to the mentally ill only about the turn of the century and a separate building, called the "New York Lunatic Asylum," was not opened (and then only to paying patients) until 1808.[5]

Apparently no effort was made to separate the mentally ill from criminals until 1827. In that year "An Act respecting Lunatics" prohibited the overseers of the poor, into whose care the civil mentally ill were now to be committed, from lodging them in a jail or even "in the same room with any person charged with or convicted of an offense."[6] The following year the Revised Statutes were enacted, repealing each of these laws.[7] The new procedures, however, still called for poorhouse confinement of civil patients.[8]

During this period there appear to have been some transfers of mentally ill prisoners from the first state prison (Newgate) to the New York Asylum,[9] but it was difficult to find room for them.[10] In 1825 it was reported that there were some 819 men-

[4] N.Y. Laws 1788, ch. 31. The act was passed over Governor George Clinton's veto based upon objections to other of its provisions, 2 Messages from the Governors 284 (Lincoln ed. 1909) (hereinafter cited as "Messages").

[5] Deutsch, *op. cit. supra* note 1, at 97098, 10 History 102.

[6] N.Y. Laws 1827, ch. 294, § 2.

[7] N.Y. Laws 1828, ch. 21, § 1(31), (525).

[8] I R.S. 634 (Part I, ch. 20, tit. 3). On the origin and development of the New York poorhouse system see Fensterstock, History of New York Social Welfare Legislation, in McKinney's N.Y. Soc. Welfare Law, pp. IX–XLIV.

[9] Administrative order transfers from Newgate Prison were authorized by N.Y. Laws 1818, ch. 211, § 9, at the suggestion of Governor DeWitt Clinton, 2 Messages 945. It was repealed by N.Y. Laws 1828, ch. 21, § 1(79).

[10] 2 Messages 945–46; 8 History 298.

tally ill persons in New York State, including 263 privately cared for in asylums, 208 in "gaol or supported by charity," and 348 "insane paupers at large, a terror to others, and suffering, in addition to mental derangement, all the privations attending penury and want." [11] However, "the condition of those under poor-house regulations, or confined in gaols, is, if possible, worse." [12]

Anxious for the relief of the poor insane not eligible[13] for admission to the Lunatic Asylum in New York, Lieutenant Governor Throop in 1830 proposed the establishment of "an asylum for the gratuitous care and recovery" of the insane poor.[14] He reminded the legislature of his proposal the following year, noting that "the ordinary poor-house provision is calculated rather to secure them from mischief, than to administer to their comfort." [15] A legislative committee investigated the problem,[16] and in 1834 Governor Marcy urged "vigorous action," especially since it was a "well-authenticated fact, that of recent cases under the treatment of the best regulated asylums, eighty and sometimes ninety patients in a hundred, have been restored. . . ." [17] He again raised the subject in his 1835 message to the legislature[18] which in 1836 finally provided for a state lunatic asylum[19] ultimately to be located at Utica[20] and designed for "the care and treatment of one thousand lunatics" in four buildings.[21] On January 4, 1842, Governor Seward announced that the asylum was ready to receive patients,[22] and the legislature in April made

[11] 3 Messages 293; see 8 History 297.

[12] 3 Messages 293.

[13] See Deutsch, *op. cit. supra* note 1, at 102.

[14] 3 Messages 293–94.

[15] Id. at 346.

[16] Id. at 378–79.

[17] Id. at 452. On the reliability of such statistics, however, see Deutsch, *op. cit. supra* note 1, at 145–57.

[18] 3 Messages 516.

[19] N.Y. Laws 1836, ch. 82.

[20] See 3 Messages 676.

[21] Id. at 713. See also id. at 859.

[22] Id. at 935. But see 4 Messages 43 (Annual Message of Governor Bouck in 1843).

provision for its organization and administration.[23] It opened on January 16, 1843.[24]

The Utica asylum was not to be limited to the care of civilly committed patients. The legislature more than responded to the governor's suggestion that "prudence, justice and humanity recommend that persons acquitted of crimes on the ground of mental aberration, should be brought under sanitary discipline." [25] The 1842 act provided for hospitalization (at the new asylum) of mentally ill persons confined under indictment, criminal charge, sentence, or "under any other than civil process," and, if their "insanity in any degree continues," those acquitted of crimes and misdemeanors.[26] The law, however, was not universally observed. For example, William Freeman languished two years in jail awaiting recovery of his sanity to be tried for murder,[27] and many mentally ill prisoners remained in prison instead of being removed to the new Utica asylum. Sing Sing prison reported that 31 mentally ill prisoners were being kept there in 1844.[28]

2. *Auburn Asylum: 1859–1892*

By 1855, because "their presence was very objectionable to the ordinary inmates," plans were being made for a separate asylum to house mentally ill prisoners of both sexes.[29] Meanwhile, it was decided to remove all prisoners from Utica to a prison without delay,[30] but two years later, the legislature revised its plans and allowed females to remain there.[31]

In 1859 Governor Morgan reported that there were 13 men-

[23] N.Y. Laws 1842, ch. 135.

[24] 4 Messages 77.

[25] 3 Messages 935. (Footnote omitted.)

[26] N.Y. Laws 1842, ch. 135, §§ 31, 32, 34.

[27] See generally Dain, Concepts of Insanity in the United States, 1789–1865, 199–200 (1964); cf. Freeman v. People, 4 Den. (N.Y.) 9 (1847).

[28] 8 History 298.

[29] See text accompanying note 64, *infra.*

[30] N.Y. Laws 1855, ch. 456.

[31] N.Y. Laws 1857, ch. 144, § 3.

tally ill prisoners at Auburn Prison, 21 at Sing Sing and three at Clinton.[32] Fortunately however, the new "Asylum for Insane Convicts" located near the prison at Auburn was "nearly ready for use, and is creditable to Christian civilization and humanity."[33] Opened in February, 1859,[34] it received 59 patients that year, nearly exhausting its capacity of 64 inmates. According to Governor Morgan:

The establishment of a separate institution for insane convicts is to a certain extent an *experiment,* but there is reason to believe it will prove successful. The excellence and completeness of the accommodations make the support of its inmates a source of considerably increased expense.[35]

In 1861 the legislature directed the removal of all mentally ill male prisoners from the Utica asylum to the new Auburn asylum.[36] Female prisoners continued to be sent to the Utica asylum (under the 1842 law) until 1865 when its superintendent suggested that the practice be halted.[37] The legislature that year prohibited their transfer to Utica, and ordered all there to be returned to the female facilities at Sing Sing or Clinton prisons.[38]

[32] 5 Messages 77.

[33] Id. at 78.

[34] 5 Messages 272. See generally N.Y. Laws 1858, ch. 130; 5 Messages 166.

[35] 5 Messages 167. See generally W. D. Lewis, *op. cit. supra,* note 3, at 281–285. It has been noted that the first superintendent (Edward Hall) of the asylum "plainly believed that their treatment should be designed not to punish but to cure, and . . . in addition to receiving counseling, schooling, and religious advice, the inmates could play dominoes, draughts, cards and quoits. They were also given music therapy and permitted to putter about in a garden which was provided for them. Hall even went so far as to advocate that the state erect a gymnasium and bowling alley for their use. Once again New York was assuming the role of penological pioneer, being the first state to provide separate facilities for the criminally insane." Id. at 282. (Footnote omitted.)

[36] N.Y. Laws 1861, ch. 63 (including those whose sentences had meanwhile expired).

[37] 5 Messages 583.

[38] N.Y. Laws 1865, ch. 353, § 2.

Two years later they were made eligible for admission to a new female section at the Auburn Asylum.[39]

By October 1868, "there were 180 insane convicts received [at Auburn] . . . of whom 81 were discharged, six escaped and seventeen died." [40] In 1869 the name of the Auburn institution was changed [41] to an asylum for "Insane Criminals" rather than "Insane Convicts." The reason was simple: it would no longer house only convicted prisoners. Criminal-order patients (that is, persons acquitted of a crime by reason of insanity and defendants becoming currently mentally ill prior to sentencing), both formerly committed to the Utica asylum under the 1842 act,[42] could now be committed to the Auburn Asylum, in the court's discretion, if the crime charged were murder, attempted murder, or arson. Persons in these classes previously committed to Utica could be transferred to Auburn by court order issued upon the application of the asylum superintendent.[43] Convicted and unconvicted criminal-order patients were once again being confined together as they had been (in jails) in colonial times, and as they were in the early civil asylums. Gradual elimination of their separation, made completely possible (except as to lesser offenders sent to civil hospitals from county jails and penitentiaries) only as of 1867 by opening of a female department at the Auburn Asylum, was already underway two years later. Contemporary comment did not recognize it, however, and in 1870 still boasted that the laws were "maintaining here, as in the outside world, a distinction between those who have been convicted of crime and those who have not been." [44]

After 1874 Auburn was authorized to accept mentally ill inmates of county penitentiaries.[45] Its function was again extended

[39] N.Y. Laws 1867, ch. 113, § 2.

[40] The Law of Insanity, 1 Albany L.J. 428, 430 (1870).

[41] N.Y. Laws 1869, ch. 895, § 3.

[42] See text accompanying note 26, *supra*.

[43] N.Y. Laws 1869, ch. 895, § 2.

[44] The Law of Insanity, 1 Albany L.J. 428, 431 (1870).

[45] N.Y. Laws 1874, ch. 446, tit. 1, art. 2, § 24. On their origin and development see Preiser, Survey of the New York State Sentencing Structure as of 1963, in State of N.Y. Temp. Comm'n on Revision of

in 1884 to include patients administratively transferred from the new State Reformatory at Elmira, and *any* criminal order patient (i.e., defendants and persons acquitted by reason of insanity) judicially transferred from a civil hospital.[46]

Auburn had opened in 1859 with a capacity of 64 patients, and admitted 59 in its first year. Balancing its (at least initially) relatively high discharge rate, the classes of criminal order commitments that could or were required to be made to Auburn had continually expanded. As of 1882 there were 141 inmates at the Auburn asylum, including nine women.[47] In 1886 a legislative commission was appointed to find additional farm land to be used by the asylum.[48]

3. *Matteawan State Hospital: 1892–1966*

a) The Concept

By 1887 the search for additional accommodations to serve the overcrowded Auburn Asylum for Insane Criminals had narrowed down to sites at Auburn in Cayuga County, and Matteawan in Dutchess County. The commissioners appointed to make the decision reported [49] to the legislature that they had selected a 250-acre farm property near the village of Matteawan. Among the reasons for its decision were the following:

The site combines great natural beauty with capabilities for attractive development that could scarcely be excelled for the purpose of a hospital for the insane . . . ; diversity and grandeur of scenery that would be invaluable as a promoter of peaceful enjoyment and pleasurable emotions, both of which are now regarded as important elements in the treatment of the insane.

Railroad service was less than two hours distant from New York City, especially important since more than seventy per cent of the number of insane criminals admitted to the asylum at Auburn up to the pres-

the Penal Law and Criminal Code, Proposed N.Y. Penal Law, Comm'n Staff Notes, App. A (pamphlet ed. 1964).

[46] N.Y. Laws 1884, ch. 289, § 8.

[47] 7 Messages 828.

[48] N.Y. Laws 1886, ch. 192; see N.Y. Laws 1888, ch. 45.

[49] Rep. Comm'n on New Asylum for Insane Criminals (1887), N.Y. Ass. Doc. No. 48 (1888).

ent time have been residents of counties east of Albany, and of these about fifty per cent resided in New York county alone. . . .[50]

Pointing with obvious pride to

the fact that New York is the pioneer State in the matter of establishing a separate hospital [Auburn Asylum, 1859] for the care and treatment of the criminal insane,

and that only one other state had followed its lead (and that "only in a moderate way"), the commissioners suggested that

the New York State Asylum for insane criminals necessarily becomes the parent institution of its kind, and, consequently, one to which other States, several of which are now seriously considering the question of separate provision for their criminal insane, would naturally look for such information and guidance as the light of actual experience in dealing with this class might alone be expected to furnish. . . .[51]

The commissioners presented the architects' plans as

embodying therein every feature of construction and arrangement which present knowledge and experience have suggested as necessary or desirable in a criminal asylum plan.[52]

Constantly in mind were the special requirements of the class for which the asylum was designed. For example:

The commissioners . . . call the attention of the Legislature to the fact that buildings for the criminal insane require to be constructed in a more substantial and secure manner and otherwise provided with more expensive facilities for insuring the safe custody of patients than would be deemed necessary or even desirable for the ordinary insane. The walls require to be thicker and stronger, the window guards to be of steel or other metal that will resist the action of files, saws and other cutting implements; the doors, fittings, etc., must be heavier and the locks more complicated than would be required in a non-criminal asylum; also the airing courts or exercise grounds must be enclosed with masonry, whereas play grounds for the ordinary insane need but a simple board fence or, preferably, no enclosure at all.[53]

[50] Id. at 6–7.
[51] Id. at 8.
[52] Ibid.
[53] Id. at 10–11.

The plans included

two small, one-story buildings, specially constructed with reference to strength and security . . . for the isolation of a certain class of vicious and dangerous lunatics, whose presence on the ordinary wards is a constant source of danger and anxiety to the more orderly and tractable patients, as well as to the employees.[54]

In 1889 the governor reported that Auburn was inadequate,[55] and the patients were moved from Auburn to Matteawan early in 1892. As suggested by Governors Hill and Flower, the Auburn facility became a women's prison.[56] In a news article later that year the *New York Times* noted that

the State asylum at Matteawan has all the necessary qualifications for a modern hospital for the insane. It now contains nearly all of the "criminal insane" of the State.

But the most important part of the new move . . . is that referring to the separation of the criminal and non-criminal insane. The Matteawan institution has ample room for such a distinction and the [Lunacy] Commission brings forward many sufficient reasons for its support.

The two classes of patients differ widely, the criminals giving the officials much anxiety at times. They are frequently dangerous and destructive.[57]

According to the Lunacy Commission's 1893 Report,[58] the separation of patients referred to was a separation of those patients held on criminal orders (i.e., persons not fit to be tried and those acquitted by reason of insanity) from the "convict insane." The former, or "so-called 'court-cases,' " constituted a majority of the patients, and for that reason

it was deemed desirable to change its title and place it in name as well as in fact, upon a State hospital basis, and thus give to it the same standing, in the public mind, as to care and treatment of its inmates, as the other public hospitals for the insane.[59]

[54] Id. at 13. See also Report (1888), N.Y. Ass. Doc. No. 82 (1889).
[55] 8 Messages 822.
[56] N.Y. Laws, 1893, ch. 306. See 8 Messages 822, 9 Messages 182.
[57] N.Y. Times, Nov. 3, 1892, p. 9, col. 4.
[58] 1893 Ann. Rep. State Comm'n in Lunacy, 279–89 19 N.Y. Ass. Doc. No. 97 (1894).
[59] Id. ch. 18.

At the end of its first full fiscal year (September 30, 1893) at Matteawan, the hospital reported a climb in population from 348 to 411, and the Superintendent (since 1889), Dr. H. E. Allison, was aided by two assistant physicians, one with three and one with four years' experience. Although this was the smallest medical staff in any of the existing nine state mental hospitals, the physician-patient ratio at Matteawan (1 to 128) was better than average (1 to 153). Other employees included 51 male night and day watchmen, night roundsmen and attendants, and four women attendants.

Responding the following year to a question by the Lunacy Commission, six hospitals reported use to varying extents of the "open-door" system, but at Matteawan

the "open door" system, as it is usually understood, is not practical . . . to any extent whatever, as the character of our patients forbids it, although considerable numbers of them in charge of attendants are employed at work upon the farm and grounds in building roadways and in other outdoor industries. All patients are committed to this hospital by order of the court under criminal charges or are under conviction, and the open door system, therefore, is impracticable.[60]

The "character" of the patients at Matteawan was described by the Lunacy Commission:

The insane convict, as a rule, is constantly bent on effecting his escape from custody. This is especially true of those who have committed crimes against property. Not infrequently his native cunning and ingenuity are seemingly intensified by his mental disease; hence the exceeding difficulty in keeping this class in penal custody in an institution like the one at Matteawan, which is structurally a hospital rather than a prison. Then, too, the fact that convict patients do not wear the prison garb while in the hospital—it being impracticable to have them wear the striped uniform of the prison owing to the presence of the unconvicted patients—furnishes to them an additional incentive and opportunity to escape. It is well known that since the opening of the Matteawan Hospital escapes and attempted escapes therefrom have been of increasing frequency, despite the unceasing efforts of the hospital officers to prevent the same. On the other hand, the class of in-

[60] 1894 Ann. Rep. State Comm'n in Lunacy 270, 18 N.Y. Ass. Doc. No. 97 (1895).

mates held on criminal orders and improperly designated "insane criminals," who, under the influence of mental disease, have committed acts of violence—homicide and the like—which, had they been done by sane persons, would have been criminal, are usually not difficult to keep in custody, and do not require to be controlled by the rigid rules of discipline and restricted environment that is absolutely necessary in the case of the convict insane. In fact, were it not for their dangerous tendencies this class of patients might properly and safely be kept in an ordinary hospital for the insane.[61]

b) The Origin of Dannemora State Hospital: 1893–1900

The hospital's population was almost at peak capacity, and was expected to exceed it before the expiration of the year partly because the 1890 State Care Act,[62] enacted after the hospital was designed, "necessitated the transfer to Matteawan of all patients held on criminal orders [i.e., defendants], etc. in the other hospitals. . . ."[63] The increase in patients was already barring realization of the planned and publicized "separation by building" of the convict and non-convict insane. The Lunacy Commission's exposition of the problem, leading ultimately to construction of Dannemora State Hospital, summarizes the history of the "separation" concept:

The establishment of the State Asylum for Insane Criminals at Auburn, in 1859, was the first instance in any State or country of a separate institution specially devoted to the care and treatment of insane criminals. At that time, and for many years thereafter, the number to be provided for was comparatively small and there was no serious objection to caring for the two classes in the same institution. In fact, at that time the number was not sufficient to warrant maintaining these two classes in separate institutions, while the esablishment of the Asylum for Insane Convicts at Auburn and the transfer thereto from the other State hospitals of all insane convicts then confined therein *and whose presence was very objectionable to the ordinary inmates,* afforded a much-needed relief to these latter institutions. The original asylum for insane criminals was designed only for insane convicts and was accordingly located on grounds adjacent to the Auburn State Prison; subsequently, in 1869, the scope of the institution was wid-

[61] Id. at 72–73.
[62] N.Y. Laws 1890, ch. 273.
[63] State Comm'n in Lunacy, *supra* note 60, at 71.

ened by a statute which provided for the admission thereto of the class of patients referred to as being held on criminal orders and who were designated "insane criminals," in contra-distinction to "insane convicts," and since that time the practice of caring for the two classes in the same institution has prevailed. Before the number of these two classes of patients became sufficiently large to justify providing for them in separate institutions, the objection to their association was more theoretical than practical, despite the difference in their legal status. But with the large increase in numbers since the Matteawan State Hospital was opened, the population having doubled in three years, while the transfers to it [of criminal-order patients from civil hospitals because of the space problem caused by the 1890 State Care Act] are steadily increasing, embarrassments in administration have arisen, owing to a mixed population which renders it extremely difficult to apply to all its members the same rules and regulations.[64]

The commission envisioned three possible solutions to the problem: (1) transfer of term-expired prisoners to civil hospitals; (2) more construction at Matteawan, and (3) a new institution for prisoners on the grounds of a state prison. It discarded the first solution because

many of the convict patients whose terms have expired belong to the criminal class and have been devoted to a life of criminal conduct, so that even though their sentence may have expired and they are legally no longer convicts, their presence in the other State hospitals would be *objectionable*.[65]

New construction at Matteawan was not feasible because of the size of the plant at that time, but the third alternative was suggested as the most satisfactory and farsighted course—to erect a suitable building,

susceptible of extension from time to time on the grounds of one of the State prisons, and to remove thereto all convict patients who are still under sentence [i.e., not term-expired patients], as well as those who become insane while in penal institutions. Such a building would

[64] Id. at 71–72. (Emphasis added.)

[65] Id. at 73. (Emphasis added.) The commission thereupon noted that, "in fact, it was mainly for this reason that the practice which formerly prevailed, of transferring them to these institutions on expiration of sentence, was discontinued." Ibid.

provide for the safekeeping and proper care of all insane convicts, many of whom are habitual criminals, often of a dangerous character, and whose chief desire is to escape from custody. It could, if deemed desirable, be subject to visitation by the commission; and such patients as should continue insane after expiration of sentence and should be determined to be proper subjects therefor, could be transferred, on the approval of the Commission, to the Matteawan State Hospital. The carrying out of this plan would also, for several years to come, supply at Matteawan the additional accommodations which will be necessary to provide for patients, held on criminal orders and for such patients as might be transferred there from the proposed prison asylum after the expiration of sentence.[66]

The year, however, was 1894, and Dannemora State Hospital would not be ready until 1900. Asked if his medical staff were "sufficient" to effect recovery in curable cases, the superintendent asked for "one additional junior assistant." [67] Another suggestion he made that year was to become a familiar refrain if not indeed a lament, in Annual Reports *up to 1965*—the problem of recruiting and retaining competent assistants:

The salaries and allowances of medical officers are sufficient to secure competent and qualified physicians, but are not sufficient to retain such men for any great length of service. The staff here consists of two assistant physicians. During the past five years . . . 3 resigned and 1 was transferred to a similar service at the Hudson River State Hospital, at an increase of salary. Of the present staff, now in service, one has been connected with this hospital for the period of six, and the other for a period of twenty months.[68]

Still better than average (1 to 171), the physician-patient ratio at Matteawan (1 to 144) reflected the increased admissions.[69] The yet doubtful validity of including the superintendent in computing the ratio was raised by his own description of his routine as of 1894:

As a rule the medical care of the patients is delegated to the assistant physicians who are directly in charge of the wards. The medical super-

66 Ibid.
67 Id. at 188.
68 Id. at 192–93.
69 Id. at 321.

intendent, however, always sees and examines each admission; and subsequently each case under treatment or presenting any unusual features is daily reported to him in the form of written notes and by verbal reports. In addition, the superintendent visits the wards from time to time, though not with regularity, and examines each patient therein, both as to his mental and physical condition; and should the condition of the patient warrant it, calls the attention of the visiting physician thereto. He also sees in consultation such cases as the physician in charge of the ward may consider as unusual or in which he desires consultation. The undertaking of all surgical operations and the treatment of violently excited patients or patients who are critically ill, is determined upon and guided largely by the medical superintendent in conference with the assistant physicians on their various wards.[70]

The superintendent described the hospital's procedures on admitting new patients as including (1) examination of the patient and the paperwork by the superintendent, (2) entering the salient points of his history and the nature and circumstances of his crime in the "Case-Book," (3) logging the admission in a Register, Time-Book, Ward Sheets and daily notebook, (4) ward assignment "largely determined by his condition," (5) physical examination and personal interviews, and (6) a period of special observation in a room "off the isolation ward" equipped with a "ceiling aperture," but this last was unnecessary in most cases "as the nature of their disease is unmistakable from the first." [71] Elsewhere it was noted that "the proportion of cases received, who are actually maniacal, is small." [72] Also in 1894 the hospital reported that outdoor recreation in the airing courts was "largely left to the devices of the patients" and that, although there had been a "school for patients" during the last years at Auburn, none had yet been organized at Matteawan.[73]

Five "insane convicts" escaped from Matteawan in April 1895, but were promptly recaptured partly because "the tramping season has not yet fairly opened" and they could not pass themselves off in a rural area as "common tramps." [74] The incident

70 Id. at 198–99.
71 Id. at 238–39.
72 Id. at 251.
73 Id. at 255.
74 N.Y. Times, April 18, 1895, p. 4, col. 4.

occasioned an editorial in the *New York Times* on the "much more serious aspect" of the case:

There is not the slightest reason to believe that any of them, except Quigley, was in the least degree insane . . . [and the other four distrusted Quigley because he "was a little off"].
Now, the law of the State does not provide for any proper inquisition in respect to a convict suspected of insanity. . . . [The prison physician's certificate, supporting administrative transfer to Matteawan] may mean nothing more than that the physician finds, or that his warden finds, that the prisoner is a refractory and troublesome person whom it would ease the labors of physician or warden to have transferred. . . . Any course of treatment proper to lunatics would be intolerable and might be maddening to sane men. . . . It is intolerable that sane criminals should be treated by the State of New York as insane criminals.[75]

Two days later the *Times* again labeled it a "gross abuse to put a sane man in an insane asylum," whether claims of "the cruelties practiced at Matteawan may or may not be true."[76] The brutality issue was again aired in an 1895 habeas corpus application by a time-expired prisoner, but it was reportedly met by a "keeper's" explanation that "force was sometimes necessary."[77]

Whether in reaction to the abuses alleged in the newspapers or simply as part of its generally liberal approach to insanity commitments, the 1896 Insanity Law replaced administrative transfers of prisoners with judicial orders based on an impartial medical examination.[78] (When Dannemora opened in 1900, however, transfers of male felons to it would once again be placed on an administrative basis,[79] but other prisoners would continue to be transferred to Matteawan only on judicial process.)

In 1896 Governor Morton noted that Matteawan had not solved the Auburn overcrowding after all, and recommended erection

[75] Ibid.
[76] N.Y. Times, April 20, 1895, p. 4, col. 4.
[77] N.Y. Times, April 28, 1895, p. 11, col. 5.
[78] N.Y. Laws 1896, ch. 545, § 97.
[79] N.Y. Laws 1899, ch. 520, § 9.

"at Dannemora of a plain and substantial asylum." [80] By 1897 the *Times* reported that Matteawan was "alarmingly over-crowded," with "more than 100 men sleeping in corridors"; the condition was partly attributable to the inability to find space in civil hospitals for time-expired prisoners, and, even if space could be made, to find prisoners whose transfer would not be "objectionable" on the ground they were "habitual criminals." [81] Dr. Allison was quoted on the subject:

About 26 per cent of all our cases today [620] consists of just such detained patients whose terms of imprisonment expired some years ago, and yet who are still insane and dangerous to be at large. Quimbo Appo, for instance, one of the first Chinamen to enter the United States under the early treaty provision of trade, and who has since committed four homicides, would manifestly be an unsafe person to release. Having been declared insane during his last term of imprison-ment, which expired long ago, he has been kept fourteen years over his time, and still possesses very strong delusions, and is yet an active man for his years. Similar reasons exist for the detention of other like cases. It is an excellent measure of safety for the community and a

[80] 9 Messages 657: "The State Hospital at Matteawan, designed and built for this class of inmates ["insane criminals"], has been occupied only three years, but it is found too small for its uses. The old asylum at Auburn contained only about 250 inmates, but this new hospital was built with a capacity for 550 patients. It already has 534 inmates, and with the rapid ratio of increase will be overcrowded within a few months. . . . It is urged by the State Commissioners in Lunacy and by the Superintendent of State Prisons, that there should, as a matter of public policy, and of physiological propriety, be a sepa-ration of the convicted and unconvicted classes. To this end, as well as with a view of relieving the congested condition of the hospital at Matteawan, I recommend . . . the erection . . . at Dannemora, of a plain and substantial asylum, to accommodate insane convicts undergoing sentence, and such of those who have served their sen-tences as it is not deemed advisable to retain in the same building with those who have not been convicted." Id. at 656–57.

In response to the Governor's request, the 1896 legislature appro-priated funds for the erection at Dannemora "of buildings adapted to the requirements of three hundred insane convicts." N.Y. Laws 1896, ch. 949.

[81] N.Y. Times, Aug. 28, 1897, p. 2, col. 1.

very good statute, but it crowds the capacity of the hospital. There is no other weeding process, however, so serviceable to the public as that which eliminates from society the dangerous insane convict and keeps him in safe custody.[82]

The superintendent noted in the course of the interview that one state prisoner in sixty becomes insane each year, but "over 20 per cent of . . . [life-sentence] cases finally become inmates of this hospital, a large majority becoming permanently insane." The admissions from penitentiaries were fewer because their short sentences do not allow "prolonged medical observation." Commitment of defendants acquitted by reason of insanity and those unfit to be tried was a "fruitful source of increase." Such "court cases" accounted for about 50 percent of the patients, and he offered proof that such admissions were not a "cloak under which the penalty for the offense is tactfully avoided":

It is a fact that the average length of confinement in criminal cases which have been declared insane by courts considerably exceeds, excluding life sentences, the average length of time served by convicts in the three great State prisons.[83]

The interview was ended by Dr. Allison's observation that "the life of a medical Superintendent in an overcrowded hospital for the criminal insane is not altogether free from anxiety." [84]

Dannemora was nearly ready by January 1900, but the conditions at Matteawan required "constant watchfulness" because 719 patients were housed in buildings whose capacity was 550.[85] In October the press reported a "revolt" at Matteawan.[86] The 752 patients had heard a "rumor" of a "large draft" about to be made to Dannemora, now completed, and since "nearly all of them live in New York" and would not receive as many visits upstate, they "objected seriously." Dr. Allison explained that overcrowding had made it necessary "to compel some 200 or more of the patients to sleep on blankets on the floor in one of

[82] Ibid.
[83] Ibid.
[84] Ibid.
[85] N.Y. Times, Jan. 29, 1900, p. 7, col. 6.
[86] N.Y. Times, Oct. 22, 1900, p. 1, col. 3.

the long corridors."⁸⁷ Twenty patients in one such corridor had attacked eight "keepers" who were watching them, and seven had escaped but four were returned the next day.⁸⁸ Finally, in November 1900, the convicted male felons with at least six months' sentence yet to serve were transferred to Dannemora.⁸⁹

c) Matteawan 1900–1918

Notwithstanding the draft to Dannemora, the population of Matteawan kept rising while capacity remained constant at 550.⁹⁰

⁸⁷ Ibid.

⁸⁸ N.Y. Times, Oct. 23, 1900, p. 7, col. 1.

⁸⁹ Dannemora State Hospital had been authorized by N.Y. Laws 1896, ch. 949, named by N.Y. Laws 1897, ch. 395, § 2, and was organized under N.Y. Laws 1899, ch. 520.

⁹⁰ See, e.g., 1902 Ann. Rep. State Comm'n in Lunacy 138, 13 N.Y. Ass. Doc. No. 62 (1903). In 1902, Governor Odell had urged the legislature to consider "the care of the insane criminals . . . because the maintenance of two such prisons, namely at Matteawan and Dannemora, should no longer be continued. The Dannemora site could be used to better advantage than for the care of insane criminals. The per capita expense at both of these institutions is too great and they are too elaborate for criminals. This department should be placed under the control of the State Commission in Lunacy, because it could be managed much more economically than at present. There should be no further appropriations for the hospital at Dannemora, because the difficulty in reaching it by rail renders the cost of maintenance too high. Such additions as may be needed in the future should be made at Matteawan where facilities for transportation and ease of access make it much more desirable than Dannemora." 10 Messages 342–43. (Italics and footnote omitted.)

Only the year before he had condemned the "great extravagance in the matter of buildings and equipments" in the entire state hospital system whose total such investment was $20,000,000 (or $909 per capita, there having been some 22,088 patients on October 1, 1900. 10 Messages 224–25.

A decrease in per capita annual maintenance expense from $178 to $165 had been effected "by an arbitrary reduction in the number of employees, and has not seemed to cause any *serious* impairment in the proper administration of the various hospitals." Id. at 225.

Transfers to Matteawan of civilly committed patients with criminal records[91] helped swell its population after 1904. The daily average population in 1906 was 667 [92] and in 1907 was approximately 693.[93] A census as of September 30, 1907, showed that 76 patients were there for one year or less, 170 for 1–5 years, 172 for 5–10 years, 141 for 10–15 years, 98 for 15–20 years, 28 for 20–30 years, and 11 for 30 years or more.[94]

In August 1913, Harry K. Thaw, who had been acquitted of the murder of Sanford White on grounds of insanity, was the twentieth patient to escape from Matteawan,[95] achieving the release that repeated habeas corpus applications[96] had been unable to effect. In October of that year, Dr. Raymond F. C. Kieb, the new Superintendent, reported 864 patients and great overcrowding.[97] Little appears to have been done except to watch the numbers grow higher. The census high point in 1918 was 920 patients in an expanded certified capacity of 657.[98] In his report for 1918, Dr. Kieb noted that admissions of "tramps and vagrants" from county jails and penitentiaries had been reduced, probably because of the wartime manpower shortage.[99]

(Emphasis added.) The Governor aspired to "be liberal, but not extravagant." Id. at 226.

[91] N.Y. Laws 1904, ch. 525, § 2 (continued as N.Y. Correc. Law § 412 until repealed by N.Y. Laws 1965, ch. 524). See Chapter II, *supra*.

[92] 1906 Ann. Rep. State Comm'n in Lunacy 297, 7 N.Y. Ass. Doc. No. 22 (1907).

[93] 1907 Ann. Rep. State Comm'n in Lunacy 401, 5 N.Y. Ass. Doc. No. 24 (1908).

[94] Id. at 414.

[95] N.Y. Times, Aug. 18, 1913, p. 3, col. 1; Aug. 22, 1913, p. 2, col. 1; Aug. 24, 1913, § 5, p. 1, col. 1.

[96] See, e.g., People ex rel. Peabody v. Chanler, 133 App. Div. 159, 117 N.Y. Supp. 322 (2d Dep't 1909), aff'd. mem., 196 N.Y. 525, 89 N.E. 1109 (1909).

[97] N.Y. Times, Oct. 25, 1913, p. 15, col. 3.

[98] 1918 Ann. Rep. Sup't State Prisons 367, 50 N.Y. Leg. Doc. No. 134 (1919).

[99] Id. at 369.

Then too, lesser offenders in New York City institutions were being detained there until expiration of sentence instead of being sent to Mateawan.[100] That allowed subsequent civil commitment to other state hospitals and reduced the admission rate. Insanity acquittals had "greatly decreased in recent years," but pre-trial commitments (section 836) "show an increase."[101] The overcrowding could be reduced by transfers to civil hospitals of some of the more than 300 time-expired prisoners, and 52 such cases were so transferred in 1918. However, even more "could be safely transferred . . . , but unfortunately a number of our superintendents are unwilling" to accept them.[102]

That year and for many years thereafter Dr. Kieb recommended erection of special buildings to house the convicted misdemeanants and petty offenders collecting in such large numbers at Matteawan:

the so-called misdemeanant type . . . belong to the wandering class, and the usual crime charged is vagrancy or disorderly conduct. . . . It is claimed that they are a troublesome factor in other hospitals, but it is questionable whether this institution was intended for their treatment. . . . [A] separate group of buildings . . . for our misdemeanant insane . . . would permit a general rearrangement of our population and provision might then be made for the transfer to this hospital by the State Hospital Commission of those [in civil hospitals] . . . who are held under criminal orders, and of those exhibiting homicidal and dangerous tendencies.[103]

The physician-patient ratio in 1918 ("including superintendent and internes") was 1 to 227 [104] but the recovery rate,

low in comparison with the so-called civil hospitals . . . must be expected as the percentage of recoverable types of psychoses committed to a hospital for the criminal insane is decidedly lower.[105]

[100] Ibid.
[101] Id. at 370. See Chapter III, *supra.*
[102] Id. at 371.
[103] Id. at 367–68.
[104] Id. at 399.
[105] Id. at 376.

Of 28 "court cases" discharged during the year, 14 had died and six were released on habeas corpus.[106] Two of the remaining eight patients, whose recovery was certified by the hospital, had been at Matteawan only 11 months and three months (forgery) respectively, but six of the 14 deceased court cases were accused of murder or assault and had been at Matteawan for from 20 to 48 years.[107] The only murder case returned for trial in 1918 had been discharged on a writ of habeas corpus.[108]

Because of overcrowding, no public sightseeing of the hospital had been allowed. However, Dr. Kieb believed that:

While the present emergency may warrant the exclusion of the general public, it would seem that limited visitation might be permitted. This hospital is widely known and naturally many odd and erroneous opinions in reference to the nature of the institution exist. Tourists and strangers come with the idea that it is a prison with patients locked in cells, whereas the actual surroundings and the presence of patients in large open wards reading, chatting, and playing games or exercising in the court yard causes them to leave with a far different opinion.[109]

d) The Year 1919

Dr. Kieb reported an improved physician-patient ratio of 1 to 176,[110] but warned that living quarters for the medical staff "are appallingly inadequate" and would cause resignations.[111] Unless higher salaries and better living conditions were provided

[106] Id. at 381.

[107] Id. at 381–82.

[108] Ibid. Concerning two patients released on habeas corpus it was stated that "marked improvement had been noted and they would have been discharged if they had not been held on criminal orders." Id. at 377.

[109] Id. at 394.

[110] 1919 Ann. Rep. Sup't State Prisons 369, 43 N.Y. Leg. Doc. No. 143 (1920). In the same report the following fact was noted about Dannemora State Hospital: "During the period of the war the work of the hospital has suffered because of an unsufficient number of physicians on the staff. Staff meetings have been discontinued for a time, as at present we have on duty one physician exclusive of the superintendent." Id. at 394.

[111] Id. at 329.

for the medical staff, it would be increasingly difficult to interest "the most promising type of physicians" in working at Matteawan.[112] Patient overcrowding was still terrible and the hospital was still receiving pre-trial commitments of petty offenders (vagrants and disorderly persons) who properly should be sent to civil hospitals.[113] The odd result of the various commitment laws was the hospital's inability to accept many civil patients proposed for transfer to Matteawan (under early forms of N.Y. Correc. Law § 412) as ex-convicts still manifesting "criminal tendencies":

Our provisions for safe treatment of the dangerous and homicidal type of patient have been seriously taxed and we cannot accept patients of this type from other hospitals until proper accommodations are provided for our present population.[114]

Seventy-one percent of the hospital's convict population were time-expired cases eligible for transfer but "overcrowded conditions which exist in all of the civil hospitals" made transfer "impossible." [115] Dr. Kieb raised, in 1919, a subject which is still of concern almost half a century later—the staff

endeavored to release every case where such action could be taken without menacing the public peace and safety. Our organic law has no provision for parole and naturally our attitude toward release must be conservative owing to the type of patients under treatment. I believe that some system of parole should be provided and that cases discharged as well as paroled should be under the jurisdiction of an after-care agent. With such a safeguard we could exercise a more liberal policy and questionable cases could have a trial as free social units. . . . [If] we did not follow a highly conservative policy some cases with a psychopathic makeup would probably be classified as recovered.[116]

The superintendent's report for 1919 was replete with references to his parole and aftercare proposals. The same proposal was

[112] Id. at 353.
[113] Id. at 329, 333.
[114] Id. at 334. See N.Y. Correc. Law § 412, note 91, *supra*, and Chapter II, *supra*.
[115] Ibid.
[116] Id. at 343.

made in Dannemora's Annual Report as to time-expired male felons.[117]

e) The Year 1921

Inadequate staff-housing had caused the predicted losses of valuable personnel and continued to be a major problem.[118] Although the physician-patient ratio remained fairly constant (1 to 178),[119] the medical staff was plagued with resignations and turnover; better housing and more pay were still necessary.[120] Patient overcrowding became "more alarming" each year despite transfers to civil hospitals of "over two hundred of the so-called harmless misdemeanants in recent years."[121] Although pre-trial commitments of indicted defendants were increasing, the superintendent was pleased because early commitment led to early recovery.[122] Minutes of the pre-trial sanity hearing became "a most important part of the history" of those cases.[123] Unfortunately, however, the hospital still received pre-trial commitments of petty offenders charged with "violation of some social ordinance" and who should be committed directly to civil hospitals.[124] There were four transfers of criminal-order patients and ex-prisoners from civil hospitals that year,[125] and fortunately a bill that would have expanded transfers to include any dangerous civil patient had been vetoed.[126] (It would ultimately be enacted in 1932.[127]) Parole facilities were again discussed,[128] and, indicating perhaps the hospital's sensitivity about its public image, the superintendent noted that

[117] Id. at 386.

[118] 1921 Ann. Rep. Sup't State Prisons 339, 3 N.Y. Leg. Doc. No. 12 (1922).

[119] Id. at 379.

[120] Id. at 366.

[121] Id. at 340.

[122] Id. at 343.

[123] Ibid.

[124] Id. at 344.

[125] Id. at 345.

[126] Ibid.

[127] See Chapter II, *supra* at note 43 (N.Y. Mental Hygiene Law § 85).

[128] Sup't State Prisons, *op. cit. supra* note 118, at 354.

the hospital has been opened daily to the public for visitation and inspection. Many have availed themselves of the opportunity and while some were impelled by morbid curiosity I feel that the hospital has greatly benefited. Most people are not conversant with the fact that the institution is operated as a hospital, not a prison, and they leave with a favorable impression with the standard of care and treatment of our patients.[129]

f) The Year 1922

The Superintendent of State Prisons reported to the legislature that overcrowding at Matteawan was "a serious menace"; there were 932 patients with space for 657—"an overcrowding of 41.85 per cent."[130] Dr. Kieb reported the remarkable fact that since February, 1922,

our staff has consisted of *three* physicians besides the superintendent. This number was not considered sufficient twenty years ago when the population of the hospital was not much more than half of the present.[131]

Plagued again with resignations ("in practically every instance the question of proper housing had direct bearing")[132] and unable to recruit competent replacements, the hospital allowed two second- and third-year medical students to perform minor routine medical tasks—"such is our exigency, however, that we are grateful for any help that we can secure."[133] Despite these woeful inadequacies, public visiting was still encouraged to dispel the mistaken notion that Matteawan was "a dingy prison with all of the patients locked in single cells, unoccupied and unable to talk with others."[134]

Pre-trial commitments of indicted and other defendants were increasing, but there were practically no commitments of female felons in recent years—the decline being attributed to the earlier

[129] Id. at 375.
[130] 1922 Ann. Rep. Sup't State Prisons 10, 22 N.Y. Leg. Doc. No. 119 (1923).
[131] Id. at 373. (Emphasis added.)
[132] Id. at 342.
[133] Id. at 373.
[134] Id. at 383.

recognition of illness and commitment as a pre-trial patient, as well as improved standards in prison work and recreation conditions—and the "so-called prison psychosis" was in decline.[135] Although only two civil transfers were received in 1922, Dr. Kieb took occasion to note that

the argument is frequently advanced that we should receive troublesome cases from other hospitals in exchange for a suitable case from our own population. Such an arrangement would be impractical and impossible as we are not able to properly classify our cases at the present time owing to the general overcrowding.[136]

Reorganization of the Institution for Defective Male Delinquents at Napanoch that year afforded some relief to Matteawan.[137] Forty patients "showing evidence of mental deficiency without symptoms of psychosis" were transferred to Napanoch, but "this represented an accumulation of years" and future transfers would be infrequent. Only one was returned to Matteawan, having later developed evidence of a psychosis, but it was precisely in anticipation of that possibility that the Napanoch legislation permitted retransfer. Apparently most of the mental defectives had come to Matteawan as pre-trial cases, and although no longer psychotic still could not be returned to court "when the history showed that commitment had been made on account of mental deficiency." All but one had adjusted to the new surroundings at Napanoch "without serious conflict." [138]

Condemning "the dangerous overcrowding," Dr. Kieb declared that "all will agree [that conditions] are worse than they have been since the hospital was originally opened on the 2nd day of February, 1859. . . ." [139] Efforts to transfer patients to civil hospitals were largely "fruitless" because of overcrowding there also.[140] It was felt that a parole system would help, would be "a sociological experiment worth trying and . . . an easy

135 Id. at 348–49.
136 Id. at 349, 351.
137 N.Y. Laws 1922, ch. 230. See Chapter II, *supra*, at note 71.
138 Sup't State Prisons, *op. cit. supra* note 130, at 351, 358, 363.
139 Id. at 341–43.
140 Id. at 359.

matter to establish a definite and workable system." [141] Discussion of parole, however,

calls attention likewise to the *advisability of social workers for this hospital.* Most of our patients come from greater New York and in many cases we are not able to obtain reliable histories. If we had one or two competent social workers they could collect much valuable data and likewise supervise [*sic*] paroled cases. In a few instances we have been assisted by after care agencies of other hospitals but I feel that our problems are different and so important that I feel we should have our own definite system. The term expired misdemeanant should at least have the benefit of a parole with an opportunity to demonstrate his power of adjustment. [142]

g) The Year 1923

Despite its ten years of protest, Matteawan was "the most overcrowded" state hospital in New York. [143] Overcrowding reached 57 percent on the male wards, [144] and a "daring escape of four patients exemplified the danger." [145] The situation warranted stopping further admissions "until new wards are available." [146] Fifty men slept on mattress-covered floors, and corridors became dormitories. [147] Yet vexed by staff housing problems, the Matteawan superintendent bluntly declared that "the standard of the medical service has been lowered. . . ." [148] At times during the year there had been only four physicians in service, and the most favorable physician-patient ratio achieved during the year was 1 to 190. [149] Addressing himself more directly

[141] Ibid.

[142] Id. at 359–60. (Emphasis added.) The first appointment of a social worker was not made until 36 years later (1958). See text accompanying note 231 *infra.*

[143] 1923 Ann. Rep. Sup't State Prisons 291, 20 N.Y. Leg. Doc. No. 98 (1924).

[144] Id. at 331. There were 837 men in space authorized for 549, but used by 261 men 30 years earlier. Ibid.

[145] Id. at 293.

[146] Ibid.

[147] Id. at 331.

[148] Id. at 291.

[149] Id. at 331.

to the legislature than to the Superintendent of State Prisons, he noted:

the people do not hesitate to criticize the hospital but it is their representatives that are jeopardizing the service by failing to provide livable quarters and a salary large enough to attract the best type of medical men for State Hospital service.[150]

Needless to say, parole and aftercare were again raised.[151]

h) The Year 1924

At last plans were being made for new male facilities, a referendum having approved a substantial bond issue.[152] It would take several years to complete the project, however. New patient housing was welcomed, but did nothing to relieve the staff housing problem or prevent further resignations. Criticizing inadequate consideration of "safe custody" in the new pre-trial observation procedures[153]—calling for examination in a hospital—Dr. Kieb suggested that the planned construction at Matteawan would make feasible a system of conducting all pre-trial mental examinations there.[154] Parole was again discussed.[155]

Between February 1859 and July 1924, some 5,058 patients had been committed to the Auburn-Matteawan institution: 3,427 "convicted" and 1,631 "unconvicted," and a cumulative table of "crimes committed by those admitted since opening" [156] was published. Since historically the institution was primarily an asylum for prisoners, it is not surprising that less than one-third of its patients were shown to have been pre-trial or acquittal cases. It is interesting to note that most "murders" were apparently within that smaller group, as were most assault, arson, and sodomy cases. However, the analysis of the "misdemeanant insane" indicated the infrequency of pre-trial commitments of tramps,

[150] Id. at 293.
[151] Id. at 307.
[152] 1924 Ann. Rep. Sup't State Prisons 10, 20 N.Y. Leg. Doc. No. 111 (1925).
[153] Id. at 301.
[154] Ibid. See Chapter III, *supra*.
[155] Id. at 312.
[156] Id. at 345–50.

vagrants, prostitutes, drunkards and disorderly persons. That, of course, was consistent with Dr. Kieb's statements concerning post-trial transfers of these "social offenders" from local jails and penitentiaries. Robbers, thieves and burglars accounted for more than one-third of all patients and less than 25 percent of these patients were pre-trial or acquittal commitments.

i) The Year 1925

Two more physicians had resigned because of the unsolved staff housing problem.[157] Their replacements operated "under a serious handicap by reason of a limited knowledge of English" which, happily, they were rapidly overcoming.[158] Apparently, however, there was a substantial period during the year when only four of six physicians at Matteawan could, assuming they found the time, effectively communicate with the 975 patients hospitalized for treatment.[159] Notwithstanding this, the superintendent repeated his suggestion that all pre-trial cases be observed at Matteawan; needless to say, he also repeated himself on the parole question.[160]

j) The Years 1926–1927

In February 1926, the Hughes Commission on Reorganization of the State Government filed its report, recommending, among other changes, creation of two new state departments: Correction and Mental Hygiene.[161] All prisons were proposed as suitable for operation within the Department of Correction but

Napanoch, and the Matteawan State Hospital, each of which would seem to present peculiarly and exclusively problems of mental treatment . . . should be operated under the new Department of Mental Hygiene.[162]

As to the proper place for Matteawan in particular:

[157] 1925 Ann. Rep. Sup't State Prisons 324, 21 N.Y. Leg. Doc. No. 117 (1926).
[158] Ibid.
[159] Id. at 330.
[160] Id. at 292.
[161] State of N.Y., Public Papers of Gov. Alfred E. Smith 597, 632–39 (1926).
[162] Id. at 637.

There has been considerable doubt as to the proper place for the Matteawan State Hospital. This institution receives patients under direct commitment from the courts who have been adjudged to be insane while under criminal charges, either before or after indictment, after conviction before sentence is imposed, or where acquitted on the grounds of insanity. It also receives patients from penal institutions who are serving sentences for misdemeanors of one year or less, but no felons, except female prisoners from the Auburn State Prison for Women who are transferred to this institution. On the whole, it appears that the problems of this institution are primarily such as should be treated under the Department of Mental Hygiene, and we accordingly recommend that it be so transferred.[163]

The recommendation was made despite the commission's recognition "that the criminal acts of the inmates" raised a serious question.[164] The commission proposed to assign Dannemora to the Department of Correction, however, because it "is so closely identified with the custody of criminals serving terms for felonies. . . ." [165] The proposals were enacted on creation of the new Mental Hygiene and Correction Departments in 1926.[166] Inexplicably, however, in 1927 Governor Smith approved a bill which removed Matteawan from the Department of Mental Hygiene and restored it to the prison authorities—the Department of Correction.[167]

k) The Year 1928

Male overcrowding was being solved,[168] and Governor Smith addressed the legislature on the other urgent needs of Matteawan:

I am calling to your attention a situation at Matteawan State Hospital that in my opinion requires our immediate attention. This institution is severely handicapped by lack of proper quarters for employees and urgently requires an addition to the Women's Group.

[163] Id. at 638.

[164] Id. at 633.

[165] Id. at 639.

[166] N.Y. Laws 1926, Chs. 584, 606.

[167] N.Y. Laws 1927, Ch. 426, § 4 (adding a new § 11 to the Mental Hygiene Law).

[168] N.Y. Times, April 19, 1926, p. 7, col. 2 (a "new annex" to accommodate 320 patients expected to be ready early in 1927).

As to the Employees' Home, married couples have only a small room, without any sanitary conveniences, and there are no rooms at all available for single male employees. When the new group was constructed, it was planned to house employees in a separate building, so that no provision exists in the new group for these employees. The only alternative, therefore, is residence in the city of Beacon, two miles from the hospital, without transportation facilities. The employees are required to be on duty at 5:45 A.M. and the Commissioner of Correction finds it impossible to recruit satisfactory employees on the low salary basis when they are confronted with the problem of walking this distance, disagreeable at all times and intolerable in rainy and stormy weather. It is proposed to provide housing for fourteen married couples and twenty-six single men.

As to the addition to the Women's Group, the housing situation for women patients is the most serious in the State when the type of patient is taken into consideration. The census today is 167 inmates, with a certified capacity of 108; and this population must of necessity increase as most of the patients admitted are suffering from chronic types of mental illness. The assaultive and homicidal patients from other hospitals are received by direct court commitments, after exhibition of dangerous tendencies, and there is no provision for housing this type of women patients. Near riots have been precipitated and immediate relief is imperative or we may at any moment look for a calamity.[169]

The necessary funds were appropriated.[170]

l) The Year 1930

The Great Depression arrived in one of Matteawan's best years since 1893. New additions had reduced overcrowding to a mere 38 patients over capacity (1,113), and the new staff housing, it was hoped, would provide "more stability in the personnel." [171] There had been no resignations during the year. The physician-patient ratio was down to 1 to 166, and the patient population was also changing:

[169] State of N.Y., Public Papers of Gov. Alfred E. Smith 149–50 (1928).

[170] N.Y. Laws 1928, ch. 631.

[171] 1930 Ann. Rep. Comm'n'r Correc. 311, 313, 20 N.Y. Leg. Doc. No. 85 (1931).

There is a natural tendency for gradual increase in court cases. Ten years ago the convicts outnumbered court cases in spite of several large transfers of the former to civil hospitals. Court cases have few avenues of release and are usually charged with more serious offenses. They have accumulated until they now constitute over sixty per cent of the population.

For the past five years court cases have also outnumbered the convicted class in admissions and one may anticipate that the change will be progressive. It is a trend which I believe is in keeping with the purpose of the hospital, and I look forward to the time when the institution will be devoted entirely to the care of cases entrusted to it by the courts until they become mentally restored and can stand trial. The convicted misdemeanant, I trust, will be either committed direct to a civil hospital, or to an institution devoted to that class alone.[172]

m) The Year 1931

Overcrowding was "largely eliminated," but of some 452 prisoners under treatment, sentences had expired in 294 or 65 percent of the cases, and "a large percentage could safely be transferred" to civil hospitals "as they have not exhibited vicious or dangerous tendencies."[173] Parole was still desirable,[174] and the physician-patient ratio was reported down to 1 to 147 despite three more resignations.[175] Equally important, however, was the need to provide Matteawan with "proper security from outside attack." Although "the institution functions primarily as a hospital . . . safe custody is essential." The security issue had been brought to a head by an incident in December 1930. Although

[172] Id. at 313.

[173] 1931 Ann. Rep. Comm'n'r Correc. 307, 310, 19 N.Y. Leg. Doc. No. 85 (1932).

[174] Id. at 316.

[175] Id. at 323, 334. The hospital told of a defendant who, if convicted, would have been a fourth offender. He was committed to Matteawan as unfit to be tried, but was returned to court as a malingerer. He was acquitted by reason of insanity and was again sent to Matteawan (under N.Y. Code Crim. Proc. § 454). The patient was "jubilant" since the hospital recognized that "detention of a sane person is illegal and this patient must be returned to society." Id. at 310.

escapes *from* Matteawan were not unheard of—8 escapes were reported for this year alone—one patient not only broke out this year, but actually returned to *break into* Matteawan to help six other patients to flee.[176]

n) The Years 1932–1944

After 1931, Matteawan's annual reports were no longer published.[177] Between 1931 and 1945 the population of Matteawan grew from 1,195 to 1,543. Only in 1942 and 1944, war years, did the census decrease.[178] Problems facing New York State during the thirties and into the war years were by no means unique. The national plight of mental hospitals has been described by Deutsch:

The Great Economic Depression that started with the stock market crash in 1929 and lasted almost a decade sharply reversed the generally upward trend in mental hospital standards witnessed during the previous half century. When state budgets were drastically curtailed, institutions for the mentally handicapped felt the pinch first and worst. Construction projects were scrapped for years.

· · ·

A report on "State Hospitals in the Depression" prepared by the National Committee for Mental Hygiene in 1934, revealed that three-fourths of 104 institutions included in the survey were overcrowded and that one-fourth had been forced to close their doors against new admissions. Long waiting lists were found in a number of states, while in some states many men and women patients were confined for lengthy periods in jails because of mental hospital overcrowding.

· · ·

Existing institutions underwent serious deterioration; for years in some states not a penny was appropriated for repairs. Budgets for personnel,

[176] Id. at 318.

[177] Apparently there has been no publication of the annual reports made by Matteawan (or Dannemora) since 1931. They are not found in the New York Legislative Documents after 1932. The committee's staff was granted access to the hospital's own carbon copies of its typewritten reports, and studied those for the years 1945 to 1965. The reports are made by the superintendent to the Commissioner of Correction (N.Y. Correc. Law § 405 [5]) as of March 31 of each year. Hereafter the footnote references to the reports will be simplified, with a notation only to the year made, as follows: M. S. H. Ann. Rep. (March 31, 1945).

[178] See Table 1.

food, and upkeep were cut to the bone. Staffs were demoralized; patients despaired; curative ideals were forgotten in the desperate push for mere physical survival.

. . .

A New York State Senator in 1943 made public serious charges against a particular hospital after a personal visit. The Governor then appointed a Moreland Act Commission to investigate the management and affairs of the State Mental Hygiene Department and the institutions operated by it. The Commission's resulting report, published in 1944, was a severe indictment of long-standing defects in the entire system that shocked the people of a state that had prided itself on its pre-eminent place in mental hygiene.[179]

The New York investigation[180] singled out as the "outstanding deficiency" the fact that mental hospitals had "become principally custodial institutions rather than hospitals in the true sense of the word." The heart of the problem was "the lack of adequate professional care of the patient." Personnel shortages in civil hospitals were an "alarming" 31 percent among physicians, 32 percent among ward employees, and 17 percent among other employees. The commission's investigation did not extend, apparently, to the conditions at Matteawan since it was then, as now, operated by the Department of Correction, not Mental Hygiene. That there is no reason to assume those conditions to have been significantly better than civil hospitals, in New York or elsewhere, is painfully clear from the Annual Reports of Matteawan Superintendents in the post-war years. The problems and disappointments had begun to collect and grow worse not more than five years after the first flush of excitement and hope for the new and expensive hospital at Matteawan. Overcrowding, staff shortages, escapes, and claims of maltreatment created a poor public image which no amount of tourist sightseeing could restore to its former pride. Economic disaster did not help, nor did the Second World War. Scandal in civil hospital administration brought reform, and money was spent—but apparently not much was spent at Matteawan. While the civil institutions were being restored in the

[179] Deutsch, The Mentally Ill in America 446–50 (2d rev. ed. 1949). (Footnote omitted.)

[180] State of N.Y., Public Papers of Gov. Thomas E. Dewey 376–460 (1944).

post-war years to their former estate, the problems of Matteawan were largely ignored. Conditions which since 1896 had never been ideal, grew worse. Once again, the story is told by outspoken and critical Annual Reports of the hospital's superintendents, and except as otherwise noted, the following facts and quotations are taken from those Annual Reports.[181]

o) The Years 1945–1949

On January 1 there were 1,545 patients at Matteawan,[182] and the medical staff was reduced to four physicians.[183] There were seven vacancies, and one man was in military service. Unless the service were made more attractive, there would be a severe recruitment problem in the post-war years. Notwithstanding the personnel situation, diagnostic staff conferences continued to be held twice weekly, and at them all patients were presented within three months of their admission, as well as those being considered for release. During the year, 85 were admitted and 103 discharged, including 46 deaths. Occupational therapy was "necessarily limited due to the type of inmates cared for," but effort was made usefully to employ about the hospitals all whose mental state permitted it. There were no concerted efforts at escape by large groups, but three escaped while on outside activity with "little or no supervision."

Population was still climbing in 1946, but the year was "marked by a grave lack of personnel, particularly on the medical staff . . . which has consisted of only three or four physicians." [184] As a result, "it has been impossible to give the individual attention to the patients which is so necessary in the care and treatment of the mentally ill."

Psychiatric service would have to be made more attractive if only to accommodate the increased admission which could be anticipated on disbanding of the armed forces and the post-war economic chaos. Until recently prohibited by the Civil Service Law, physicians at Matteawan and Dannemora could look for-

[181] See note 177 *supra*. Reports will be cited only once for each year.

[182] See Table 1.

[183] M. S. H. Ann. Rep. (March 31, 1945).

[184] M. S. H. Ann. Rep. (March 31, 1946).

ward to promotion within the larger Department of Mental Hygiene. The professional interchange had been good for both types of institutions, but even on a more practical level the new rule created a "decidedly dreary" promotion outlook for younger men considering service in Correction hospitals. Unless the law were amended, there would be little possibility of obtaining competent medical staffs at Matteawan and Dannemora. Under the added burden of the removal of preferential pay for the less pleasant service in the Correction hospitals, they "will gradually revert to custodial care." Although badly pressed for isolation units caring for the assaultive and homicidal type of patients, new projects had been approved and it was hoped that construction would start soon.

By 1947, returning servicemen and women had made it easy to recruit custodial personnel, but the "greatest problem" still was obtaining competent medical personnel.[185] The following year an amendment to allow interdepartmental promotions was under discussion, and it was reported that "the general standard of care and treatment of the patients has improved." [186] Transfers of "quiet and well behaved" patients to civil hospitals relieved some of the overcrowding at Matteawan, but admissions were still increasing, and

we continue to receive disturbed, assaultive and homicidal patients, with no adequate provision for their care. A great many of them must be cared for in open wards. . . .

The authorized construction was urgently needed.

The same tales were told in 1949: recruitment problems, need for promotional interchange, four staff vacancies, rising admissions, and overcrowding (male, 18%; female, 22%).[187] Hopefully, someone would do something about new facilities for disturbed and female patient housing.

p) The Years 1950–1959

The new decade, marking almost 60 years at Matteawan, brought with it some prospect of improvement and new notoriety.

185 M. S. H. Ann. Rep. (March 31, 1947).
186 M. S. H. Ann. Rep. (March 31, 1948).
187 M. S. H. Ann. Rep. (March 31, 1949).

Contracts had finally been awarded for construction of facilities for 44 female patients, for disturbed patients, and for a much-needed dining room.[188] However,

this added construction will increase our housing capacity by 179, which would not take care of our overcrowding even if it were available as of the present date. Therefore immediate consideration should be given to construction of additional housing for male patients in the Reception Hospital Building which has been included in our budgetary requests for several years.

Some 170 patients were admitted in 1950, and 149 were discharged, including 55 deaths. The plight of the medical staff, in whose hands was placed the responsibility to treat and ultimately to release the patients, was described by the superintendent:

It is interesting to note that twenty-five years ago with a daily average population of 953, the Medical Staff consisted of five physicians. Today, with a daily average population of 1,690 we still have the same number of physicians on the Staff and there have been prolonged periods when the number was reduced to four.

It was recognized that the civil hospitals were also having trouble recruiting, but it was "particularly difficult" at Matteawan "because of the dangerous type of patient" to be treated. The Personnel Committee of the Department of Mental Hygiene in an "ill-considered" action had rejected a proposal which would have permitted interdepartmental movement, and staff housing was inadequate.

Operating under these conditions, the staff had released on March 5, 1950, a young man named William H. Jones. Five days later he stabbed seven persons in Brooklyn, killing four of them.[189] Within a week the conditions at Matteawan became part of an attack on the incumbent administration's conservative use of the state's Post-War Reconstruction Fund available for expansion of mental hospital facilities.[190] A New York City councilman called for a major investigation of "the parole and release system" at

[188] M. S. H. Ann. Rep. (March 31, 1950).
[189] See cases cited in notes 199, 202 infra.
[190] N.Y. Times, March 13, 1950, p. 3, col. 3.

Matteawan.[191] No immediate investigations appear to have been made.

The following year Matteawan reported [192] that with only four physicians on the staff "the standards of care and treatment have necessarily suffered." It was "most difficult to fill" vacancies despite a finally won amendment of the Mental Hygiene Law (section 5) allowing interdepartmental movement. Unfortunately the new law did not include "physicians in the Senior Supervisory or Supervisory group, and these are the positions which are most difficult to fill." Another difficulty with filling these positions was that the canvassing of applicants was done by the Civil Service Commission. As a result, the superintendent had "little or no possibility of personal contact with the candidate," some of whom did not have a clear idea of the nature of Matteawan, apart, perhaps, "from having been instrumental in having someone committed" to it.

In 1952 new male housing was again urged for immediate consideration.[193] Medical staff problems of course continued. A higher salary scale was needed "if we expect to accord our patients proper scientific care and treatment." Moreover, three staff houses for physicians had been "requested for several years" and needed serious consideration so the hospital could offer suitable quarters to such applicants as might appear. No progress had been made in extending the interdepartmental promotional range.

On July 28, 1952, two patients escaped and stole cars, but were recaptured in New York City.[194] Prompted by "a recent widely publicized murder committed by a former patient at a Federal hospital," on August 2, 1952, Governor Dewey requested the Mental Hygiene Council to "undertake a thorough review" of release procedures in public and private mental hospitals.[195]

[191] N.Y. Times, March 15, 1950, p. 39, col. 5.

[192] M. S. H. Ann. Rep. (March 31, 1951).

[193] M. S. H. Ann. Rep. (March 31, 1952).

[194] M. S. H. Ann. Rep. (March 31, 1953).

[195] N. Y. S. Mental Hygiene Council, Statement and Report Concerning a Study of Release Procedure for Mental Patients in New York State 2 (Dec. 7, 1954), in State of N.Y. Public Papers of Gov. Thomas E. Dewey 831–57 (1954).

Meanwhile, a Dutchess County grand jury investigated the Matteawan escape, visited the hospital, and in September, 1952, returned a presentment reporting no evidence of neglect, but at the same time recommending a series of improved security devices: (1) more attendants, particularly at night, (2) a 24-hour ground patrol with vehicles or horses and a modern communication system, (3) improved communication systems within the buildings, (4) an organized police road-block plan, (5) a training program for attendants, and (6) extension of existing fences.[196] The Commissioner of Correction promised "careful study and thorough consideration" of the recommendation that more attendants be added to Matteawan.[197]

In the same month as the grand jury's presentment was reported, the press carried new stories relating to Jones' four homicides. The lawsuit brought by one of Jones' victims came to trial in September, 1952, and her counsel claimed to be able to prove that the Matteawan staff was so "badly overworked" that one physician "had to care for eight wards and 500 patients."[198] At the trial the Superintendent of Matteawan "admitted," according to the trial court, that "the diagnosis ultimately arrived at was erroneous" but "the mistake could not have been avoided."[199] He also testified that "two psychiatrists were doing the work of six. 'The doctors were over-worked and the institution was understaffed.' "[200] On February 4, 1953, the state lost a judgment of $40,712 in the Jones litigation, the court finding negligence in a premature release,[201] but it was later reversed by the Appellate Division on the ground that the state was not "legally responsible in damages for an honest error of professional judgment made by qualified and competent persons. . . ."[202]

[196] M. S. H. Ann. Rep. (March 31, 1953).

[197] N.Y. Times, Sept. 16, 1952, p. 22, col. 3.

[198] N.Y. Times, Sept. 4, 1952, p. 15, col. 3.

[199] St. George v. State of N.Y., 203 Misc. 340, 348, 118 N.Y.S. 2d 596, 603 (Ct. Cl. 1953).

[200] Id. at 347, 118 N.Y.S. 2d at 602.

[201] Id. at 348–50, 118 N.Y.S. 2d at 604–05.

[202] St. George v. State of N.Y., 283 App. Div. 245, 248, 127 N.Y.S. 2d 147, 150 (3d Dep't), aff'd. mem., 308 N.Y. 681, 124 N.E. 2d 320 (1954).

In his report for the 1952–53 fiscal year,[203] Superintendent McNeill had little favorable news to report. The population was still climbing inexorably toward the 2,000 mark. Resignations by two newly appointed physicians barred any improvement in the medical service, and none of the long-sought recruitment devices were available. Additional staff housing was still up in the air. The hospital had been attempting to obtain professional approval for a residency in psychiatry but it had failed partly because of limited training facilities, and lack of a hospital pathologist, psychologist and social workers. Such a program would help recruit younger men into the service. Having asked for them in 1952, the hospital in 1953 won approval for the necessary new positions, but could only fill the psychologist position, and that only on a temporary basis. The superintendent sifted through the grand jury's security recommendations and (probably encouraged by his commissioner's earlier promise of serious consideration) he requested funds for various changes. The most significant request was for 80 *custodial* positions. The fence extension was considered impractical (but is currently being effected). A training program of 20 lectures was begun in January 1953.

Two months into the next fiscal year, on June 7, 1953, three patients escaped by sawing through window bars.[204] Again a Dutchess County grand jury investigated because of the "public furor created by repeated escapes from institutions" in that county. More security devices and more custodial personnel were urged, as well as compliance with its earlier recommendations. Electric-eye searches and checks of all autos and visitors for weapons were recommended, as well as a new building for patients—this latter because it would be less expensive than replacing old bars in existing facilities (estimated possible cost for new bars, excluding masonry work, was between $844,000 and $2,000,000). In September, 1953, a system of continuous vehicular patrol of the hospital grounds was instituted; a police booth was erected at the main entrance and all other gates were closed to the public. Twelve armed safety personnel were added, as well as a safety supervisor. In April, 1954, 25 new positions were al-

203 M. S. H. Ann. Rep. (March 32, 1953).
204 M. S. H. Ann. Rep. (March 31, 1954).

lotted to the ward service. Additional telephones were installed in the dormitories, but the electric eye was omitted as impractical. All of these improvements in the *security* of the hospital were reported as achieved in less than two years after they were requested. However, the Annual Report (1954) in which they were related still told of the familiar *medical* needs of the institution.

Salary differentials and promotions were essential. Staff housing was still inadequate despite its having been pointed out "for a number of years"—it had still not been approved by the Division of the Budget. It was

most difficult to keep up the standards of care and treatment due to the shortage on the Medical Staff and the fact that we have had an increased admission rate. This is in great part due to the fact that the Code of Criminal Procedure, particularly Section 662-b, was amended last year, making it mandatory that the courts commit all cases under indictment to this hospital, rather than allow them a choice of a commitment to a civil hospital . . . or to this hospital. At the time this law was proposed, I called to the attention of the Department some of the objectionable features which I felt were involved in the law, and also pointed out that this would necessarily mean an increase in our population and would result in overcrowding to a dangerous degree.

. . .

Further housing for male patients is imperative. The amendments . . . have caused an increase in the rate of admissions, the present capacity of the hospital being 1615 and as of March 31, 1954, the census was 1920. A budgetary request has been made for additional housing for 450 male patients and unless this construction is undertaken in the immediate future, the overcrowding will result in serious consequences. I would therefore urge that the Department give every possible attention to the speeding up of the construction requested.

Part of the problem behind the inability to recruit physicians was the type of work:

The psychiatric work in an institution of this nature is not as satisfying as it is in that of the civil hospitals. A high percentage of our patients are paranoid individuals who resent any attempt to make a sympathetic approach and are prone to take the law into their own hands, and not abide by the rules and regulations. We have in the past contacted qualified psychiatrists in the Department of Mental Hygiene relative to the possibility of a transfer or even a promotion, but this has been refused, mainly because they can receive the same remuneration in a much more pleasant and satisfying environment.

During the year the hospital also contacted 24 upstate counties and posted notices in the Academy of Medicine, but the efforts generated no results. One of the few satisfactions of the year was the success in achieving "good results" from purposefully installing two of the five new television sets "on disturbed wards."

On December 22, 1954, Governor Dewey made public[205] a summary report of the Mental Hygiene Council's study of mental hospital release procedures.[206] They were found to be "fundamentally sound and conscientiously administered." [207] The statutory framework was "legally, medically and socially sound." [208] The consultants visited Matteawan and Dannemora, and received "full and descriptive details of release procedures and special problems." [209] Discharge and "follow-up" was a medical matter, not legal.[210] Personnel standards in all hospitals should constantly be improved, but there was "a country-wide shortage of psychiatric specialists" in all classes of employees.[211] The release systems in the state

can and should be continuously improved by measures to increase knowledge of the conduct of the patients while on convalescent status and after discharge . . . by continuing to provide better standards and ratios of personnel; by extending still further the program in the hospitals for the criminal insane; by ultimately transferring these hospitals to the Department of Mental Hygiene. . . .

.   .   .

Except for such statutory amendments as would be required to accomplish a transfer of certain institutions from the Department of Correction to the Department of Mental Hygiene . . . it is believed that further improvements in release machinery can be quickly and effectively accomplished by departmental regulation.[212]

[205] N.Y. Times, Dec. 23, 1954, p. 26, col. 6.
[206] N.Y.S. Mental Hygiene Council, op. cit. supra note 195.
[207] Id. at 9.
[208] Id. at 11.
[209] Id. at 5.
[210] Id. at 6.
[211] Ibid.
[212] Id. at 9, 11.

The report listed a variety of recommendations, some already "accomplished," some "in progress" and others "long-term objectives." Among those already accomplished were (1) additional positions for assistant directors at the larger hospitals to facilitate diagnosis, treatment and release; (2) new positions for "release officers" (psychiatrists); (3) proposed legislation creating local mental health boards; (4) reorganization of follow-up and after-care services in New York City; (5) changes in release procedures of the Department of Mental Hygiene.[213]

In addition to several relating solely to the civil hospitals, the following "recommendations in progress" concerned the Correction hospitals:

1. Arrangements have been made between the Department of Mental Hygiene and the Department of Correction to provide in part for the transfer of eligible patients to institutions in the Department of Mental Hygiene so that following their release the social service staffs of the latter institutions can follow the patients.
2. The consultants recommended that in order to improve the service in the institutions for the criminal insane a method be developed for the interchange of medical personnel between the institutions of the two departments by mutual agreement. Inasmuch as individuals of professional status are involved, a number of difficulties have been encountered, although some steps leading to professional interchange have been taken.[214]

If these recommendations seemed to be stop-gap measures, requiring Matteawan, for example, to forego having its own social workers, it was obviously because the "long-term objectives" included transfer to Mental Hygiene of Dannemora, Matteawan, Napanoch and Albion:

The placing of mental institutions under the same administrative control will facilitate the transfer of difficult criminal cases, provide better medical care for the criminal insane, promote recruitment of professional staff by providing better opportunities for rotation through various types of institutions, and foster research in medical jurisprudence and criminal psychopathology. The placing of criminal insane and defective delinquents in a department other than that controlling the

213 Id. at 12–13.
214 Id. at 13–14.

civil mental hospitals occurs in very few states. The experience of states that have had separate administrative control has been unsatisfactory from the standpoint of rehabilitation and treatment of the criminal insane.[215]

Once Dannemora and Matteawan are transferred to Mental Hygiene that department

should develop [for those hospitals] better quotas with special reference to psychiatrists, social workers, psychologists, nurses, attendants and medical stenographers, so that better treatment, better follow-up and better records can be maintained.[216]

In the text of the actual *Study* itself, as distinguished from the summary "report" thereon released by the Governor, it had been noted that, statewide, "release procedures are usually initiated by the ward psychiatrist," [217] and that "case records, which are essential to the continuity of treatment and release consideration, were found to be of uneven quality." [218] At Matteawan and Dannemora: "the whole small staff participated in release consideration"; "observation of clinical conferences at both institutions revealed high-level professional judgment from a clinical point of view"; Matteawan had "only three fully available psychiatrists carrying an impossibly heavy load"; Dannemora "was about twice as well off, but still woefully understaffed"; "the present professional atmosphere is one of overburdened deadly isolation" and "recruitment of professional staff appears at a chronic standstill." [219] Notwithstanding these problems, the 1953 amendment of section 662-b of the Code of Criminal Procedure —mandating commitment to Matteawan of all mentally ill *indicted* defendants—appeared "sound" when it was considered that "many of these patients require" maximum-security custody and "their relatively small number would not unduly burden the

[215] Id. at 14–15.
[216] Id. at 14.
[217] Study of Release Procedures in New York Mental Hospitals 19 (1953).
[218] Id. at 30.
[219] Id. at 32.

181

correctional institutions." [220] The study also made observations concerning release of defendants,[221] persons acquitted by reason of insanity,[222] time-expired prisoners,[223] after-care[224] and habeas corpus.[225]

[220] Id. at 41. It was also noted that in civil hospitals "these patients require special handling in regard to security [and] . . . cannot usually participate in the same therapeutic program as the others." The new law should afford "considerable relief" from such problems. Id. at 21. See Chapter III, *supra*.

[221] Id. at 42. It is "extremely difficult for the prosecutors to obtain a conviction" of patients civilly admitted to civil state hospitals pursuant to sections 872 and 873 because of the "practical, though not a legal presumption" of insanity at the time of the crime. "The sections are said to be used frequently to avoid serving prison terms. With this realistic circumstance in mind, considerable thought should be given by the directors of the institution to return a patient to the court upon a finding that he is no longer in such a state of insanity as to be unable to stand trial. The statutes indicate that the primary responsibility is upon the court to determine whether the defendant should then be released to the community. As a practical matter, the responsibility to the community must be, in some measure, taken by the director in such a release, since the provision for return to the court in many cases is a mere formality in returning him to the community." Ibid. (Presumably, reference was made to patients indicted after they were ordered hospitalized.)

[222] Id. at 43. Patients committed upon acquittal under section 454 of the Code of Criminal Procedure "might represent the most potentially dangerous group under consideration," but "since ordinarily when they are committed . . . for homicide or a crime of violence they are rarely released," they did not constitute a major problem. Ibid.

[223] Id. at 44. Release of time-expired prisoners from Matteawan and Dannemora "create some serious problems" of which "the most serious . . . is the complete omission of any provision for after care for such patients." The lawsuit resulting from Jones' four homicides (see text accompanying notes 189 and 198–202, *supra*) "demonstrated clearly" the need for "caution, adequate information, and sound judgment in the discharge of a patient in this category." Ibid.

[224] See note 223, *supra*.

[225] Id. at 45. Although habeas corpus is "widely used" by criminal

Between 1951 and 1955, the medical staff at Matteawan increased from five psychiatrists to 10, and although there were still no social workers, there was a clinical psychologist on the staff after 1953.[226] The usual requests and suggestions as to the *medical* situation were repeated in 1955.[227] Two physicians were living off-grounds because of inadequate housing as to which "nothing concrete" had yet been done. The hospital had also been denied the additional (second) dentist it required with a daily average population of 1,940, up by 71 over the prior year. The certified capacity was still 1,615 and overcrowding on the male wards "reached serious proportions." The hospital had also been denied four additional security patrolmen despite its protest that adequate security required them.

By the following year (1956), the number of psychiatrists had dropped from 10 to 8, just as population inevitably increased to 1,988 (certified capacity still 1,615).[228] Equally serious was the fact that some

members of the Medical Staff who are not licensed and who are not familiar with the English language cannot be adequately trained [in forensic psychiatry]. It is of the utmost importance that testimony be presented to the courts in such a manner that potentially dangerous individuals are not released into society. The very fact that the psychiatrist appears and testifies against the release of our patients accentuates the feelings of hatred and revenge against them, and the psychiatrist is not infrequently included in the patients' delusional formation.

The same old problems of the medical staff were discussed except that now four physicians were living off the grounds. It was noted that it was "impossible to fill" social-worker and occupational-therapy positions. An associate pathologist had been added to the staff during the year, however (the first in 30 years), as well as another dentist. The hospital still was denied the additional patrolmen and firemen it had sought for several years.

---

order patients, "available information reveals that relatively few obtain release in this fashion." Ibid.

[226] M. S. H. Ann. Rep. (March 31, 1955).

[227] Ibid.

[228] M. S. H. Ann. Rep. (March 31, 1956).

Male overcrowding continued, but plans for new construction were almost complete. Compensating the overcrowding to some degree, perhaps, was the success in using tranquilizers. Serpasil was used in 149 cases which were among the "most difficult management problems, both from a psychiatric and behavior standpoint." Some improvement was found in 77 percent of the cases, and 42.4 percent were "markedly improved." According to the superintendent,

many of these patients have been institutionalized for years and have been subject to electroshock and other procedures, without benefit. Although the drug did not cure, it enabled the psychiatrists to establish a healthier relationship with a number of patients who have been resistant to previous attempts and regimes.

The civil hospitals were also experiencing "quite satisfactory" results in the use of tranquilizers—civil releases climbed 3,000 above the prior year's rate—and the success was reported to have "brought about a drastic change in outlook for the mental hygiene program." [229]

The next year (1957) was "the first year in the past decade where the discharges [249] from . . . [Matteawan] have exceeded the admissions [246]." [230] There were no changes in the medical staff (eight) which included three diplomates of the American Board of Psychiatry and Neurology, as well as three psychiatrists who were not licensed to practice medicine. A clinical laboratory operated by the pathologist appointed the prior year was approved by the state, but preferential pay was still lacking as well as new staff housing. The "psychological Department" at Matteawan consisted of one senior clinical psychologist added during the year. The daily average population was 2,000. There was still no social worker and there were vacancies in occupational therapist and O.T. aides (and, as to the latter, "due to the required standards and low salary"). There was difficulty in filling ward-attendant positions on a permanent basis because appointments were made from a combined attendant and guard list which allowed transfers back and forth between

[229] N.Y. Times, April 6, 1956, p. 27, col. 7; Jan. 30, 1957, p. 11, col. 3; N.Y.S. Journal of Medicine, June 15, 1956 (Matteawan).
[230] M. S. H. Ann. Rep. (March 31, 1957).

prisons and the two hospitals in the Department of Correction. The training programs for the two positions "differ widely in detail" and transfers involved retraining. As to physicians:

We have made numerous contacts in an endeavor to obtain the services of licensed physicians, even though they were not psychiatrists, with the idea in mind that they could be trained, but so far we have been unsuccessful and due to the shortage of psychiatrists throughout the State institutions, we have been unable to obtain any acceptances when certified lists were circularized.

.   .   .

The psychiatric standards of the hospitals must be maintained unless we are willing to accept the criticism of the committing courts and the public in general. The committing courts, on frequent occasions, advised the relatives of our patients that they are not being sent to prison but are being sent to a hospital for care and treatment of the mentally ill, and the public in general, because of the great publicity given to psychiatry in recent years, demands that modern methods of care and treatment be made available to the patients.

.   .   .

This year one hundred and ten days were spent in the courts by members of the Staff. Unless we are able to obtain qualified men, the hospital will gradually lose its standing and become simply a custodial institution.

Because the single social-worker position was still vacant, the psychiatrists themselves tried to collect as much information as possible about patients in their care. Contact would be made with the committing court, the district attorney, and any institution in which the patient had earlier been confined:

When this information has been assembled, the patient is presented by summary before a Staff conference where the patient is examined by the group. Following the patient's dismissal a general discussion of psychodynamics, diagnosis, prognosis and treatment is held and a treatment program outlined.

Such meetings were held twice weekly and another "special Staff conference is called when a board of three Diplomates in Psychiatry meet with the Superintendent to consider the possible discharge of any case."

In the last two years of another decade in the life of a now 100-year-old "experiment," the medical staff climbed back up to the 1955 figure (ten). The social-worker position was filled in

1958 on a temporary basis.[231] Three physicians on the staff had "little or no training in psychiatry and are not licensed to practice medicine in New York State." The decade closed the way it had opened—too many vacancies, recruitment difficulty and other familiar problems. One favorable trend that appeared to be in progress was a perceptible increase in the number of patients transferred or committed to civil hospitals. For example, in the five-year period from 1950 to 1954, a total of 78 patients were thus removed from Matteawan. In the three-year period from 1956 to 1958, some 91 patients were removed.

q) The Years 1960–1966

Little had changed. Nothing is said about the Blain Commission's recommendations to Governor Dewey.[232] There were 13 psychiatrists at Matteawan,[233] but, once again, the medical-staff problem:

The fact that we have been unable to recruit qualified psychiatrists has been called to the attention of the Department [of Correction] on many occasions. I am of the opinion, unless some action is taken to establish a preferential wage scale for the various positions on the Medical Staff of this hospital, we will have to continue to operate with psychiatrists who are not qualified.

Because of the fact that we have so much medico-legal work and are so closely involved with the courts, it is essential that we have qualified psychiatrists who are able to examine and give expert testimony in the courts.

. . .

There continues to be an acute shortage of staff houses, although we were allowed one staff cottage this year. We have had applications by physicians which we were unable to accept because of lack of suitable housing for themselves and their families.

In 1961 there was no reason for the superintendent to amend his complaint:[234]

Granted, there is a shortage of psychiatrists throughout the country. The shortage is particularly evident in a hospital of this type. Those

[231] M. S. H. Ann. Rep. (March 31, 1958).
[232] See text accompanying notes 195 and 206–25, *supra*.
[233] M. S. H. Ann. Rep. (March 31, 1960).
[234] M. S. H. Ann. Rep. (March 31, 1961).

psychiatrists who had proper training and a good background are not interested in the care and treatment of the criminal insane.

It is my opinion that unless some such [preferential] classification is approved, the standard of care and treatment of the patients will gradually deteriorate.

A new annex to the Reception Building opened in February, but would only "in part relieve the overcrowding on the male wards" since wards housing approximately 150 patients had been closed pending rehabilitation. The average daily population for the year was 2,002, and there were still 13 psychiatrists at Matteawan.

The following year (1962) the daily average population rose to 2,063.[235] There were 12 psychiatrists, and

if one were to look back in the records prior to 1943 . . . we would find that [preferential pay] . . . was a common practice at that time and was quite productive.

Again the daily average population climbed now to 2,117 (1963) with 14 psychiatrists. Recruitment was soon eased by an urgent problem in the Department of Mental Hygiene:[236]

In December of 1962 civil hospitals which were recognized for training of their psychiatric staff suddenly were informed that recognition would be withheld if they continued to employ unlicensed physicians or physicians who had not passed the B.C.F.M.G. and as a result we were fortunate in obtaining the services of two psychiatrists from [a civil hospital]. . . . Soon after the first of the year we also obtained another Senior Psychiatrist. . . . These Senior Psychiatrists are not licensed to practice medicine in the State of New York, and this is a handicap to the administration of this hospital.

The hospital was "being pressured by Justices of the Supreme Court to return every possible recovered patient to the committing court." There were other pressures:

In addition, we are often criticized for holding patients who were arrested for insignificant offenses and have been retained at the hospital for many years because they have been obviously mentally ill. [For these reasons] . . . a survey was started in December 1962, and with the cooperation and approval of the Department of Mental Hy-

[235] M. S. H. Ann. Rep. (March 31, 1962).
[236] M. S. H. Ann. Rep. (March 31, 1963).

giene increasing numbers of patients were referred for evaluation as to suitability for care in a civil hospital.

Examination of prospective transfers was made "bi-weekly or monthly" by an assistant commissioner of the Department of Mental Hygiene. Fifty-four patients went to Hygiene institutions during the year, and although the hospital anticipated a higher rate of transfers out, it recognized in a new amendment to section 85 of the Mental Hygiene Law[237] the possibility of "larger numbers of dangerously mentally ill patients being certified from civil hospitals" to Matteawan.

Preferential pay would still "provide better and more adequate psychiatric care," but at least two new staff houses were available, and three more "tentatively provided" by the 1963 legislature were "much needed." Another psychologist was needed as well as an "Educational Supervisor to better organize and direct an educational therapy program." The education program apparently was a joint effort by the "psychology Department" and "patient teachers." The hospital needed "a certified teacher."

On March 31, 1964, there were 14 psychiatrists at Matteawan.[238] The situation was good, and it was bad:

During the past year all psychiatric positions have been filled. However, many [four] of our psychiatrists do not possess a license to practice medicine in either another state or New York State. This constitutes a weakness about which we can do little at the present time.

Subtle pressure to release patients was sustained, and the transfer survey had been continued. The hospital was grateful to Hygiene for accepting 117 patients during the year, not only because it reduced "the temporary overcrowding" to a not "excessive" level, but also because it afforded "a defense to organizations such as the Civil Liberties Union and the Bar Association, which sometimes lack understanding of our problem." The give and take involved in transfers between civil hospitals and Matteawan was a serious matter. Transfers of "dangerous" civil patients to Matteawan were at an all-time high. As many section

[237] See Chapter II, supra.
[238] M. S. H. Ann. Rep. (March 31, 1964).

85 patients were received in the previous two years (49) as in the next earlier five years combined:

On frequent occasions we are able to say to Mental Hygiene that we are prepared to look after the difficult, dangerous type of patient, but in return we shall expect that they will receive our quiet, non-aggressive patient who no longer has legal entanglements.

Once again preferential pay was requested, and the hope was expressed "that Public Works will soon be able to let the contract for at least two additional homes for psychiatrists," because "this fringe benefit helps to staff our hospital." The situation was probably not as bad as in 1894 when outdoor recreation was "largely left to the devices of the patients" themselves,[239] but what was also needed in 1964 was a "recreation supervisor and until this position is provided by the Division of the Budget we continue to provide as much recreation as possible for our patients."

As of March 31, 1965, the hospital staff was still handicapped by "several" unlicensed physicians, a "substantial need for preferential pay," a "vitally needed" addition of two psychologists, and a need for "a professionally trained recreation supervisor." Contracts had been awarded, however, for three new staff residences.[240]

In its most current annual report (March 31, 1966),[241] the hospital noted the "crisis" which resulted from the *Baxstrom*[242] decision and the fact that despite the "slowly dropping census" (803 patients discharged during the fiscal year), "about the same number of patients were produced" on writs of habeas corpus. Of 292 appearances, five writs were sustained. There had been no change in the psychiatric staff of the hospital, but three custodial positions had been reclassified for the Social Service Department. The request for an additional psychologist was re-

[239] See text accompanying note 73 *supra*.

[240] M. S. H. Ann. Rep. (March 31, 1965).

[241] M. S. H. Ann. Rep. (March 31, 1966).

[242] Baxstrom v. Herold, 383 U.S. 107 (1966). See Chapter II, *supra*.

peated since only one position was "granted by the budget," as well as that for a trained recreation supervisor. The hospital's educational program was described as putting the "main emphasis" on the "elementary level." An institutional teacher had been appointed, and he supervised eight inmate-teachers who "almost exclusively" taught the male students, and volunteer correction officers who, aided by two part-time inmate-teachers, taught the female students.

A note in closing. Matteawan was the result of a search for additional farm land that had begun in 1886. The hospital now reports that "since the spring of 1966 no patients have been assigned to the farm. All farm work is now being done by paid employees." Finally, in addition to (but separate from) its mentally ill patients, Matteawan now is expected to care for mental defectives and narcotics addicts.[243] The slack created by *Baxstrom* is fast being taken up.

[243] See Chapter II, *supra*, at note 71.

APPENDIX B

NEW YORK LEGISLATION AFFECTING MENTALLY ILL PRISONERS: 1842–1965

1. Utica Asylum: 1842–1858

In the 1842 [1] Act organizing the first "State Lunatic Asylum" at Utica, the omnibus criminal-insanity section[2] authorized the removal of a mentally ill prisoner "to the asylum, where he shall remain until restored to his right mind," and until a court believed his discharge to be "safe, legal and right." The provision that if on his recovery "the period of his imprisonment shall have expired he shall be discharged," impliedly authorized confinement after the expiration of his sentence. Because prisoners were merely one of many classes of persons covered by the section, and because only one procedure was set forth, they could be transferred to the asylum only after "a careful investigation" by a county judge who could choose to be aided by the testimony of "two respectable physicians and other credible witnesses," and possibly a jury.[3] Whether because this judicial procedure was considered too formal, or simply because the Utica Asylum was too inconvenient or too crowded, it is clear that not all mentally ill prisoners were removed to the asylum.[4]

In 1846, provision was made for mandatory transfer of a mentally ill prisoner in a state prison to the Utica Asylum for as "long as he shall continue insane," making explicit the authority granted by implication in 1842 to retain a prisoner after sentence.[5] In its major prison legislation of 1847,[6] the legislature provided

---

[1] For earlier legislation see Appendix A, *supra*, at notes 1–24.
[2] N.Y. Laws 1842, ch. 135, § 32, 42.
[3] N.Y. Laws 1842, ch. 135, § 32.
[4] See Appendix A, *supra*.
[5] N.Y. Laws 1846, ch. 324, § 1.
[6] N.Y. Laws 1847, ch. 460, §§ 14, 96–100.

that the 1842 rules for judicial commitments of mentally ill persons "under sentence of imprisonment" should be "construed" to apply to prisoners in *county jails*. A male or female prisoner in a *state prison*, however, now could be transferred to Utica by administrative order if the prison physician reported he was "so far insane as to render him dangerous, or an improper subject of prison discipline." If "no such report shall have been made," and if the warden or chaplain believed the criterion was met in a particular case, they could request an examination by a "justice of the peace and two practising physicians." If by majority vote they certified the prisoner mentally ill, the warden was obliged to transfer him to Utica.

Only one year later, the procedure was changed, placing the decision to transfer a state prisoner in the hands of a prison inspector who would "fully" investigate and hear the "testimony of at least two physicians"; if the transferred prisoner were still mentally ill at expiration of sentence, he could now be removed to a county poorhouse if further care at Utica would not benefit him.[7]

2. *Auburn Asylum: 1858–1893*

The 1858 Act organizing the Auburn Asylum,[8] apparently seeking to make use of such experts as were available, provided again a rather clumsy procedure (but now again administrative rather than judicial). By this time there were prisons at Sing Sing, Auburn and Clinton,[9] each designed to serve different parts of the state and thereby to save the expense and bother of distant transportation.[10] If the physicians at any one of these prisons believed a prisoner mentally ill, he was to notify the prison inspectors who would make a full examination of the prisoner, and cause him to be examined by one of the physicians of the State Lunatic Asylum at Utica. If the inspectors were satisfied that the prisoner was insane, or if there were "probable cause to believe"

[7] N.Y. Laws 1848, ch. 294.

[8] N.Y. Laws 1858, ch. 130.

[9] See N.Y. Laws 1847, ch. 460, §§ 29, 84.

[10] See, e.g., 2 Messages from the Governors 855 (Lincoln ed. 1909) (hereinafter cited as "Messages").

him insane, they were required to order the prison warden "forthwith to convey" him to the new asylum at Auburn. If when "restored to reason" the prisoner's sentence had not yet run, he was to be transferred to nearby Auburn Prison to finish it. If he was still mentally ill on expiration of his sentence, he could not be discharged unless he had relatives willing and able to satisfy the asylum superintendent of their "ability to maintain" him and to execute a written indemnification against his becoming a public charge.[11]

The legislature had overlooked prisoners transferred to the Utica Asylum after 1842 and whose terms of sentence had expired before the 1855 recall. In 1861 it remedied its oversight by requiring the Utica superintendent "as soon as practicable" to send all *male* prisoners to the Auburn Asylum, "whether their term of sentence shall have expired or not," and such prisoners were declared subject to the discharge rules enacted in 1858.[12]

In 1863 the legislature (1) abandoned the requirement that prospective transfers first be examined at Utica, (2) made the administrative transfer of mentally ill prisoners discretionary with the prison authority rather than mandatory (perhaps taking into account either the capacity of Auburn Asylum or the possibility of convenient prison confinement of some patients), and (3) expanded the discharge rules to include those enacted in 1848.[13] Now, if his sentence had expired, a prisoner still mentally ill could be released to his home county if (a) he were "harmless and will probably" remain so and is "not likely to be improved by further treatment," or (b) if he were "manifestly incurable and can probably be rendered comfortable at the county alms house," or he could be discharged to his relatives or friends if (c) they "will undertake, with good sureties for his peaceful behavior, safe custody and comfortable maintenance without further public charge. . . ." In any event, no patient was to be detained after expiration of sentence except upon a *court order* to be issued after hearing the opinion of "two respectable physicians" that he was still mentally ill. Thereafter the inmate would be detained

[11] N.Y. Laws 1858, ch. 130, §§ 8, 10.
[12] N.Y. Laws 1861, ch. 63, § 1.
[13] N.Y. Laws 1863, ch. 139.

until "recovered of his insanity" or sooner released to county or family as described above.[14]

The 1863 legislation was, apparently, another attempt to shift to the counties the responsibility of providing for friendless mentally ill former prisoners. Its requirement of a judicial rather than administrative order to justify post-expiration confinement was a distinct but shortlived improvement.

In 1865 the Utica Superintendent suggested that mentally ill female prisoners should no longer be transferred from prison to his asylum.[15] Responding to his request, the legislature that year prohibited their further transfer to Utica, and ordered all there to be removed within three months to the female facilities at either Sing Sing or Clinton Prisons.[16] Two years later, however, the Inspector of State Prisons was authorized to transfer them to the female department of the Auburn Asylum. Their later disposition would be governed by the Auburn rules for males, except that on recovery before expiration of sentence they would go to "the female State Prison at Sing Sing" rather than to nearby Auburn Prison.[17]

In 1874 the legislature attempted to consolidate and revise the various laws governing the mentally ill, including those relating to "commitment of the insane by criminal process." [18] Prisoners serving sentences in county *penitentiaries*[19] could now be forthwith transferred to the Auburn Asylum instead of to a hospital, but only under a court order issued upon "satisfactory evidence" of insanity.[20] (Likewise, the three classes of acquittal and pre-conviction defendants eligible for hospitalization at Auburn still were entitled to judicial process before commitment

---

[14] N.Y. Laws 1863, ch. 139, § 2.

[15] 5 Messages 583.

[16] N.Y. Laws 1865, ch. 353.

[17] N.Y. Laws 1867, ch. 113, § 2.

[18] N.Y. Laws 1874, ch. 446, tit. 1, art. 2.

[19] On their origin see Preiser, Survey of the New York State Sentencing Structure as of 1963, in State of N.Y. Temp. Comm'n on Revision of the Penal Law and Criminal Code, proposed N.Y. Penal Law, Comm'n Staff Notes, App. A (pamphlet ed. 1964).

[20] N.Y. Laws 1874, ch. 446, tit. 1, art. 2, § 24.

or transfer there.[21]) Transfer of state prisoners was continued on an administrative basis, however, by simple restatement[22] of the 1858 Act as amended. That the emphasis in 1874 was upon consolidation and not revision is clear, as noted elsewhere, from its restatement[23] of the original 1842 provisions respecting judicial transfers of persons "under sentence of imprisonment." The consolidation was, in short, a conglomeration of overlapping and inconsistent provisions.

In 1875, besides tidying up some of the mess enacted at the previous session,[24] the legislature dropped the word "Lunatic" from the asylum's title and restored the 1858 rule that administrative transfers of mentally ill state prisoners were mandatory, rather than discretionary (as changed in 1863).[25] The post-expiration rules, retained in 1874, were now modified. A court order (required since 1863) was no longer necessary to detain a mentally ill prisoner who had served his sentence but who did not qualify for a "harmless" or "incurable," etc., release. He was now to "be retained in said asylum until adjudged a fit subject to be discharged by the [new] State Commissioner in Lunacy." [26]

After 1884, Auburn was also to receive administrative transfers from the new State Reformatory at Elmira, judicial transfers to Auburn of any criminal-order patient (i.e., mentally ill defendants) in a civil hospital were authorized, and the provisions for release of prisoners still mentally ill were completely revised.[27] The inmate whose sentence had expired but who remained mentally ill could be retained at the asylum until (1) the medical

[21] N.Y. Laws 1874, ch. 446, tit. 1, art. 2, §§ 22, 23. See Appendix A, *supra*, at notes 41–44.

[22] N.Y. Laws 1874, ch. 446, tit. 8, §§ 9, 10.

[23] N.Y. Laws 1874, ch. 446, tit. 1, art. 2, § 26. See note 2, *supra*.

[24] See N.Y. Laws 1875, ch. 574. Female convicts were governed by the Auburn rules as amended rather than as enacted, and penitentiary transfers were not returned to state prisons. N.Y. Laws 1875, ch. 574, § 13.

[25] N.Y. Laws 1875, ch. 574, § 13, amending N.Y. Laws 1874, ch. 446, tit. 8, § 10.

[26] N.Y. Laws 1875, ch. 574, § 13, amending N.Y. Laws 1874, ch. 446, tit. 8, § 12.

[27] N.Y. Laws 1884, ch. 289, §§ 8–9.

superintendent considered it "safe" to return him to the county poor-authorities or (2) with approval of the State Commissioner in Lunacy, he discharged the inmate to relatives or friends willing to stake money on his later "peaceable behavior, safe custody and comfortable maintenance without further public charge. . . ." Therefore, the "harmless" insane and those with interested and financially able relatives or friends were still eligible for removal from Auburn, but "incurables" who could not safely be kept by the county would have to remain there.

3. *Prisoners at Matteawan: 1893–1965*

The new hospital as reorganized [28] at Matteawan in 1893 was to be used

for the purpose of holding in custody and caring for (1) such insane persons as may be committed to said institution by courts of criminal jurisdiction, and (2) for such convicted persons who may be declared insane while undergoing sentence at any of the various penal institutions of this state.[29]

The administrative transfer provision, last amended in 1884, was restated, but now applied to transfers from county "or other penal institutions" as well.[30] Lesser offenders in county jails (as distinguished from penitentiaries) would no longer go to civil hospitals. The warden was to act on the opinion of his institution's physician, and transferred prisoners were to be kept there until recovered "or [otherwise] legally discharged." Those remaining mentally ill after sentence could still be discharged under the 1884 rules as restated and modified.[31] Clearly reflecting the 1890 State Care Act and the opening of expanded civil state mental hospitals, authority to make "safe" releases to county poor-authorities was deleted and discretionary administrative transfers to civil asylums by the State Commission in Lunacy were authorized; release to the care of "relatives or friends" was continued. Those detained at Matteawan after sentence could ulti-

[28] See Appendix A, *supra.*
[29] N.Y. Laws 1893, ch. 81, §§ 1–5.
[30] N.Y. Laws 1893, ch. 81, § 9.
[31] N.Y. Laws 1893, ch. 81, § 9.

mately be discharged by its superintendent as recovered.[32] If "restored to his right mind" before his sentence expired, the prisoner was to be administratively transferred to prison on the basis of a certificate by the asylum superintendent.[33]

While Dannemora State Hospital was being built,[34] the 1893 Matteawan legislation was incorporated into the new Insanity Law of 1896.[35] Some changes were made in transfer procedures and post-expiration retention. (It is interesting to speculate to what extent, if any, the new restrictive transfer procedures and liberal release procedures were attributable to the overcrowding at Matteawan, or to recent editorial criticism of "gross abuse" in administrative transfers.[36] They may just as well have been part of the fruit of Governor Hill's earlier call for more "safeguards" in insanity proceedings generally and more enlightened release procedures for those supportable by relatives or able to earn their own living.[37])

The warden seeking to transfer a prisoner to Matteawan now had first to request a court-ordered examination by "two legally qualified examiners in lunacy" other than the prison's own physicians. The examiners' certificate that the prisoner was mentally ill would support the warden's further request for a judicial order to transfer to Matteawan.[38] This provision was reminiscent of the judicial procedures of the original 1842 act with traces of the 1858 effort to bring the expertise of the Utica physicians into the decision. In fact, the 1842 law was still on the books, and in 1897 it was amended to require the same examination, but this statute was primarily used in pre-conviction cases and only nominally applied to prisoners.[39]

Prisoners detained at Matteawan after expiration of sentence could now be discharged on the superintendent's own decision

[32] Ibid.
[33] N.Y. Laws 1893, ch. 81, § 10.
[34] See Appendix A, supra, at note 62 et seq.
[35] N.Y. Laws 1896, ch. 545, art. IV.
[36] See Appendix A, supra, at note 76.
[37] 8 Messages 485.
[38] N.Y. Laws 1896, ch. 545, art. IV, § 97.
[39] See Chapter III, supra, at notes 6–13.

that the convict was "reasonably safe to be at large," and discharge to relatives willing and able to accept responsibility was facilitated by removal of surety requirements; those prisoners who "shall have recovered" before their sentences expired would, of course, still be removed to prison.[40]

In 1899 male felons were removed from Matteawan to Dannemora which would thereafter house males becoming mentally ill while serving sentences in state institutions, or while serving a sentence longer than one year in a county penitentiary.[41] In 1904, the Matteawan organic act finally caught up with the changes made since 1893, and its purposes thereafter included the custody and care of *all* mentally ill female prisoners and males serving sentences less than one year.[42] Its judicial transfer procedures, dating from 1896, were not abandoned, however, even though the Dannemora legislation had meanwhile resorted to administrative transfer.[43] In 1912 non-felony transfers were enlarged to include those serving either one year or less, or a (perhaps larger) sentence for a misdemeanor.[44]

The Matteawan legislation was moved into the Prison Law in 1927,[45] and that was renamed the Correction Law in 1929.[46] The statutes then were given their present numeration as sections 400–13. Ten years later, section 408 (governing judicial transfers) was amended in minor respects[47] and then in 1943 was wholly repealed and a new section substituted.[48] Thereafter the allegedly mentally ill prisoner, or someone on his behalf, was to receive at least one day's written *notice* of the application (based on the findings of a court-ordered examination) to send him to Matteawan. If the prisoner's relative or friend, or the court itself, demanded a *hearing*, it had to be held either before a

[40] N.Y. Laws 1896, ch. 545, art. IV, § 98, 99.
[41] N.Y. Laws 1899, ch. 520, §§ 8–9.
[42] N.Y. Laws 1904, ch. 525.
[43] See text accompanying note 62, *infra*.
[44] N.Y. Laws 1912, ch. 121; see 1912 Ops. Att'y Gen. 147.
[45] N.Y. Laws 1927, ch. 426, § 14.
[46] N.Y. Laws 1929, ch. 243, §§ 1–2.
[47] N.Y. Laws 1939, ch. 160.
[48] N.Y. Laws 1943, ch. 382.

judge or a referee and would be followed by an order of commitment or a written explanation for refusal to commit. The validity
of any transfer previously made was not to be affected.

In 1948, a new paragraph "1-a" was added to section 408, providing for administrative transfers of *any* convicted prisoner in a
New York City facility to Bellevue or Kings County Hospital for
the initial transfer examination,[49] to be followed by a hearing and
commitment to Matteawan. The following year, at the instance
of the Sheriff's Association, and although the Department of
Correction believed it "superfluous," section 408 was amended
specifically to include transfers from county jails (as well as
from prison, penitentiary, workhouse, reformatory or other correctional institution).[50]

After minor amendment of sections 408 and 410 in 1955 [51] and
of section 408 in 1957,[52] further revision was made in 1960. To insure time for a relative to retain counsel and appear in the proceedings, the prisoner and a wider class of relatives were now
entitled to *three* days notice served by the sheriff; a personal
examination of the prisoner by the judge was required, and interim commitment to Matteawan was authorized.[53]

In 1961, sections 400 (purpose) and 408 (admissions) were
further amended to "cure an obvious defect in existing commitment procedures" by making possible the commitment to Matteawan, instead of to Dannemora, of youthful offenders, wayward
minors and juvenile delinquents. They otherwise were

> required by law to be thrown with hardened insane felons, while other
> insane adults serving shorter sentences receive the quite different treat-
> ment of being sent to an institution [Matteawan] more conducive to
> recovery.[54]

[49] N.Y. Laws 1948, ch. 447.

[50] N.Y. Laws 1949, ch. 146; N.Y. Legislative Annual 36 (1949).

[51] N.Y. Laws 1955, ch. 794, §§ 16–17.

[52] N.Y. Laws 1957, ch. 267.

[53] N.Y. Correc. Law § 408, as amended by N.Y. Laws 1960, ch.
528; N.Y. Legislative Annual 512 (1960).

[54] N.Y. Correc. Law §§ 400, 408, as amended by N.Y. Laws 1961,
ch. 157; N.Y. Legislative Annual 41–42 (1961). See text, *infra,* at
note 69.

After 1962, only the prisoner was entitled to personal service of notice under section 408, and others such as friends or family could be served by registered mail.[55] That change, contemplated since 1960,[56] had been opposed on the ground that

the bill's possible abridgement of the prisoner's right to effective representation at a commitment hearing outweighs the marginal administrative convenience which the measure may achieve.[57]

However, the governor pointed out that the personal service provision had been "at times, particularly burdensome" and that in any event the Civil Practice Act provided for a total notice period of six days when served by mail.[58] In 1965 the legislature amended section 409 so that post-expiration transfer to a civil hospital would now be made by the Commissioner of Correction (rather than Mental Hygiene) with the consent of the Commissioner of Mental Hygiene.[59]

Summary of Matteawan Procedures
Relating To Prisons as of July 1, 1965:[60]

Admission: Judicial commitment based on notice and a hearing under N.Y. Correc. Law § 408.

Retention: If still "insane" at expiration of sentence the patient could be retained under section 409 without any further judicial proceedings.

Discharge: (a) If still "insane" at expiration of sentence, but "reasonably safe to be at large," the patient could be discharged under section 409 to relatives or

[55] N.Y. Correc. Law § 408, as amended by N.Y. Laws 1962, ch. 799.

[56] See N.Y. Legislative Annual 512 (1960).

[57] Ass'n of the Bar of the City of N.Y., Report of Comm. on State Legislation 145–48 (1962).

[58] N. Y. Legislative Annual 381 (1962).

[59] N.Y. Laws 1965, ch. 879.

[60] Subsequent developments, principally the decision in Baxstrom v. Herold, 383 U.S. 107 (1966), are discussed in the body of the report. See Chapters I, II, *supra.*

friends "willing to comfortably maintain him, without further public charge."

(*b*) If "recovered" prior to expiration of sentence, the patient could be administratively transferred under section 410 to his original place of confinement.

(*c*) If "recovered" after expiration of sentence, the patient could be discharged by the superintendent under section 409.

(*d*) Any time-expired patient who was "not recovered" (and not "reasonably safe to be at large") could be transferred to a civil hospital by the Commissioner of Correction with the Mental Hygiene Commissioner's consent.

(*e*) Mental defectives not mentally ill could be transferred under section 410 by the Commissioner of Mental Hygiene before or after expiration of sentence.

4. *Prisoners at Dannemora: 1899–1965*

Its erection authorized in 1896, named in 1897,[61] the new institution was organized in 1899 under the predecessor statute of Correction Law Section 375,

for the purpose of confining and caring for such *male* prisoners as are declared insane [*a*] while confined in a state prison or reformatory, or [*b*] while serving a sentence of more than one year in a penitentiary.[62]

Convicted male felons with at least six months' sentence to be served were to be transferred from Matteawan to Dannemora, and, thereafter, directly from prison to Dannemora on a prison physician's certificate to its warden that the inmate was mentally ill. Transfer procedure was back to its mid-century form. The three-year-old approach of the Insanity Law, with its judicial procedure and impartial experts, was abandoned in favor of simple administrative action, just as the 1842 procedure had been

[61] N.Y. Laws 1897, ch. 395, § 2.
[62] N.Y. Laws 1899, ch. 520, § 1. (Emphasis added.)

changed in 1847. Strangely, however, the legislature reverted to the 1863 requirement that no prisoner be *detained* after expiration of sentence except upon a court order. It had been abandoned in 1875, but was now restored with some minor changes: two "examiners in lunacy" displaced "two respectable physicians," and the institution physicians were disqualified from proving their own claim. Prisoners detained at Dannemora after sentence could be discharged by the superintendent on recovery, and in the meantime they could be transferred by a Lunacy Commission order "to any institution for the insane." That such institution likely was Matteawan rather than a civil asylum may be inferred from Governor Morton's earlier statement of the uses to be made of Dannemora and Matteawan, and became clear in statements of the Lunacy Commission itself.[63] The unrecovered prisoner whose sentence had expired could be discharged to friends or family by the superintendent if he were "reasonably safe to be at large." Those who did recover before their sentence had expired would, as usual, be returned administratively to prison on the superintendent's certificate.

In 1912, Dannemora's name was shortened by deletion of the phrase "for Insane Convicts," and its purposes were amended to limit transfers to male *felons* and to exclude misdemeanants serving more than one year in a penitentiary; they would be sent to Matteawan.[64] In 1933 defective male felons at Napanoch were made subject to transfer to Dannemora.[65] Notice and an opportunity to be heard in the post-expiration-retention proceeding was held to be impliedly required by section 384, and, to conform the statute to those requirements, the procedure for retaining inmates whose sentences had expired was amended in 1948.[66] To avoid illegal detention during the "two or three weeks" needed to recommit, and to legitimatize the current practice of applying

[63] See Appendix A, *supra.*

[64] N.Y. Laws 1912, ch. 121, § 10; see note 44, *supra.*

[65] N.Y. Laws 1933, ch. 150.

[66] N.Y. Laws 1948, ch. 377; see Troutman v. New York, 273 App. Div. 619, 79 N.Y.S. 2d 709, (3d Dep't 1948); cf. People ex rel. Morriale v. Branham, 291 N.Y. 312, 52 N.E. 2d 881, (1943), adhered to on reargument, 292 N.Y. 127, 54 N.E. 2d 331 (1944).

prior to expiration of sentence,[67] the institution's director was thereafter to apply within 30 days prior to expiration of the term for a court-ordered examination, and, if the inmate were found mentally ill, for a further order (to be issued in accordance with the hearing procedures of section 408 dealing with retention of prisoners at Matteawan) committing him to Dannemora.

In 1950, further change was made in sections 375 (purposes) and 383 (admissions). Previously, only mentally defective *felons* could be transferred from Napanoch to Dannemora; lesser offenders who became psychotic were sent to Middletown State Homeopathic Hospital, but that practice involved discharge from the Department of Correction, and, on recovery, a court action to recommit to Napanoch. To avoid the *"considerable expense and inconvenience"* of court action, the department proposed transfer to Dannemora as a "satisfactory solution to the problem." [68] The purpose and transfer provisions were amended [69] to include broad new classes of mental defectives subject to transfer to Dannemora: (1) felons transferred to Napanoch under section 439; (2) youths over 16 convicted of a "criminal offense" and committed to Napanoch under section 438; (3) youths over 16, convicted of a misdemeanor, imprisoned, and transferred to Napanoch under section 438-a; (4) certain 15-year-old juvenile delinquents, committed to the Elmira Reception Center under section 61 (for a major felony) and later transferred to Napanoch as mental defectives under section 438-b; (5) youths between 16 and 21, convicted of any offense or crime, or adjudged juvenile delinquents, wayward minors, youthful offenders, disorderly persons or vagrants, committed to the Elmira Reception Center under section 61, and later transferred to Napanoch as mental defectives under section 438-b; (6) youths over 16 in civil institutions for mental defectives, found to be dangerous and committed to Napanoch under section 438 (and N.Y. Mental Hygiene Law § 135); (7) youths over 16 committed to Napanoch, as unable to stand trial, under N.Y. Code Crim. Proc. 662-b,

[67] N.Y. Legislative Annual 37 (1948).

[68] N.Y. Legislative Annual 51 (1950).

[69] N.Y. Laws 1950, ch. 229; but see text accompanying note 54, *supra*.

872, and N.Y. Correc. Law § 438; (8) inmates of Napanoch retained under section 440 after the expiration of their terms.

The discharge provisions and those governing retention and ultimate disposition of term-expired patients were completely rewritten in 1961.[70] According to Governor Rockefeller, the new law would

facilitate the transfer from Dannemora to a suitable Mental Hygiene institution of patients no longer under criminal sentence who are completely suitable for care and treatment in a civil institution setting. The bill will thus improve the chance of ultimate recovery for such patients. Placement of such mentally ill patients will be based upon a complete medical assessment of their individual backgrounds and conditions.[71]

Hereafter, *retention* was to be effected by a civil commitment procedure as under the Mental Hygiene Law (section 74) for "a person not in confinement on a criminal charge." If satisfied the inmate "may require care and treatment in an institution for the mentally ill," the court would commit him to the custody of the Commissioner of Mental Hygiene

to be placed in an appropriate state institution of the Department of Mental Hygiene or of the Department of Correction as may be designated for the custody of such person by agreement between the heads of the two deparments.

Once placed either in a Correction or a Mental Hygiene facility, he might again thereafter be administratively transferred to another. Those who had already been detained at Dannemora under the former rules would be deemed to have been placed there by the Commissioner of Mental Hygiene under the new provisions if a valid order of retention were obtained before September 1, 1961. These men were also eligible for transfer to any appropriate civil hospital.

An inmate of Dannemora after the 1961 changes, could be *discharged* on expiration of his term if "reasonably safe to be at large," or be recommitted. If recommitted, he could be transferred to a civil hospital and then back to Dannemora. Thereafter he could be discharged by the Commissioner of Mental

[70] N.Y. Laws 1961, ch. 429.
[71] N.Y. Legislative Annual 443 (1961).

Hygiene (1) upon recovery, or (2) if discharge would "not be detrimental to the public welfare, or injurious to the patient," and (3) could be granted convalescent status. If a request for discharge were refused, the patient could apply to a court of record for an order (1) discharging him, or (2) conditionally releasing him (subject to revocation within five years). The court entertaining the application could appoint two "disinterested psychiatrists" to examine the patient.

Prompted perhaps by a 1961 decision of the New York Court of Appeals upholding the administratively transferred time-serving inmate's right to seek relief by habeas corpus, the following year (1962) the legislature gave its close attention to the *transfer* procedure under section 383.[72] In accordance with the prior recommendations of this committee,[73] administrative transfers were abandoned in favor of court-ordered independent medical examinations followed by a *hearing*. In New York City, however, administrative transfers to Bellevue or Kings County Hospitals for examination of felons imprisoned in city institutions[74] (a similar bill having been vetoed in 1915 by Governor Whitman because of overcrowding at Bellevue and unfavorable effect on other patients[75]), was permitted, as well as on-premises examination by examiners secured by the warden. If the prisoner were reported mentally ill, the prison warden would apply to a court of record for an order committing the man to Dannemora. Three days' notice of that application would be served on the prisoner and on his nearest relative, or, failing such, any known friend. If either the prisoner or anyone on his behalf demanded a hearing, or if the court itself decided to hold a hearing, the application would be heard, after further notice thereof, within five days of the return date of the application unless "regularly adjourned." Testimony from either side would be heard and the court could personally examine the prisoner. If it preferred, the court could refer the matter to a referee to hear and report. If

[72] N.Y. Laws 1962, ch. 393; see People ex rel. Brown v. Johnston, 9 N.Y. 2d 482, 174 N.E. 2d 725, 215 N.Y.S. 2d 44 (1961).

[73] Mental Illness and Due Process 244–52, 256 (1962).

[74] N.Y. Correc. Law § 383, as amended by N.Y. Laws 1962, ch. 393.

[75] State of N.Y., Public Papers of Governor Whitman 91 (1915).

the court ultimately decided that the prisoner was mentally ill, it would forthwith commit him to Dannemora where he would remain "until legally discharged." The court refusing to commit was to "certify in writing his reasons for such refusal." If the prisoner required immediate hospitalization at Dannemora he could be forthwith committed on the court's order prior to termination of the proceedings.

In 1965, section 384 was amended to provide its own hearing procedure without reference to the Mental Hygiene Law rules. Instead, an order of retention under the revised procedure was to be "deemed a civil commitment." [76]

Summary of Dannemora Procedures as of July 1, 1965:[77]

Admission: Judicial orders based on notice and a hearing under section 383 of the Correction Law.

Retention: Judicial recommitment based on notice and a hearing under section 384 (as amended in 1965). Later transfers to civil hospitals at discretion of Commissioner of Mental Hygiene. Discharge of recommitted patients governed by N.Y. Mental Hygiene Law 87 (3) authorizing discharge upon recovery or by convalescent status. Right to seek judicial discharge or conditional release on refusal of commissioner to act.

Discharge: (*a*) If patient is "recovered" before expiration of sentence, he returns to prison under section 386.

             (*b*) If, on expiration of sentence, a patient "is still mentally ill," has not been recommitted, and is "reasonably safe to be at large," the director may discharge him under section 385.

[76] N.Y. Laws 1965, ch. 540, § 4.
[77] See note 60, *supra.*

APPENDIX C

TABLE 1

MATTEAWAN STATE HOSPITAL
ANNUAL* POPULATION 1925–1966

Year	M	F	Total	Year	M	F	Total
1925	827	148	975	1948	1415	236	1651
1926	860	152	1012	1949	1448	242	1690
1927	888	158	1046	1950	1495	249	1744
1928	925	168	1093	1951	1540	245	1785
1929	948	179	1127	1952	1566	239	1805
1930	982	191	1173	1953	1653	244	1897
1931	1011	184	1195	1954	1704	251	1955
1932	1037	184	1221	1955	1731	260	1991
1933	1067	182	1249	1956	1750	268	2018
1934	1109	183	1292	1957	1690	259	1949
1935	1133	183	1316	1958	1723	263	1986
1936	1174	191	1365	1959	1732	264	1996
1937	1216	204	1420	1960	1738	266	2004
1938	1241	206	1447	1961	1823	267	2090
1939	1302	207	1509	1962	1845	271	2116
1940	1334	209	1543	1963	1703	250	1953
1941	1346	223	1569	1964	1543	238	1781
1942	1338	221	1559	1965†	1495	240	1735
1943	1354	221	1575	1966‡			683
1944	1335	210	1545				
1945	1335	208	1543				
1946	1376	230	1606				
1947	1403	240	1643				

* As of December 31. *Source:* Dr. W. Cecil Johnston, Director, Matteawan State Hospital.

† As of March 31 (M.S.H. Ann. Rep.).

‡ As of December 20.

TABLE 2

Types of Commitments to Matteawan State Hospital, 1940–1966

	1940	1941	1942	1943	1944	1945	1946	1947	1948	1949	1950	1951	1952	1953
Mentally Ill Def'ts														
N.Y. Code Crim. Proc. § 659	47													
§ 662-b		46	42	21	34	38	50	58	78	82	74	91	119	77
§ 662-b (trsfr)					3				1			1	3	3
§ 870	15	9	9	8	11	12	16	12	5	9	7	7	7	12
§ 872								4	14	15	7	5	5	12
§ 872 (trsfr)											2			
§ 875														
Insanity Acquittals														
§ 454	2	1	1	1		1			1	1	2			1
Prisoners														
Corr. L. § 408	50	88	60	33	41	17	31	42	44	51	60	50	63	41
§ 412	2				2		1	3	2	7	5	1	3	11
§ 384														
Civil Patients														
M.H.L. § 85	3	10	8	10	10	17	15	12	10	11	13	9	11	11
§ 85 (trsfr)														
§ 135														
"Illegal"			(1)					(3)	(3)					
	119	154	121	73	101	85	113	131	155	176	170	164	211	168

TABLE 2 continued

	1954	1955	1956	1957	1958	1959	1960	1961	1962	1963	1964	1965	1966
Mentally Ill Def'ts													
N.Y. Code Crim. Proc. § 659													
§ 662-b	116	124	131	114	137	142	147	173	162	175	136	135	149
§ 662-b (trsfr)	8	2	1		1	1	1						
§ 870													
§ 872	40	23	31	27	20	9	26	25	36	48	42	47	85
§ 872 (trsfr)	5	3	6	2	3	6	5	3	3	1	4	4	4
§ 875	16	14		14	12	10	6	5	2	2	15		3
Insanity Acquittals													
§ 454	1	1	1	1				1	2	2		1	3
Prisoners													
Corr. L.													
§ 408	44	53	63	73	69	106	77	73	93	87	108	97	73
§ 412	16	10	19	8	6	11	2	8	3	2	7	3	1
§ 384											4	3	
Civil Patients													
M.H.L.													
§ 85	18	13	5	7	3	6	10	19	9	27	22	15	18
§ 85 (trsfr)								1					
§ 135													
"Illegal"												1	
	264	243	257	246	251	291	274	308	308	344	338	306	336

Source: Annual Reports of M.S.H. (by fiscal years ending March 31).

TABLE 3

MATTEAWAN STATE HOSPITAL
CENSUS *

		1962	1964	1965	1966
Mentally Ill Defts					
N.Y. Code Crim. Proc.	§ 662-b	1167	907	811	500
	§ 872	239	228	225	6
	§ 873			1	
	§ 875	37	35	25	2
Insanity Acquittals					
N.Y. Code Crim. Proc.	§ 454	7	7	9	8
Civil Patients					
N.Y. Mental Hg. Law	§ 85	170	196	199	107 †
	§ 135			1	1
Prisoners					
N.Y. Corr. Law	§ 408	95	85	84	59
(serving time)					
Former Prisoners					
N.Y. Corr. Law	§ 408	370	269	231	
(time-expired)					
	§ 412	57	59	54	
(civil hosp. transfers)					
	§ 384			4	2
(Dannemora transfers)					
TOTALS		2,142	1,790	1,642	683

Source: Dr. W. Cecil Johnston, Director, Matteawan State Hospital.
* As of November 1 each year, except 1966 as of December 20.
† Applications were being prepared for permission to retain at Matteawan approximately 70 of these patients. See Chapter II.

TABLE 4

Crime	Number	Percentage
Disorderly Conduct	26	
Vagrancy	19	
Public Intoxication	13	
Tramp	6	
	64	19.6%
Grand Larceny	11	
Petit Larceny	52	
	63	19.3%
Assault	52	
Homicide	8	
	60	18.4%
Youthful Offender	37	
Wayward Minor	14	
Juvenile Delinquent	1	
	52	15.9%
Unlawful Entry	20	
Burglar's Tools	4	
Burglary	2	
	26	7.9%
Dangerous Weapon	9	2.7%
Narcotics	8	2.7%
Miscellaneous†	44	13.5%
TOTALS	326 ‡	100.00%

* *Source:* based on raw data collected by Dr. W. Cecil Johnston, Director, Matteawan State Hosp., by special alphabetical census of a fluctuating patient population over the period July 1 to October 1, 1965.

† Includes arson, robbery, sodomy, indecent exposure, endangering health, impairing morals, carnal abuse, indecent pictures, fraudulent check, parole violation, contempt, malicious mischief, abandonment, non-support, municipal ordinance, criminally receiving, and violation of Motor Vehicle Law.

‡ Includes 71 under sentence and 255 time-expired.

TABLE 5

MATTEAWAN STATE HOSPITAL
DISPOSITION OF PATIENTS DISCHARGED
1960–1966

	1960	1961	1962	1963	1964	1965	1966
To committing court	97	108	74	175	259	179	254
To other institutions in Dep't of Correc. to complete sentence	40	32*	11	38	55	40	37
To county jails, penitentiaries, etc. to complete sentence	17	6	3	21	36	39	37
To community, relatives, friends, etc.	20	41	24	8	26	20	54
Transferred to other (civil) hospitals by order of Dep't Ment. Hyg.	42	24	53	54	117	115	367
Deported	5	1	1	—	—	1	—
Returned to native state†	6	9	6	—	—	—	—
Committed to other mental hospitals or V.A. hospitals	5	7‡	—	13	14	14	7
By court order (habeas corpus)	3	—	4	1	4	2	5
Without psychosis¶	—	—	—	—	2	1	—
Died	60	45	50	56	41	30	32
To Salvation Army	—	—	—	—	—	—	8
Repatriated	—	—	—	—	—	—	2
TOTALS	295	273	226	366	554	441	803

Source: Annual Reports of M.S.H. (by fiscal year ending March 31).

* Includes 1 man returned to Sing Sing; probably an illegal commitment.

† Covered by line 8 after 1962.

‡ Includes 1 imbecile sent to a state school.

¶ Disposition not indicated.

TABLE 6

MATTEAWAN STATE HOSPITAL
DISPOSITION OF PATIENTS DISCHARGED *
1940–1964

	1940	1950	1960	1964
Returned to committing courts	11	15	110	140
Returned to correc. inst.	6	24	41	61
Discharged to community, relatives, friends	5	19	36	23
Returned to jails, penitentiaries, etc.	4	4	19	94
Transferred and committed to other (Dep't Ment. Hyg.) hospitals	9	11	27	142
Returned to other hospitals (V.A., out-of-state, etc.)	7	6	14	14
Returned on court order (habeas corpus)	4			2
Discharged as dead	53	41	50	32
TOTAL DISCHARGED	99	120	297	508

Source: Dr. W. Cecil Johnston, Director, Matteawan State Hospital.
* By calendar year.

TABLE 7

MATTEAWAN STATE HOSPITAL
CONDITION OF PATIENTS DISCHARGED
1940–1965

	1940	1945	1950	1955	1960	1964	1965
Recovered	25	29	62	107	172	375	361
Much improved	14	5	11	13	12	9	27
Improved	6	10	10	19	30	21	93
Unimproved	5	6	10	7	19	106	288
Without psychosis	1	—	1	2	2	2	2
Transferred	2	7	*	*	*	*	*
Died	44	46	55	46	60	41	32
TOTALS	97	103	149	194	295	554	803

Source: Annual Reports of M.S.H. (by fiscal year ending March 31).
* Included in other classes.

213

TABLE 8

MATTEAWAN STATE HOSPITAL

LENGTH OF RESIDENCE BY YEAR AND TYPE OF ADMISSION *

OCTOBER 1, 1965

Year Admitted	Total	Pre-trial				Prisoners		Civil				
		CCP 662	CCP 872	CCP 873	CCP 875	Serv-ing	Ex-pired	MHL 85	CL 412	Acquit-tals	CL 384	MHL 135
1901	1	1										
1910	1	1										
1914	1									1		
1915	1	1										
1916	1	1										
1917	3	3										
1918	2	2										
1919	1	1										
1921	5	3					1		1			
1922	2	2										
1923	3	2							1			
1924	2	2										
1925	6	5					1					
1926	7	3	2				2					
1927	7	4	2				1					
1928	2	1					1					
1929	13	10	1				2					
1930	8	6					2					
1931	9	6					3					
1932	6	5					1					
1933	11	7					4					
1934	15	8	1				5		1			
1935	12	9					2	1	1			
1936	17	14					1	2				
1937	23	15	2				4	2				
1938	13	7					5	1	2			
1939	17	4	5				6	1				
1940	19	10					2					

214

TABLE 8 continued

1942	16	5	4		1		1	5	1			
1943	23	8	4				4	6				
1944	15	6	4				1	4				
1945	23	10	2				3	8		3		
Sub-totals 20 years or longer†	306	172	35		1		56	33	6	3		
1946	33	18	5				4	6	1			
1947	36	18	4				9	4	2			
1948	42	21	6				6	7	1			
1949	35	18	5				6	4				
1950	31	21	2				3	5	1			
1951	38	21	1				7	8	2			
1952	40	16	5				13	4	4			
1953	52	24	8				5	9	5			
1954	46	21	5		1		5	6	5			
1955	44	22	5		4		8	3	2			
1956	44	17	8		1	1	5	4	3			
1957	49	23	6		7		12	2	4			
1958	68	29	6		3	2	17	7		2		
1959	64	38	8		2		14	4				
1960	74	32	6			2	13	17	4			
1961	81	48	9				14	6	4			
1962	116	57	18				12	25	2		1	
1963	103	46	14		3	7	25	14	5	1	1	
1964	165	67	24		4	22	14	17	3	2		
1965	187	91	40	1		37	7	11				1
TOTALS	1,654	820	220	1	26	71	255	196	54	8	2	1

* Source: based on raw data from an alphabetical census of a fluctuating patient population over the period July 1, 1965 to October 1, 1965 made by Dr. W. Cecil Johnston, Director, Matteawan State Hospital.

† As of September 16, 1966 there were only 93 patients remaining who had been at Matteawan since 1945 or earlier. The total population had been reduced to 838 patients. See Chapter III and Table 9.

TABLE 9

MATTEAWAN STATE HOSPITAL
LENGTH OF RESIDENCE BY YEAR
AND TYPE OF ADMISSION *
SEPTEMBER 16, 1966

Year Admitted	Total	Pre-conviction			Prisoners	Patients		Acquittals
		CCP 662	CCP 872	CCP 875	Serving time 408 CC	MHL 85	MHL 135	CCP 454
1917	1	1						
1925	1	1						
1926	1	1						
1927	5	5						
1929	5	5						
1930	2	2						
1931	1	1						
1932	1	1						
1933	3	3						
1934	1	1						
1935	5	5						
1936	4	2				2		
1937	3	2				1		
1938	2	2						
1939	2	2						
1940	10	7				1		2
1941	6	5				1		
1942	7	3		1		3		

216

TABLE 9 *continued*

	Total							
1943	11	6				5		
1944	8	5				3		
1945	14	8				6		
Sub-totals for 21 years or longer	93	68	1			22		2
1946	13	8	1			4		
1947	19	15				4		
1948	18	11	1			6		
1949	14	12				2		
1950	16	12				4		
1951	18	11				7		
1952	13	10				3		
1953	18	10	1			7		
1954	17	11	1			5		
1955	14	12				2		
1956	11	8				3		
1957	18	15	1			2		
1958	29	20	1	1	1	5		1
1959	32	28	1			3		
1960	41	22	1		1	16	1	
1961	31	25			2	4		
1962	60	42	1			17		
1963	46	33	1			11		1
1964	77	50	2	1	8	14	1	1
1965	118	78	1	1	15	22		1
1966	122	64	1		34	21		2
TOTAL	745	497	14	3	61	162	2	6
GRAND TOTAL	838	565	15	3	61	184	2	8

* *Source:* Dr. W. Cecil Johnston, Director, Matteawan State Hospital.

217

TABLE 10

DANNEMORA STATE HOSPITAL
ANNUAL POPULATION *
1925–1965

1925	565	1936	925	1947	1117	1958	1381
1926	575	1937	954	1948	1098	1959	1378
1927	615	1938	1003	1949	1085	1960	1368
1928	654	1939	1049	1950	1109	1961	1349
1929	693	1940	1138	1951	1144	1962	1227
1930	697	1941	1172	1952	1210	1963	1134
1931	744	1942	1222	1953	1288	1964	1101
1932	777	1943	1223	1954	1362	1965	1067
1933	791	1944	1198	1955	1381		
1934	856	1945	1146	1956	1358		
1935	886	1946	1143	1957	1368		

* As of March 31 (*Source:* Dr. R. E. Herold, Director of D.S.H.)

TABLE 11

DANNEMORA STATE HOSPITAL
SOURCE OF ADMISSIONS
1955–1965

	1955	1960	1962	1963	1965
Attica Prison	19	27	27	9	11
Auburn Prison	30	18	11	18	9
Clinton Prison	26	61	137	60	69
Eastern Correc. Inst.	50	31	27	10	13
Elmira Reception Center	2	4	7	6	4
Elmira Reformatory	19	12	11	15	11
Green Haven Prison	9	23	12	15	12
Great Meadow Correc.	10	4	3	16	8
N.Y.S. Voct. Inst.	2	2	2	2	0
Sing Sing Prison	30	25	23	17	14
Walkill Prison	3	2	1	1	0
Woodbourne Correc.	5	3	4	0	0
N.Y.C. Penitentiary	4	4	2	0	0
TOTALS	209	216	267	169	151
1st Admissions	164	134	147	98	75
Readmissions	45	82	120	71	76

Source: figures supplied by Dr. R. E. Herold, Director of Dannemora State Hospital for 1955, 1960 and 1965 (other years from Annual Reports of D.S.H.).

218

TABLE 12

DANNEMORA STATE HOSPITAL
RELEASES
1955–1965

	1955	1960	1962	1963	1965
Attica Prison			6	3	
Auburn Prison			9	1	4
Clinton Prison	95	116	183	140	117
Eastern Correc. Inst.	23	32	21	15	7
Elmira Reception Ctr.	7	2	4	3	
Elmira Reformatory	14	17	6	11	4
Green Haven Prison			7	8	
Great Meadow Correc. Inst.					
N.Y.S. Voc. Inst.				1	
Sing Sing Prison					
Walkill Prison					
Woodbourne Correc. Inst.	2				
N.Y.C. Penitentiary	1	3	2	2	
TOTALS	142	170	238	186	132
To civil hospitals in					
Dep't Mental Hygiene	12	21	118	40	14
By death	29	30	27	30	26
By court order			2	1	9
By custody of relatives			2		
Matteawan State Hospital					3
By own custody	3		2		
Transfer to V.A. and out-of-state hospitals	4	1	4	3	1
GRAND TOTALS	190	226	389	262 *	185

Source: figures supplied by the Hospital Director for 1955, 1960 and 1965 (other years from Annual Reports of D.S.H.).

* Includes 1 deported and 1 returned to N.Y.C. Department of Correction.

TABLE 13

DANNEMORA STATE HOSPITAL
CLASSIFICATION OF PATIENTS BY CRIME *
November, 1965

Crime	Under Sentence C.L. 383	Time-Expired C.L. 384	TOTAL
Robbery	152	120	272
Burglary	47	93	140
Assault	30	88	118
Grand Larceny	32	72	104
Manslaughter	54	28	82
Murder	78	–	78
Rape	11	13	24
Arson	11	10	21
Drugs	9	9	18
Concealed weapon	3	11	14
Sodomy	9	5	14
Carnal abuse	5	3	8
Forgery	3	5	8
Incest	2	2	4
Extortion	3	–	3
Criminally receiving	1	2	3
Kidnapping	2	–	2
Maiming	2	–	2
Felonious escape	2	–	2
Bigamy	–	1	1
TOTALS	456	462	918

* Source: Dr. Ludwig Fink, Ass't Dir., D.S.H.

APPENDIX D

OPERATION BAXSTROM AFTER ONE YEAR*

By Robert C. Hunt, M.D. and E. David Wiley, LL.B.

On February 23, 1966, the Supreme Court of the United States held that Johnnie K. Baxstrom was denied equal protection of the laws by the statutory procedure under which he was held at the Dannemora State Hospital (*Baxstrom v. Herold,* 383 U.S. 107). This is an institution of the New York State Department of Correction for "insane criminals," persons declared mentally ill while serving a criminal sentence. Baxstrom had been certified as insane and transferred to Dannemora in June, 1961, while serving a sentence in a state prison. When his maximum sentence expired in December, 1961, Baxstrom was civilly committed to Dannemora under the provisions of section 384 of the Correction Law, which gave procedures for retaining persons found still mentally ill on expiration of sentence.

The Supreme Court in effect held section 384 to be in violation of the equal protection clause of the Fourteenth Amendment: (1) by failure to grant the right to "the jury review available to all other persons civilly committed in New York," and (2) by "civil commitment to an institution maintained by the Department of Correction beyond the expiration of his prison term without a judicial determination that he is dangerously mentally ill such as that afforded to all so committed except those like Baxstrom nearing the expiration of a penal sentence."

Compliance with the Supreme Court decision required immediate administrative moves. Baxstrom was only one of about 400 patients held at Dannemora under section 384 which had just

* A version of this appendix appeared in the American Journal of Psychiatry 124 (1968), pp. 974–78. Reprinted by permission. Read at the annual meeting of the American Psychiatric Association, Detroit, Michigan on May 11, 1967.

been struck down. An additional 250 patients at the Matteawan State Hospital of the Department of Correction were in a similar situation, held after expiration of sentence for an offense less than a felony. Furthermore, the legal minds involved felt that the principles of the *Baxstrom* decision might apply to several hundred more patients held under other statutes at Dannemora and Matteawan. With the first 650 there could be no question; they had to be discharged from the Correction hospitals as quickly as possible, and there was immediate urgency about 24 patients under section 384 at Dannemora who had writs of habeas corpus pending.

A conference in Albany on March 8 worked out broad outlines of procedure to admit these patients to civil state hospitals of the Department of Mental Hygiene on new civil certifications as they were discharged from the Correction hospitals. Correction people were responsible to identify *Baxstrom* cases, screen them as to the need for further hospital care, get records and other paper work completed, and have the patients examined, certified, and transported. We in Mental Hygiene were responsible to allocate each patient to one of the eighteen civil hospitals, and to make preparations for the reception, care and treatment of the patients.

On March 11 a team of four Mental Hygiene psychiatrists screened the 24 Dannemora patients with pending writs. From this experience, a method was worked out for rapid survey and allocation of the larger groups. The Correction hospital people organized their records so that Mental Hygiene agents could see at a glance the data they needed: the patient's place of residence, his family residence and interest, any dangerous tendencies requiring special precautions. By March 23 the entire backlog of 652 identified *Baxstrom* patients had been surveyed and allocated; the Correction hospitals had completed their formidable administrative preparations and were ready to move patients as rapidly as the Mental Hygiene hospitals could take them. Meanwhile, the civil hospitals had been notified of the impending influx, and of the approximate numbers they could expect.

The guiding principle in the distribution was to send each patient to the hospital serving his district of residence. This was not always simple. Often the residence of record was just where he happened to be on arrest, while his lifelong home was in another part of the state. Much of the difficulty in allocation stemmed from three-fourths of the patients' being from New York City, where there was the least readily available space to accommodate them. Five of the eight hospitals serving the city were so crowded that they could take only token numbers. Half of the entire load was concentrated on the three large hospitals on Long Island: Central Islip, Kings Park, and Pilgrim. The upstate hospitals took residents of their own districts, but also helped relieve the pressure on the metropolitan area by taking the patients with unknown or out-of-state residence, and New York City residents who appeared to have no interested family or friends.

The actual transportation of the patients began in the middle of March. By the end of the month 388 had been moved, and another 323 during April. Thereafter the flow was less, the total number reaching 969 by the end of August when the *Baxstrom* deck was arbitrarily closed to further additions. The small continuing flow of patients from Correction to Mental Hygiene since then is regarded as normal routine.

The final *Baxstrom* deck swelled beyond the original 652 in a variety of ways. There were several groups in the Correction hospitals under statutes not specifically upset by the *Baxstrom* decision, but thought to have the same legal principles involved. Then on July 1, 1966, a new statute for the first time gave to persons under sentence in Dannemora and Matteawan the same right to earn time off for good behavior as enjoyed by other prisoners. This immediately created another 100 patients eligible for a civil hospital even though the maximum sentences had not expired.

The civil state hospitals receiving the *Baxstrom* patients were reminded that these were now "civil cases, with nothing in their legal status requiring special security measures. Ward placement, precautions, treatment and disposition will be determined by the clinical condition, giving due consideration to any dangerous tendencies in accordance with standard practice." Two of the hospitals receiving large numbers, about 150 each during

223

March and April, set up special wards for the processing of the *Baxstrom* patients. One of these had anticipated maintaining such a special unit indefinitely. It was quickly evident, however, that there was no clinical need for this, and both special units were disbanded as the patients reached the end of their initial 60-day observation period. In all other hospitals the *Baxstrom* patients were admitted and studied in the regular reception services and given ward assignments like anyone else. By the end of May all had been absorbed into the hospital populations, scattered through different wards, and at least one-fourth of them were known to reside on open wards.

There were staff anxieties at all levels when the *Baxstrom* operation was first announced. Union officials protested against what they considered a dangerous move, and demanded that there be special training and special pay before working with *Baxstrom* patients. This quickly subsided with assurances that most of these patients should present no special management problems, and that any who proved too difficult for a civil hospital would be committed to Matteawan. The sudden influx of new patients did create some staffing problems, and these were eased by an emergency allocation of additional attendant positions for those hospitals receiving large numbers.

In the neighborhoods surrounding the civil hospitals there were also some flurries of anxiety. With one exception, these died down with explanation and reassurance. Serious public reaction occurred in just one town, as a reactivation of panic from an event of eight years before. This also subsided in time, but only after a great deal of difficult educational work with the community.

At the end of the first year the most striking news is that there is no news. None of the hospitals has any particular problems to report. The hospital directors all use similar terms in conveying that the *Baxstrom* patients are no more problem than anyone else, that nobody any longer thinks of them in any special way, that no lists are kept and that one never hears any reference to this group by staff or patients. One hospital reported ward staffs requesting their share of *Baxstrom* patients because they had turned out to be such good workers. The great majority of these

224

patients were long-term schizophrenics, well stabilized and adjusted to hospital routines.

At the end of February, 1967, of the 969 *Baxstrom* patients, 702 were in hospital. There had been 176 discharges, 147 of these to the community and the remainder to other hospitals. There had been 62 placements on convalescent care, 10 transfers out, and 24 deaths. A few were on escape, leave, or family care. It had been anticipated by some officials that as many as one-fourth of the *Baxstrom* patients might prove too dangerous for civil hospitals. As it has worked out, just seven have been found difficult enough to warrant committing them to Matteawan on a judicial determination that they were dangerous. Of those released, there is a record of one subsequent arrest, for petit larceny.

Nearly all of the patients were admitted to the civil hospitals on two-physician certificates good for only 60 days, after which the patients must be released or converted to some other form of admission. Almost half of the *Baxstrom* patients, some 454, elected to remain in hospital on voluntary or informal status. Court-ordered retention was used for the others who remained.

A development for the civil hospitals, related to the *Baxstrom* decision, is a change in the disposition of indicted defendants found to be so mentally ill as to be incapable of standing trial. Until recently all such persons were committed to the Matteawan State Hospital under section 662-b of the Code of Criminal Procedure, to be held there until restored to sanity, at which time they are returned to the court for criminal proceedings. A new statute effective in September, 1965, committed these to the Commissioner of Mental Hygiene, to be placed either in Matteawan or in a civil hospital, depending upon how dangerous they were thought to be. In the first ten months under this statute, 148 such patients were admitted, 33 of them (22 percent) to civil hospitals, the others to Matteawan. In August, 1966, there was a shift in concepts of danger, and in the next six months, of the 61 such admissions, 37 (61 percent) were to civil hospitals. There was considerable staff anxiety at first, but this has also subsided with experience, and none of the hospitals reports any particular problems. The potentially more dangerous character disorders tend to have transitory psychotic episodes which clear up so that the patients become defendants again, to be sent back to the court for disposition. Those with more serious psychotic illness tend to settle into an amenable patient role under treatment.

The *Baxstrom* operation, which at first loomed up as a major convulsion, a year later has virtually disappeared from everyone's consciousness in the civil state hospitals. For Dannemora and Matteawan, however, the consequences have been more profound. The personnel from the beginning felt their jobs threatened by the drop in patient population. The Dannemora State Hospital, with its patient population dropping from 994 on February 28, 1966, to 487 six months later, has had a freezing of 35 hospital officer positions. The liberated space facilitated a significant new development, however. The 1966 legislature enacted the Clinton Prison Diagnostic and Treatment Center on the Dannemora grounds. The hospital itself can take only those prisoners certified as mentally ill. The new center is designed to serve inmates with mental and emotional problems who may not be certifiable, by offering intensive diagnostic and treatment services, while also serving as a research and training center. The center has been organized and is in operation, with its professional program directed by the McGill University Department of Forensic Psychiatry. The first 50 inmates were received in October, 1966, and another 50 in March, 1967. It is planned to expand this to accommodate 150 to 200.

At Matteawan, the patient population dropped from 1,465 on February 28, 1966, to 804 in October. This resulted in the freezing of 200 hospital officer positions. No jobs were lost, however; there were already 167 vacancies, and the remaining excess members were assigned to positions in the treatment area. The vacant space made possible another move, the establishment of the Beacon Institution for Defective Delinquents, on their grounds. These individuals had before this been in a separate institution at Napanoch. This move is expected to make possible an improved program for the defective delinquents by using the existing staff and facilities at Matteawan, while liberating the Napanoch facility for badly needed additional reformatory space.

A number of new statutory developments have taken place since the *Baxstrom* decision. Some have been referred to above. In May, 1966, the state's highest court cited *Baxstrom* in holding that an indigent mental patient in a habeas corpus proceeding is entitled to counsel as a constitutional right (*People ex. rel. Rogers v. Stanley*, 17 N.Y. 2d 256). Later in the year the legislature enacted provisions for assignment of counsel and appointment of expert witnesses at state expense for indigent persons in proceedings which might result in loss of liberty for mental illness. Also enacted that summer was authority for the Department of Correction to operate halfway houses, and a whole new system of discretionary relief of first offenders from the forfeitures and disabilities automatically imposed by law on convicted persons. While all these legislative measures cannot be attributed solely to the effects of the *Baxstrom* decision, it can be said that they were initiated by the social and legal philosophies which were developing to produce *Baxstrom,* and that the *Baxstrom* decision itself was a catalytic and accelerating force.

The clinical experience with these "insane criminals" and "criminally insane" raises questions concerning the need and the wisdom of placing such persons in special security facilities just because of their legal status. Most of the *Baxstrom* patients had been eligible for transfer to civil hospitals by consent of the Commissioner of Mental Hygiene long before the Supreme Court decision. Most of them had been examined at least once, often several times, by experienced psychiatrists from Mental Hygiene and had been denied transfer on grounds of being too disturbed or potentially dangerous. Yet over 99 percent of them did well in civil hospitals when the court decision compelled the move. This would appear to be another instance of institutionalized expectations putting blinders on our perceptions.

The decision has also had a profound effect upon thinking and planning in legal and governmental circles concerning the use of prison-type facilities to confine the mentally ill. There is now almost unanimous questioning of the constitutionality of so confining any mentally ill persons other than (1) convicted prisoners under sentence, or (2) non-prisoners found too dangerous for a civil hospital by judicial procedure with all the due process and procedural safeguards to which any person is entitled.

Ironically enough, Johnnie K. Baxstrom is not himself a living beneficiary of the new developments. Late in May, 1966, he was discharged from a civil state hospital by court order after a jury trial, despite the testimony of a hospital psychiatrist that his release would be tantamount to a death sentence. Two weeks later, Baxstrom died in status epilepticus as predicted.

SUMMARY

1. A decision of the U.S. Supreme Court resulted in the movement of 969 "insane criminals" and "criminally insane" from the hospitals of the New York State Department of Correction to the civil state hospitals of the Department of Mental Hygiene during the period March to August, 1966.
2. After one year there have been no significant problems with the patients. All have been absorbed into the general patient population, many reside on open wards, over 200 have been released, and only seven have been certified as too dangerous for a civil hospital.
3. The experience has stimulated a variety of administrative and legislative moves toward liberalizing and improving the state's programs for the mentally ill and for offenders.
4. The clinical experience raises questions concerning the need and the wisdom of placing the mentally ill in special security facilities just because of their legal status.
5. Legal circles are questioning the constitutionality of confining any mentally ill person in a prison-type facility unless there has either been conviction for an offense, or special danger established by judicial determination with full due process.

APPENDIX E

SELECTED STATUTES

1. Prisoners

CORRECTION LAW

§ 375. Establishment and purposes of the Dannemora State Hospital

§ 383. Commitment of mentally ill prisoners to the Dannemora state hospital

§ 384. [Old section—repealed 1966] Certification of mentally ill prisoners after the expiration of their terms

MENTAL HYGIENE LAW

§ 87(3). [Old section—repealed 1966] Discharge of certain patients committed under correction law

CORRECTION LAW

§ 385. Disposition of mentally ill prisoners at expiration of terms

§ 386. Prisoners on recovery to be transferred to prison

§ 400. Establishment and purpose of the Matteawan state hospital

§ 408. Commitment of mentally ill prisoners to the Matteawan state hospital

§ 409. Disposition of mentally ill prisoners after expiration of term of imprisonment and any other patients who are neither prisoners nor charged with crimes

§ 410. Prisoners on recovery to be transferred to prison

2. Civil Patients

CORRECTION LAW

§ 412. [Old section—repealed 1965] Transfers from other state hospitals to Matteawan state hospital

MENTAL HYGIENE LAW

§ 72.   Admission on certificate of two physicians
§ 73.   Court authorization to retain a patient
§ 74.   Review of court authorization to retain a patient
§ 85.   Proceedings for certification to Matteawan state hospital of certain dangerous mentally ill patients of state hospitals in the department
§ 88.   Mental health information service

3. Defendants

CODE OF CRIMINAL PROCEDURE

§ 454.   When defendant acquitted on the ground of insanity, the fact to be stated in the verdict and the judgment. Commitment of defendant
§ 658.   Court order for examination as to sanity of defendant
§ 659.   Examination as to sanity; by whom made
§ 660.   Method of examination
§ 661.   Procedure; powers of examiners; subpoenas
§ 662.   Reports to court
§ 662-a. Hearings before the court
§ 662-b. Procedure where defendant is found to be in a state of idiocy, imbecility or insanity
§ 662-c. Procedure where defendant is not found insane
§ 662-d. Return of bail or refund of deposit of money upon commitment of defendant
§ 662-e. Costs
§ 662-f. Effect of other statutes
§ 870.   Order for examination as to sanity of a defendant
§ 871.   Procedure if defendant is subsequently indicted
§ 872.   Defendant found to be in a state of idiocy, imbecility or insanity; procedure where charged with crime
§ 873.   Defendant found insane; procedure where charged with offense not a crime and certain misdemeanors
§ 874.   Defendant found not insane; procedure
§ 875.   Procedure in criminal court of the city of New York
§ 876.   [Inconsistent laws]

CORRECTION LAW

C.L. SECTION 375

§ 375. Establishment and purposes of the Dannemora State Hospital.

The grounds and property located at Dannemora, in the county of Clinton, and the buildings erected thereon, or such parts thereof as may be designated by the Commissioner of Correction, shall continue to be known as the Dannemora state hospital. Such hospital shall be used for the purpose of confining and caring for such male prisoners as are declared mentally ill while confined in a state prison, reformatory, penitentiary or institution for male defective delinquents, who have been sentenced or committed thereto for a felony and others provided for under section three hundred eighty-three. The department of correction shall have the jurisdiction and control of such hospital; but it shall be subject to visitation and inspection of the head of the department of mental hygiene, by himself and his authorized representatives from the department of mental hygiene. As amended L. 1950, c. 229, § 2; L. 1964, c. 105, § 1, eff. March 16, 1964; L. 1966, c. 653, § 2, eff. June 21, 1966.

C.L. SECTION 383

§ 383. Commitment of mentally ill prisoners to the Dannemora state hospital.

1. Whenever the physician or the psychiatrist of any one of the state prisons, state correctional institutions, reformatories, penitentiaries or of the Eastern Correctional Institution shall certify to the warden or superintendent thereof that a male prisoner confined therein and sentenced or committed thereto for a felony or committed to or retained by the Eastern Correctional Institution pursuant to the provisions of sections four hundred thirty-eight, four hundred thirty-eight-a, four hundred thirty-eight-b, and four hundred forty of this chapter, is in his opinion mentally ill, such warden or other officer shall apply to a judge of a court of record to cause an examination to be made of such person by two examining physicians other than a physician connected with such state prison, state correctional institution, reformatory, penitentiary or of the Eastern Correctional Institution. Such physicians shall be designated by the judge to whom the application is made. An examing physician, within the meaning of this article, is a physician possessing the qualifications prescribed by the provisions of section two of the mental hygiene law. Such physicians, if satisfied, after a personal examination, that such prisoner is mentally ill, shall make a certificate to such effect.

C.L. SECTION 383 *continued*

1-a. In the city of New York, if the physician of a workhouse, city prison, penitentiary or reformatory reports in writing to the warden or other officer in charge of such institution that a prisoner confined therein, serving a sentence for a felony, is in his opinion mentally ill, the warden or other officer in charge of said institution shall either transfer said prisoner to Bellevue or Kings county hospital for observation as to his mental condition by two examining physicians or shall secure two examining physicians to make such examination in his institution. Such physicians, if satisfied from their personal examination and observation that the prisoner is mentally ill, shall make a certificate to such effect.

2. Upon such certificate of the examining physicians being so made, it shall be delivered to the warden or other officer in charge, who shall thereupon apply by petition forthwith to a judge of a court of record, annexing such certificate to his petition, for an order commiting such convict to the Dannemora state hospital. Upon every such application for such an order of commitment, notice thereof in writing of at least three days, together with a copy of the petition, shall be served upon the alleged mentally ill person, and in addition thereto such notice and copy of the petition shall be served by registered mail upon either the wife, the father or mother or other nearest relative of such alleged mentally ill person, if there be any such known relative within the state; and if not, such notice shall be served upon any known friend of such alleged mentally ill person within the state. If there be no such known relative or friend within the state, the giving of such notice shall be dispensed with, but in such case the petition for the commitment shall recite the reasons why service of such notice on a relative or friend of the alleged mentally ill person was dispensed with and in such case the order for commitment shall recite why service of such notice on a relative or friend of the alleged mentally ill person was dispensed with.

3. The judge to whom such application for the commitment of the alleged mentally ill person is made may, if no demand is made for a hearing in behalf of the alleged mentally ill person, proceed forthwith on the return day of such notice to determine the question of mental condition and if satisfied that the alleged mentally ill person is mentally ill, may immediately issue an order for the commitment of such alleged mentally ill person to the Dannemora state hospital.

4. Upon the demand for a hearing by the convict, any relative or near friend on behalf of such alleged mentally ill person, the judge shall, or he may upon his own motion where there is no demand for a hearing, issue an order directing the hearing of such application before him at a time not more than five days from the date of such order which shall be served upon the parties interested in the application and upon such other persons as the judge, in his discretion may name. Upon such day or upon such other day to which the proceedings shall be regularly adjourned, he shall hear the testimony introduced by the parties and shall examine the alleged mentally ill person, if deemed advisable in or out of court, and render a decision in writing as to

C.L. SECTION 383 *continued*

such person's mental illness. If such judge cannot hear the application, he may, in his order directing the hearing, name some referee who shall hear the testimony and report the same forthwith, with his opinion thereon, to such judge, who shall, if satisfied with such report, render his decision accordingly. If it be determined that such person is mentally ill, the judge shall forthwith issue his order committing him to the Dannemora state hospital. Such warden or other officer in charge shall thereupon cause such mentally ill person to be delivered to the superintendent of the Dannemora state hospital and such mentally ill person shall be received into such hospital and retained there until legally discharged. Such warden or other person in charge before delivering said mentally ill person shall see that he is bodily clean. At the time of such transfer there shall be submitted to the superintendent of such hospital the original certificate of conviction. If such judge shall refuse to issue an order of commitment, he shall certify in writing his reasons for such refusal.

5. When an order of commitment is made, such order and all papers in the proceeding shall be presented to the superintendent of the Dannemora state hospital at the time when the mentally ill person is delivered to such institution and a copy of the order and of each such paper shall be filed with the department of mental hygiene and also in the office of the county clerk of the county wherein the court is located which made the order of commitment. The judge shall order all such papers so filed in the county clerk's office to be sealed and exhibited only to parties to the proceedings, or someone properly interested, upon order of the court.

6. The costs necessarily incurred in determining the question of mental condition including the fees of the medical examiners, shall be a charge upon the state or the municipality, as the case may be, at whose expense the institution is maintained, which has custody of the alleged mentally ill person at the time of the application for his commitment to the Dannemora state hospital, under provisions of this section.

7. During the pendency of such proceeding, the judge may forthwith commit such allegedly mentally ill person to Dannemora state hospital upon petition and the affidavit of two examining physicians that the warden or other officer in charge is not able to properly care for such person at the institution where he is confined, and that such person is in need of immediate treatment. Added L. 1962, c. 393; L. 1964, c. 105, § 3, eff. March 16, 1964.

C.L. SECTION 384

[Note: This section was repealed by L. 1966, c. 891, § 1, eff. July 29, 1966.]

§ 384. **Certification of mentally ill prisoners after the expiration of their terms.**

1. Within thirty days prior to the expiration of the term of a prisoner confined in the Dannemora state hospital, when in the opinion of

C.L. SECTION 384 *continued*

the director such prisoner continues mentally ill, the director shall make application for his commitment. Application for commitment shall be made to a court of record or judge thereof, as that term is defined in section two of the mental hygiene law, in the county or, if application is made to the supreme court, in the judicial district where the institution is located. The application shall be made by a petition accompanied by the certificate of two examining physicians certifying to the defendant's need for institutional care and treatment. Three days notice of the application, together with a copy of the petition, shall be served upon the prisoner and upon his nearest relative or, if none, upon any known friend within the state.

If there is no demand for a hearing, the court to which application is made may, if satisfied that the prisoner is in need of institutional care and treatment immediately issue an order for the commitment of the prisoner to the custody of the commissioner of mental hygiene to be placed in an appropriate institution in the state department of mental hygiene or the state department of correction which has been approved by the heads of such departments.

If a hearing is demanded, the court shall, or it may upon its own motion, issue an order directing a hearing upon the application at a time not more than five days from the date of such order. Notice shall be served upon the parties interested in the application and upon such other persons as the court may determine. If after hearing held, the court shall grant the petition, it shall order the commitment of the prisoner to the custody of the commissioner of mental hygiene as stated above.

Commitment pursuant to this section shall be made upon blanks prescribed by the commissioner of mental hygiene and shall be deemed a civil commitment.

The costs necessarily incurred in determining the question of mental illness, including the fees of the medical examiners, shall be a charge upon the amount appropriated for the support and maintenance of the Dannemora state hospital, and be paid in the same manner as are other expenses of such hospital.

2. A patient committed to the custody of the commissioner of mental hygiene and placed in an appropriate institution in the department of mental hygiene or the department of correction pursuant to the provisions of this section may at any time during the period of his commitment be transferred to an appropriate state institution in the department of mental hygiene or in the department of correction, which has been designated for the custody of such patient by agreement between the heads of the two departments.

3. All persons retained in Dannemora state hospital pursuant to a valid order of retention issued in accordance with the provisions of this section prior to September first, nineteen hundred sixty-one shall be deemed to have been committed to the custody of the commissioner of mental hygiene pursuant to subdivision one of this section and shall be deemed to have been placed in the custody of Dannemora state hospital by designation of the commissioner of mental hy-

C.L. SECTION 384 *continued*

giene and the commissioner of correction pursuant to subdivision one of this section. Any such patient in the Dannemora state hospital may be transferred to any appropriate state institution of the department of mental hygiene or of the department of correction as may be designated for the custody of such patient by agreement between the heads of such departments. As amended L. 1948, c. 377; L. 1961, c. 429; L. 1964, c. 105, § 4; L. 1965, c. 540, § 4, eff. Sept. 1, 1965.

MENTAL HYGIENE LAW

M.H.L. SECTION 87(3)

[Note: This section was repealed by L. 1966, c. 891, § 1, eff. July 29, 1966.]

3. Discharge of certain patients committed under correction law. The commissioner shall discharge any patient committed to his custody pursuant to section three hundred eighty-four of the correction law who, in his judgment, is recovered. The commissioner shall also discharge any such patient who is not recovered, but whose discharge, in the judgment of the commissioner, will not be detrimental to the public safety or welfare, or injurious to the patient. When the commissioner is unwilling upon request to certify to the discharge of a patient committed to his custody pursuant to section three hundred eighty-four of the correction law, and so certifies in writing, giving his reasons therefor, such patient may make application for his discharge to a court of record in the judicial district of the institution in which the patient is placed. Upon a written finding by the court that there is reasonable cause to believe that the application has merit, the court may appoint two qualified disinterested psychiatrists to examine such patient, to report within sixty days, or such longer period as the court determines to be necessary for the purpose, their opinion as to his mental condition. The court may call for the presentation of such other evidence, written or oral, as it may consider necessary for the proper disposition of the application. If, on the basis of the report of such psychiatrists and such other evidence, the court is satisfied that the discharge or conditional release of such patient will not be detrimental to the public safety or welfare or injurious to the patient, it shall order his discharge, or his release on such conditions as it shall determine to be necessary. If, within five years after the conditional release of any such patient, the court shall determine that for the safety of such person or the safety of others his conditional release should be revoked, the court shall forthwith order him recommitted to the custody of the commissioner of mental hygiene and such recommitment shall be deemed to be a commitment to the custody of the commissioner of mental hygiene pursuant to section three hundred eighty-four of the correction law. All patients suitable for discharge or release under this subdivision may be granted a convalescent status in accordance with

M.H.L. SECTION 87(3) *continued*

rules prescribed by the commissioner. As amended L. 1955, c. 775, § 2; L. 1957, c. 117; L. 1960, c. 550, § 2; L. 1961, c. 105, § 2; L. 1961, c. 429, § 3; L. 1964, c. 738, § 17, eff. Sept. 1, 1965.

CORRECTION LAW

C.L. SECTION 385

§ 385. **Disposition of mentally ill prisoners at expiration of terms.**
Every prisoner in Dannemora state hospital whose sentence has expired or who is otherwise entitled to release shall be dealt with as hereinafter provided. Whenever any prisoner in Dannemora state hospital shall continue to be mentally ill the director of such hospital may apply for his admission to a hospital for the care and treatment of the mentally ill as provided in the mental hygiene law. The director may if it is his opinion that any such prisoner is so dangerously mentally ill that his presence in a hospital in the department of mental hygiene would be dangerous to the safety of the other patients therein, the officers or employees thereof, or the community, make application to a court as provided in section eighty-five of the mental hygiene law and the provisions of such section shall govern such proceedings before such court. The director of the Dannemora state hospital may discharge any prisoner at the expiration of his sentence, and who is still mentally ill, but who, in the opinion of the director, is reasonably safe to be at large. Such discharged prisoner shall be entitled to suitable clothing adapted to the season in which he is discharged, and if it can not be otherwise obtained, the business officer, or other officer having like duties shall, upon the order of the director, or of the commissioner, as the case may be, furnish the same, and money not exceeding fifty dollars, to defray his expenses until he can reach his relatives or friends, or find employment to earn a subsistence. As amended L. 1959, c. 354; L. 1961, c. 429, § 2; L. 1963, c. 713; L. 1964, c. 105, § 5; L. 1966, c. 891, § 4, eff. July 29, 1966.

C.L. SECTION 386

§ 386. **Prisoners on recovery to be transferred to prison.**
Whenever any prisoner, who shall have been confined in such hospital as a mentally ill person, shall have recovered before the expiration of his sentence, and the superintendent thereof shall so certify in writing to the warden or superintendent of the institution from which such prisoner was received, or to which the commissioner of correction may direct that he be transferred, such prisoner shall forthwith be transferred to the institution from which he came, by the superintendent of the hospital, or, if received from one of the state prisons, to such state prison as the commissioner of correction may direct; and the warden or superintendent of such institution shall receive such pris-

C.L. SECTION 386 *continued*

oner into such institution, and shall, in all respects, treat him as when originally sentenced to imprisonment. As amended L. 1964, c. 105, § 6, eff. March 16, 1964.

C.L. SECTION 400

§ 400. Establishment and purpose of the Matteawan state hospital.

The grounds, buildings and property located at Beacon in the county of Dutchess, and used for the purpose of the hospital for mentally ill criminals, shall continue to be known as the Matteawan state hospital, to be used for the purpose of holding in custody and caring for such mentally ill persons held under any other than a civil process as may be committed to the said institution by courts of criminal jurisdiction, or transferred thereto by the commissioner of mental hygiene, and for such persons as may be committed thereto pursuant to the provisions of section eighty-five of the mental hygiene law, and for such convicted persons as may be declared mentally ill while undergoing sentence of one year or less or for a misdemeanor, or upon a commitment as youthful offenders, juvenile delinquents or wayward minors at any of the various penal institutions of the state, and for all female convicts becoming mentally ill while undergoing sentence. When a person is committed to the Matteawan state hospital under the provisions of section six hundred and sixty-two-b, section eight hundred and seventy-two or section eight hundred and seventy-five of the code of criminal procedure; or section eighty-five of the mental hygiene law, a copy of the minutes of the proceedings instituted to determine his mental condition shall be furnished to said hospital. The department of correction shall have the jurisdiction and control of such hospital; but it shall be subject to visitation and inspection of the head of the department of mental hygiene, by himself and his authorized representatives from the department of mental hygiene. As amended L. 1953, c. 188; L. 1961, c. 157, § 1; L. 1964, c. 105, § 7, eff. March 16, 1964.

C.L. SECTION 408

§ 408. Commitment of mentally ill prisoners to the Matteawan state hospital.

1. Whenever the physician of the state prison for women, any county penitentiary, county jail or workhouse, any reformatory for women, or of a state reformatory or any other correctional institution, shall report in writing to the warden or other officer in charge thereof, that any person undergoing a sentence of one year or less or convicted of a misdemeanor, or adjudicated to be a youthful offender, wayward minor or juvenile delinquent, or any female prisoner confined therein is, in his opinion, mentally ill, such warden or other officer shall apply to a judge of a court of record to cause an examination to be made of such person by two examining physicians, other than a physician connected with such state prison, penitentiary, jail, reformatory or correctional institution. Such physicians shall be designated by the

judge to whom the application is made. An examining physician, within the meaning of this article, is a physician possessing the qualifications prescribed by the provisions of section two of the mental hygiene law. Such physicians, if satisfied, after a personal examination, that such prisoner is mentally ill, shall make a certificate to such effect.

1-a. In the city of New York, if the physician of a workhouse, city prison, jail, penitentiary or reformatory reports in writing to the warden or other officer in charge of such institution that a prisoner confined therein, serving a sentence for a misdemeanor or offense, is in his opinion mentally ill, the warden or other officer in charge of said institution shall either transfer said prisoner to Bellevue or Kings county hospital for observation as to his mental condition by two examining physicians or shall secure two examining physicians to make such examination in his institution. Such physicians if satisfied from their personal examination and observation that the prisoner is mentally ill, shall make a certificate to such effect.

2. Upon such certificate of the examining physicians being so made, it shall be delivered to the warden or other officer in charge, who shall thereupon apply by petition forthwith to a judge of a court of record, annexing such certificate to his petition, for an order committing such convict to the Matteawan state hospital. Upon every such application for such an order of commitment, notice thereof in writing, of at least three days, together with a copy of the petition, shall be served personally upon the alleged mentally ill person, and in addition thereto such notice and copy of the petition shall be served upon either the wife, the husband, the father or mother or other nearest relative of such alleged mentally ill person, if there be any such known relative within the state; and if not, such notice shall be served upon any known friend of such alleged mentally ill person within the state. If there be no such known relative or friend within the state, the giving of such notice shall be dispensed with, but in such case the petition for the commitment shall recite the reasons why service of such notice on a relative or friend of the alleged mentally ill person was dispensed with, and in such case the order for commitment shall recite why service of such a notice on a relative or friend of the alleged mentally ill person was dispensed with.

3. The judge to whom such application for the commitment of the alleged mentally ill person is made may, if no demand is made for a hearing in behalf of the alleged mentally ill person, proceed forthwith on the return day of such notice to determine the question of mental illness, and if satisfied that the alleged mentally ill person is mentally ill, may immediately issue an order for the commitment of such alleged mentally ill person to the Matteawan state hospital.

4. Upon the demand for a hearing by any relative or near friend on behalf of such alleged mentally ill person, the judge shall, or he may upon his own motion where there is no demand for a hearing, issue an order directing the hearing of such application before him at a time not more than five days from the date of such order, which shall be served upon the parties interested in the application and upon such

238

C.L. SECTION 408 *continued*

other persons as the judge, in his discretion, may name. Upon such day or upon such other day to which the proceedings shall be regularly adjourned, he shall hear the testimony introduced by the parties and shall examine the alleged mentally ill person, if deemed advisable in or out of court, and render a decision in writing as to such person's mental illness. If such judge cannot hear the application, he may, in his order directing the hearing, name some referee who shall hear the testimony and report the same forthwith, with his opinion thereon, to such judge, who shall, if satisfied with such report, render his decision accordingly. If it be determined that such person is mentally ill, the judge shall forthwith issue his order committing him to the Matteawan state hospital. Such warden or other officer in charge shall thereupon cause such mentally ill person to be delivered to the superintendent of the Matteawan state hospital and such mentally ill person shall be received into such hospital and retained there until legally discharged. Such warden or other person in charge before delivering said mentally ill person shall see that he is bodily clean. If such judge shall refuse to issue an order of commitment, he shall certify in writing his reasons for such refusal.

5. When an order of commitment is made, such order and all papers in the proceeding shall be presented to the superintendent of the Matteawan state hospital at the time when the mentally ill person is delivered to such institution, and a copy of the order and of each such paper shall be filed with the department of mental hygiene and also in the office of the county clerk of the county wherein the court is located which made the order of commitment. The judge shall order all such papers so filed in the county clerk's office to be sealed and exhibited only to parties to the proceedings, or someone properly interested, upon order of the court.

6. The costs necessarily incurred in determining the question of mental illness, including the fees of the medical examiners, shall be a charge upon the state or the municipality, as the case may be, at whose expense the institution is maintained, which has custody of the alleged mentally ill person at the time of the application for his commitment to the Matteawan state hospital, under the provisions of this section.

7. During the pendency of such proceeding the judge may forthwith commit such allegedly mentally ill person to Matteawan state hospital upon petition and the affidavit of two examining physicians that the warden or other officer in charge is not able to properly care for such person at the institution where he is confined, and that such person is in need of immediate treatment.

8. The notice provided for herein shall be served by the sheriff of the counties of the state of New York, the charges of such sheriff shall be a disbursement in such proceeding, or by registered mail on all persons required to be served other than the alleged mentally ill person. As amended L. 1948, c. 447; L. 1949, c. 146; L. 1955, c. 794, § 16; L. 1957, c. 267; L. 1960, c. 528, §§ 1, 2; L. 1961, c. 157, § 1; L. 1962 c. 799; L. 1964, c. 105, § 9; L. 1966, c. 496, eff. June 7, 1966.

C.L. SECTION 409

§ 409. **Disposition of mentally ill prisoners after expiration of term of imprisonment and any other patients who are neither prisoners nor charged with crimes.**

Every prisoner in Matteawan state hospital whose sentence has expired or who is otherwise entitled to release shall be dealt with as hereinafter provided. Whenever any prisoner in the Matteawan state hospital shall continue to be mentally ill at the expiration of the term for which he was sentenced the director of such hospital may apply for his admission to a hospital for the care and treatment of the mentally ill as provided in the mental hygiene law. The director may, if it is his opinion that any such prisoner is so dangerously mentally ill that his presence in a hospital in the department of mental hygiene would be dangerous to the safety of the other patients therein, the officers or employees thereof, or to the community, make application to a court as provided in section eighty-five of the mental hygiene law and the provisions of such section shall govern such proceedings before such court.

The director of Matteawan state hospital may discharge any prisoner at the expiration of the term for which he was sentenced, and who is still mentally ill, but who, in the opinion of the director is reasonably safe to be at large. Such discharged prisoner shall be entitled to suitable clothing adapted to the season in which he is discharged, and if it can not be otherwise obtained, the business officer, or other officer having like duties shall, upon the order of the director, or of the commissioner, as the case may be, furnish the same, and money not exceeding fifty dollars, to defray his expenses until he can reach his relatives or friends, or find employment to earn a subsistence. The director of the hospital may discharge any other person, who is not a prisoner, although he is still mentally ill, but who, in the director's opinion, is reasonably safe to be at large or is recovered, except those patients being retained pursuant to section six hundred sixty-two-b or eight hundred seventy-two of the code of criminal procedure against whom indictments are outstanding and a warrant is on file with the director. Any patient retained pursuant to such sections of the code of criminal procedure, who has not recovered, may upon the order of the commissioner of correction with the consent of the commissioner of mental hygiene, be transferred to any appropriate mental institution in the department of mental hygiene. Added L. 1966, c. 891, § 5, eff. July 29, 1966.

C.L. SECTION 410

§ 410. **Prisoners on recovery to be transferred to prison.**

Whenever any prisoner, who shall have been confined in such hospital as a mentally ill person, shall have recovered before the expiration of his sentence, and the superintendent shall so certify in writing to the agent and warden or other officer in charge of the institution, from which such prisoner was received or to which the commissioner

C.L. SECTION 410 *continued*

of correction may direct that he be transferred, such prisoner shall forthwith be transferred to the institution from which he came by the superintendent of the hospital, or if received from one of the state prisons, to such state prison as the commissioner of correction may direct; and the warden or other officer in charge of such institution shall receive such prisoner into such institution, and shall, in all respects, treat him as when originally sentenced to imprisonment. Any inmate not a prisoner, held upon an order of a court or judge, in a criminal proceeding, may be discharged therefrom, upon the superintendent's certificate of recovery, made to and approved by such court or judge.

Any prisoner, before or after expiration of sentence, who, in the opinion of the superintendent, is a mental defective and who does not show evidence of mental illness, may be transferred by the commissioner of mental hygiene on an application made by the superintendent, accompanied by a certificate of mental defect made by two examining physicians, or by an examining physician and a certified psychologist, as defined in the mental hygiene law. Any inmate held on the order of a court or judge in a criminal proceeding who, in the opinion of the superintendent, is a mental defective and who does not show evidence of mental illness may be transferred by the commissioner of correction to the Eastern Correctional Institution, on the application of the superintendent accompanied by a certificate of mental defect executed by two examining physicians, or by an examining physician and a certified psychologist. When such a transfer is made the superintendent shall notify in writing the district attorney of the county from which the inmate was committed and the clerk of the court making the commitment, who shall make proper record thereof. After the transfer of any such inmate he may be returned to the said hospital upon the order of the commissioner of correction, whenever in his judgment it shall appear that the said inmate is not a proper person to be detained in a state institution for mental defectives. The order of such commissioner directing the return of such inmate shall state the reasons for such return. As amended L. 1955, c. 794, § 17; L. 1964, c. 105, § 10, eff. March 16, 1964.

C.L. SECTION 412

[Note: This section was repealed by L. 1965, c. 524, § 1, eff. June 28, 1965.]

§ 412. **Transfers from other state hospitals to Matteawan state hospital.**

The commissioner of mental hygiene may, by order in writing, transfer to the Matteawan state hospital any insane inmate of another state hospital, who was held under any other than a civil process, committed thereto upon the order of a court of criminal jurisdiction or of a judge or justice of such a court; or any patient who has previously been sentenced to a term of imprisonment in any correctional institution, and who still manifests criminal tendencies, or any

C.L. SECTION 412 *continued*

such patient who has previously been an inmate of the Matteawan state hospital. All persons committed to said Matteawan state hospital shall be a charge upon the state.

MENTAL HYGIENE LAW

M.H.L. SECTION 72

§ 72. Admission on certificate of two physicians.

1. The director of a hospital may receive and retain therein as a patient any person alleged to be mentally ill and suitable for care and treatment upon the certificate or certificates of two examining physicians accompanied by an application for the admission of such person executed within ten days prior to such admission by any person with whom the person alleged to be mentally ill may reside or at whose house he may be, or the father or mother, husband or wife, brother or sister, or the child of any such person, or the nearest relative or friend available, or the committee of such person, or an officer of any well recognized charitable institution or agency or home, or any public welfare officer of the town, any town or community service officer or commissioner of public welfare, or director of community mental health services, of the city or county in which any such person may be, or in the case of the admission of any such person to a hospital operated by the state or a political subdivision thereof, by the director of such hospital. Such application shall contain a statement of the facts upon which the allegation of mental illness and need for care and treatment are based, and shall be executed under penalty of perjury but shall not require the signature of a notary public thereon. The director of the hospital where such person is brought shall cause such person to be examined forthwith by a staff physician of such hospital other than the original examining physicians whose certificate or certificates accompanied the application, and if such person is found to be in need of care and treatment he may be admitted thereto as a patient as herein provided. Such original examining physician may be the director or staff member of a hospital operated or maintained by the state or a political subdivision thereof to which it is proposed to admit such person, provided, however, that in case of admission of such person to a hospital operated by the state only one such examining physician may be on the staff thereof, and in the case of admission of such person to a hospital operated or maintained by a political subdivision of the state both such examining physicians may be on the staff thereof and in the case of admission of such person to a licensed private institution, neither such examining physician may be on the staff thereof.

2. The director shall cause written notice of such application to be given the person alleged to be mentally ill not later than five days, excluding Sunday and holidays, after such admission and such notice shall set forth such person's rights under the provisions of this section.

M.H.L. SECTION 72 *continued*

At the same time such notice shall also be given to the mental health information service and personally or by mail to the nearest relative of the person alleged to be mentally ill other than the petitioner if there be any such person known to the director, and to as many as three additional persons if designated in writing by the person alleged to be mentally ill to receive such notice.

3. If at any time prior to the expiration of sixty days from the date of admission of such patient, he or any relative or friend or the mental health information service gives notice in writing of request for hearing on the question of need for hospitalization to the director, a hearing shall be held as herein provided. The patient or person requesting a hearing on behalf of the patient may designate the county where the hearing shall be held, which shall be either in the county where the hospital is located, the county of the patient's residence or the county in which the hospital to which the patient was first admitted is located and such hearing shall be held in the county so designated, subject to application by any interested party, including the director, for change of venue to any county because of the convenience of parties or witnesses or the condition of the patient. It shall be the duty of the director upon receiving notice of such request for hearing to forward forthwith a copy of such notice with a record of the patient as defined and described in section twenty of this chapter to a court of record in the county designated by the applicant, if one be designated, or if no designation be made, then to a court of record in the county where such hospital is located. A copy of such notice and record shall also be given the mental health information service. The court which receives such notice shall fix the date of such hearing at a time not later than five days from the date such notice is received by the court and cause the patient or other person requesting the hearing, the director, the mental health information service and such other persons as the court may determine to be advised of such date. Upon such date, or upon such other date to which the proceeding may be adjourned, the court shall hear testimony and examine the person alleged to be mentally ill, if it be deemed advisable in or out of court, and shall render a decision in writing as to the mental illness and the need for retention of the patient. If it be determined that the patient is mentally ill and in need of retention for care and treatment, the court shall forthwith issue an order authorizing the retention of such patient for care and treatment in the hospital for a period not to exceed six months from the date of the order or if the patient is in a psychiatric hospital maintained by a political subdivision of the state or in a general hospital the court may order the patient transferred to the jurisdiction of the department for retention in a hospital operated by the state designated by the commissioner or to a licensed private institution for retention therein for a period not to exceed six months from the date of such order. If, however, it appears that such mentally ill person is harmless and his relatives or a committee of his person are willing and able properly to care for him, at some place other than a hospital, then, upon their written consent, the court may order the transfer of the patient to the

243

care and custody of such relatives or such committee. If the court cannot hear the application it may appoint a referee to hear and report forthwith the testimony with his opinion thereon, to the court, which if satisfied with such report shall issue its order in accordance with this subdivision.

4. If the court shall order the release of the patient, it shall state in writing its reasons for such order and such patients shall forthwith be released.

5. The department or the director of the hospital authorized to retain or receive and retain such patient, as the case may be, shall be immediately furnished with a copy of the order of the court and, if a transfer is ordered, shall immediately make provisions for the transfer of such patient. Added L. 1964, c. 738, § 5, eff. Sept. 1, 1965.

M.H.L. SECTION 73

§ 73. Court authorization to retain a patient.

1. If no application for a hearing shall have been made by a patient or by anyone on behalf of such patient within sixty days of the initial admission of such patient pursuant to this article, and if the director shall determine that the condition of such patient requires his continued retention in a hospital, he shall, if such patient does not agree to remain in such hospital as a voluntary or informal patient, prior to the expiration of sixty days from the initial admission of such patient, apply to a court of record in the county where the hospital is located for an order authorizing continued retention of such patient or for his transfer to an appropriate hospital and continued retention. The director shall cause written notice of such application to be given the patient and a copy thereof shall be given personally or by mail to the persons required by section seventy-two of this article to be served with notice of such patient's initial admission and to the mental health information service. If no application is made for a hearing on behalf of the patient within five days, excluding Sunday and holidays, from the date such notice of such application was given such patient, and if the mental health information service has not requested a hearing, the court receiving the application may, if satisfied that the patient requires continued retention for care and treatment, or transfer and continued retention, immediately issue an order authorizing continued retention of such patient in such hospital for a period not to exceed six months from the date of the order or if such patient is in a psychiatric hospital operated by a political subdivision of the state or in a general hospital, such order may direct the transfer of such patient to the jurisdiction of the department for retention in a hospital operated by the state or to a licensed private institution, to be retained therein for a period not to exceed six months from the date of such order.

2. Upon the demand of the patient or of anyone on his behalf or upon request of the mental health information service, the court shall, or may on its own motion, fix a date for the hearing of the application,

M.H.L. SECTION 73 *continued*

in like manner as is provided for hearings in subdivision three of section seventy-two of this article. The provisions of such subdivision shall apply to the procedure for obtaining and holding a hearing and to the granting or refusal to grant an order of retention by the court, except that the patient shall not have the right to designate initially the county in which the hearing shall be held.

3. If the director of a hospital in which a patient is retained pursuant to section seventy-two or subdivisions one or two of this section shall determine that the condition of such patient requires his further retention in a hospital, he shall, if such patient does not agree to remain in such hospital as a voluntary or informal patient, apply during the period of retention authorized by the last order of the court, to a court of record in the county where the hospital is located, for an order authorizing further continued retention of such patient. The procedures for obtaining any order pursuant to the subdivision shall be in accordance with the provisions of subdivisions one and two of this section. The period for continued retention pursuant to the first order obtained under this subdivision shall authorize further continued retention of the patient for not more than one year and the period for the further continued retention of the patient authorized by any subsequent order under this subdivision shall be for periods not to exceed two years each. Added L. 1964, c. 738, § 5, eff. Sept. 1, 1965.

M.H.L. SECTION 74

§ 74. Review of court authorization to retain a patient.

If a person whose retention, continued retention or transfer and continued retention has been authorized pursuant to this article, or any relative or friend in his behalf, be dissatisfied with any such order he may, within thirty days after the making of any such order, obtain a rehearing and a review of the proceedings already had and of such order, upon a petition to a justice of the supreme court other than the judge or justice presiding over the court making such order, who shall cause a jury to be summoned as in the case of proceedings for the appointment of committee for a mentally ill person where the question of fact arising upon the competency of the person is tried by a jury, and shall try the question of the mental illness of the patient so authorized to be retained, in the same manner as provided in said proceedings. Any such patient or the person applying on his behalf for such review may waive the trial of the fact by a jury and consent in writing to trial of such fact by the court. If such petition for rehearing and review be made by any other than the person so authorized to be retained or the father, mother, husband, wife or child of such person or the person with whom the person so authorized to be retained was residing at the time of the making of such order authorizing continued retention or accustomed to reside, before such rehearing or review shall be had, the petitioner shall make a deposit or give a bond, to be approved by a justice of the supreme court, for the payment of the costs and expenses of such rehearing, review and determination of the question of mental

245

M.H.L. SECTION 74 *continued*

illness by a jury as aforesaid, if the order authorizing continued retention is sustained. If the verdict of the jury, or the decision of the court when jury trial has been waived, be that such person is not mentally ill, the justice shall forthwith discharge him, but if the verdict of the jury, or the decision of the court where a jury trial has been waived, be that such person is mentally ill, the justice shall certify that fact and make an order authorizing continued retention under the original order. Such order shall be presented, at the time of authorization of continued retention of such mentally ill person, to, and filed with, the director hospital in which the mentally ill person is authorized to be retained, and a copy thereof shall be forwarded to the department by such director and filed in the office thereof. Proceedings under the order shall not be stayed pending an appeal therefrom, except upon an order of a justice of the supreme court, and made upon a notice and after a hearing, with provisions made therein for such temporary care or confinement of the alleged mentally ill person as may be deemed necessary. If a judge or justice shall refuse to grant an application for an order authorizing continued retention of a mentally ill person proved to be dangerous to himself or others, he shall state his reasons for such refusal in writing, and any person aggrieved thereby may obtain a rehearing and review and the determination of the question of mental illness by a jury in the same manner and under like conditions as from an order authorizing continued retention. Formerly § 76, amended L. 1961, c. 504, § 8; renumbered 74 and amended L. 1964, c. 738 § 6, eff. Sept 1, 1965.

M.H.L. SECTION 85

§ 85. **Proceedings for certification to Matteawan state hospital of certain dangerous mentally ill patients of state hospitals in the department.**

1. The director of any state hospital, upon order of the commissioner, upon ascertaining that any person, duly admitted to and a patient of such hospital as a mentally ill person, has committed or is liable to commit an act or acts which if committed by a sane person would constitute homicide or felonious assault, or is so dangerously mentally ill that his presence in such a hospital is dangerous to the safety of other patients therein, the officers or employees thereof, or to the community, shall forthwith make application to a court of record or judge thereof within the county wherein such state hospital is located or a justice of the supreme court in the judicial district wherein such county is located to cause an examination to be made of such person by two examining physicians, other than a physician connected with such state hospital. Such physicians shall be designated by the judge to whom the application is made. Such physicians, if satisfied, after a personal examination, that such patient has committed or is liable to commit an act or acts which if committed by a sane person would constitute homicide or felonious assault, or is so dangerously mentally ill that his presence in such hospital is dan-

M.H.L. SECTION 85 *continued*

gerous to the safety of other patients therein, the officers or employees thereof, or to the community, shall make a certificate to such effect.

2. Upon such certificate of the examining physicians being so made, it shall be delivered to the director or other officer in charge who shall thereupon apply by petition forthwith to a judge of a court of record, annexing such certificate to his petition, for an order placing such patient in the Matteawan state hospital for hospitalization. Upon every such application for such order, notice thereof in writing, together with a copy of the petition, shall be served personally upon the alleged dangerously mentally ill person, and in addition thereto such notice and a copy of the petition shall be served upon the mental health information service and upon either the wife, husband, the father or mother or other nearest relative of such alleged dangerously mentally ill person, if there be any such known relative within the state; and if not, such notice shall be served upon any known friend of such alleged dangerously mentally ill person within the state. Such service shall be at least five days in advance of the return date if service is effected personally or at least eight days in advance of the return date if service is effected by mail. If there be no such known relative or friend within the state, the giving of such notice shall be dispensed with, but in such case the petition for the commitment shall recite the reasons why service of such notice on a relative or friend of the alleged dangerously mentally ill person was dispensed with, and in such case the order for hospitalization shall recite why service of such a notice on a relative or friend of the alleged dangerously mentally ill person was dispensed with.

3. The judge to whom such application for the hospitalization of the alleged dangerously mentally ill person may, if no demand is made for a hearing by or on behalf of the alleged dangerously mentally ill person, proceed forthwith on the return date of such notice to determine the question of the dangerous mental illness of such person, and if satisfied that the alleged dangerously mentally ill person is dangerously mentally ill, may immediately issue an order placing such alleged dangerously mentally ill person in Matteawan state hospital.

4. Upon the demand for a hearing by the patient, any relative or near friend, or the mental health information service on behalf of such alleged dangerously mentally ill person, the judge shall, or he may upon his own motion where there is no demand for a hearing, fix the date of such hearing of such application before him at a time not more than five days from the date of such demand, notice of which shall be served upon the parties interested in the application and upon such other persons as the judge, in his discretion, may name. The person whose dangerous mental illness is being inquired into may be represented by counsel in any such proceedings. Upon such day or upon such other day to which the proceeding shall be regularly adjourned, he shall hear the testimony introduced by the parties and shall examine the alleged dangerously mentally ill person, if deemed advisable in or out of court, and render a decision in writing as to

such person's dangerous mental illness. If such judge cannot hear the application, he may, when fixing the date of the hearing, name some referee who shall hear the testimony and report the same forthwith, and his opinion thereon, to such judge, who shall, if satisfied with such report, render his decision accordingly. If it be determined that such person is dangerously mentally ill, the judge shall forthwith issue his order hospitalizing him in the Matteawan state hospital for a period not to exceed six months from the date of such order. Such director or other officer in charge shall thereupon cause such dangerously mentally ill person to be delivered to the Matteawan state hospital and such dangerously mentally ill person shall be received into such hospital and retained there until he is no longer dangerous to safety or until the expiration of the period of hospitalization ordered or authorized retention provided in the next subdivision whichever shall occur first, unless prior thereto he is no longer dangerous to safety whereupon he may be released as provided in section four hundred nine of the correction law or, if he is in need of continued hospitalization, he may be transferred to any hospital in the department upon the order of the commissioner. If the director of any hospital shall determine the condition of a patient so transferred requires his continued retention in a hospital, he shall if such patient does not agree to remain in such hospital as a voluntary or informal patient, prior to the expiration of sixty days from the date of such transfer, apply to a court of record for an order authorizing continued retention as provided in section seventy-three of this article. The provisions of subdivision three of such section and of section seventy-four shall apply to such orders authorizing continued retention or to subsequent orders authorizing continued retention. Such director or other person in charge of before delivering such dangerously mentally ill person shall see that he is bodily clean. If such judge shall refuse to issue an order for such hospitalization, he shall certify in writing his reasons for such refusal.

4-a. If the director of Matteawan state hospital shall determine that the condition of any patient admitted under this section requires his further retention in such hospital because of dangerous mental illness, he shall apply within six months of the effective date of this subdivision or during the period of retention authorized by the last order of the court, for an order authorizing further continued retention of such patient. The provisions of sections seventy-three and seventy-four of this article shall apply to all applications for orders authorizing retention, further continued retention and orders authorizing retention, except that the question to be determined thereon shall be the continued dangerous mental illness of such patient. If it shall be determined that the patient is no longer dangerously mentally ill the court may order the discharge of the patient or it may order the transfer of the patient to a hospital in the department, provided, however, the court in so ordering must state in writing its reasons therefor.

5. Orders for hospitalization in Matteawan state hospital pursuant to this section shall not be deemed as or received in any court in evi-

M.H.L. SECTION 85 *continued*

dence of commission of a crime by the person so ordered hospitalized, nor shall such order for hospitalization be deemed or considered as punishment for a crime.

6. The costs necessarily incurred, under this section, in determining the dangerous mental illness of such person, including fees of the examiners, fees of the medical witnesses, and any other necessary expenses allowed by the judge or justice, shall be a charge upon the county from which such person was originally certified, but in the city of New York, the judge or justice shall order such costs audited and allowed by the comptroller from the court fund, and charged to the proper county within the said city.

7. During the pendency of such proceeding the judge may forthwith order the hospitalization of such alleged dangerously mentally ill person in Matteawan state hospital upon petition and the affidavit of two examing physicians that the director or other officer in charge is not able to properly care for such person at the institution where he is confined, and that such person is in need of immediate treatment.

8. The notice provided for herein may be served by registered mail on all persons required to be served other than the alleged dangerously mentally ill person. Added L. 1963, c. 704, § 1; amended L. 1966, c. 891, §§ 2, 3, eff. July 29, 1966.

M.H.L. SECTION 88

§ 88. Mental health information service.

There is hereby created and established a mental health information service of the state of New York in each judicial department of the supreme court. The head of such service in each judicial department, and such assistants and such staff as may be necessary, shall be appointed and be removable by the presiding justice of the appellate division of such judicial department. Appointments and transfers to such service shall comply with the provisions of the civil service law and except for the head of such service in each judicial department all such positions shall be in the competitive class of the civil service. Standards for qualifications of the personnel in such service having duties requiring direct contact with patients and their immediate families shall be established in agreement with the commissioner. The mental health information service in each judicial department of the state shall perform the following duties subject to directions made and rules and regulations promulgated by the presiding justice of the appellate division of such department;

(a) Study and review the admission and retention of involuntary patients;

(b) inform such patients and in proper cases others interested in the patients' welfare concerning procedures for admission and retention and of the patients' right to have judicial hearing and review, to be represented by legal counsel and to seek independent medical opinion;

(c) in any case before a court, to assemble and provide the court

M.H.L. SECTION 88 *continued*

with all the relevant information as to the patient's case, his hospitalization, his right to discharge, if any, including information from which the court may determine the need, if any, for the appointment of counsel for the patient or the obtaining of additional psychiatric opinion;

(d) perform services for voluntary patients and informal patients similar to those required under clauses (a) and (b) of this section, as may be requested by the patient or anyone on his behalf;

(e) provide such services and assistance to patients and their families and to the courts having duties to perform relating to the mentally ill or alleged mentally ill as may be required by a judge or justice thereof and in accordance with the regulations of the presiding justice of the appellate division of each such judicial department. Added L. 1964, c. 738, § 18, eff. Sept. 1, 1965.

CODE OF CRIMINAL PROCEDURE

C.C.P. SECTION 454

§ 454. **When defendant acquitted on the ground of insanity, the fact to be stated in the verdict and the judgment. Commitment of defendant.**

(1) When the defense is mental disease or defect of the defendant, pursuant to section 30.05 of the penal law, the jury must be instructed, if they acquit him on that ground, to state the fact in their verdict and if the defendant is so acquitted the judgment shall so state. In the event of such acquittal, the court shall order the defendant to be committed to the custody of the commissioner of mental hygiene to be placed in an appropriate institution in the state department of mental hygiene or the state department of correction which has been approved by the heads of such department, and the court shall direct the sheriff if the court is located in a county outside the city of New York and the court shall direct the department of correction of the city of New York if the court is located in the city of New York, to temporarily hold the defendant pending such approval or designation of an appropriate institution in which the defendant shall be placed, and when notified by the commissioner of mental hygiene of the designated institution, the sheriff or the department of correction, as the case may be, shall forthwith cause the defendant to be delivered to the head of such institution.

(2) If the commissioner of mental hygiene is of the opinion that a person committed to his custody, pursuant to paragraph one of this section, may be discharged or released on condition without danger to himself or to others, he shall make application for the discharge or release of such person in a report to the court by which such person was committed and shall transmit a copy of such application and report to the district attorney of the county from which the defendant

C.C.P. SECTION 454 *continued*

was committed. The court may then appoint up to two qualified psychiatrists to examine such person, to report within sixty days, or such longer period as the court determines to be necessary for the purpose, their opinion as to his mental condition. To facilitate such examination and the proceedings thereon, the court may cause such person to be confined in any institution located near the place where the court sits, which may hereafter be designated by the commissioner of correction or the commissioner of mental hygiene as suitable for the temporary detention of irresponsible persons.

(3) If the court is satisfied that the committed person may be discharged or released on condition without danger to himself or others, the court shall order his discharge, or his release on such conditions as the court determines to be necessary. If the court is not so satisfied, it shall promptly order a hearing to determine whether such person may safely be discharged or released. Any such hearing shall be deemed a civil proceeding. The committed person may offer the testimony of any qualified psychiatrist at such a hearing. After such a hearing, the committed person shall be discharged, released on such conditions as the court determines to be necessary, or recommitted to the commissioner of mental hygiene. The commissioner of mental hygiene shall make suitable provision for the care and supervision by the department of mental hygiene of persons released conditionally under this section.

(4) If, within five years after the conditional release of a committed person, the court shall determine, after a hearing, that for the safety of such person or the safety of others his conditional release should be revoked, the court shall forthwith order him recommitted to the commissioner of mental hygiene subject to discharge or release only in accordance with the procedure set forth in subdivisions two, three and five of this section.

(5) A committed person may make application for his discharge or release to the court by which he was committed, and, if, after receiving a report of the commissioner of the mental hygiene department, the court considers that there may be merit in the application, the court shall follow the procedure prescribed in subdivisions two and three of this section.

(6) A defendant committed to the custody of the commissioner of mental hygiene pursuant to the provisions of this section may at any time during the period of his commitment be transferred to an appropriate institution in the state department of mental hygiene or in the state department of correction, which has been approved by the heads of such departments. As amended L. 1960, c. 550 § 1; L. 1963, c. 527; L. 1967, c. 681, § 58, eff. Sept. 1, 1967.

C.C.P. SECTION 658

§ 658. **Court order for examination as to sanity of defendant.**

If at any time before final judgment it shall appear to the court having jurisdiction of the person of a defendant indicted for a felony

C.C.P. SECTION 658 *continued*

or a misdemeanor that there is reasonable ground for believing that such defendant is in such state of idiocy, imbecility or insanity that he is incapable of understanding the charge, indictment or proceedings or of making his defense, or if the defendant makes a plea of insanity to the indictment, instead of proceeding with the trial, the court, upon its own motion, or that of the district attorney or the defendant, may in its discretion order such defendant to be examined to determine the question of his sanity. Added L. 1939, c. 861, § 2, eff. Sept. 1, 1939.

C.C.P. SECTION 659

§ 659. Examination as to sanity; by whom made.
Outside of the city of New York upon request of the court the superintendent or person in charge of a hospital supported by the state, or by any political subdivision thereof, which has been certified by the state commissioner of mental hygiene as having adequate facilities to make such examination, or the director of community mental health services, shall cause an examination of such defendant to be made. In New York city upon request of the court, the director of the division of psychiatry of the department of hospitals of such city shall cause an examination of such defendant to be made.
Such examinations shall be made as follows: Outside of the city of New York, the superintendent of the hospital or the director of community mental health services shall designate two qualified psychiatrists as defined in the mental hygiene law, of whom he may be one, to make such an examination. In New York city, the director of the division of psychiatry of the department of hospitals shall designate from the staff of such division two such qualified psychiatrists, of whom he may be one, to make such an examination; they shall be aided by an assistant corporation counsel assigned for that purpose by the corporation counsel of such city. As amended L. 1966, c. 762, § 1, eff. July 1, 1966.

C.C.P. SECTION 660

§ 660. Method of examination.
The psychiatrists so designated shall forthwith examine the defendant. Examinations may be made in the place where the defendant is detained, or, upon recommendation of said superintendent or director the court may commit the defendant for a reasonable period, not to exceed sixty days, for observation and examination to another place of detention or to such hospital as may be designated by such superintendent or director. When the defendant is committed to a hospital for examination the court, upon request of the superintendent or of the director of the division of psychiatry, as the case may be, may require the sheriff of the county where the defendant is under indictment, or in New York city the department of correction to furnish sufficient deputies or officers to guard such defendant. The state

C.C.P. SECTION 660 *continued*

commissioner of mental hygiene shall prescribe and furnish blanks for such commitment for observation and examination to a hospital supported by the state, or by any political subdivision thereof, which has been certified by the commissioner of mental hygiene as having adequate facilities to make such examination and admission shall be had only upon such blanks. When such commitment for observation and examination is made to an institution of the department of mental hygiene, the commitment shall be made to the institution serving the institutional district established pursuant to the mental hygiene law in which the court having jurisdiction of the defendant is located. Added L. 1939, c. 861, § 2; amended L. 1950, c. 525, § 24; L. 1953, c. 785, § 1, eff. July 1, 1953.

C.C.P. SECTION 661

§ 661. Procedure; powers of examiners; subpoenas.

Before commencing his duties hereunder each psychiatrist designated to make an examination ordered by the court shall take the oath prescribed by the civil practice act to be taken by referees, which shall be annexed to and made a part of the report hereinafter provided for. Such psychiatrists may continue such examination for such periods of time as may be necessary. They may examine witnesses and receive such other information relating to the subject of their inquiry as may aid them in reaching a determination and for such purpose may administer oaths and compel the attendance of witnesses and the production of books, papers and records deemed relevant or material. Subpoenas shall be issued and served by the clerk of the court having jurisdiction of the defendant upon the request of such psychiatrists. Added L. 1939, c. 861, § 2, eff. Sept. 1, 1939.

C.C.P. SECTION 662

§ 662. Reports to court.

Upon the completion of such examination of a defendant the superintendent of the hospital or director of the division of psychiatry of the department of hospitals of New York city or the director of community mental health services, as the case may be, must forthwith transmit to the court in quadruplicate a full and complete report including the findings of the qualified psychiatrists who have conducted the examination to the effect that the defendant is, or is not, at the time of such examination in such state of idiocy, imbecility or insanity as to be incapable of understanding the charge against him or the proceedings or of making his defense. If the two psychiatrists do not agree in their findings, the court may request the superintendent of the hospital or the director of said division of psychiatry or the director of community mental health services, as the case may be, to appoint a third psychiatrist to examine the defendant and submit a report to the court. The report of the psychiatrists made pursuant to this section shall not be received in evidence upon the trial of the

C.C.P. SECTION 662 *continued*

defendant but shall be filed by the court in the office of the clerk of the court where it shall be subject to inspection only on an order of the court or a justice thereof. A copy of such report shall be transmitted by the clerk of the court to the superintendent of the institution to which the defendant is committed. As amended L. 1966, c. 762, § 2, eff. July 1, 1966.

C.C.P. SECTION 662-a

§ 662-a. Hearings before the court.

The court shall cause one copy of such report to be served upon the district attorney and one copy upon counsel for the defendant. If either counsel for the defendant or the district attorney does not accept the findings of the psychiatrists and wishes to contravert them, the court shall afford counsel for the defendant and the district attorney opportunity to do so before him. Added L. 1942, c. 284, § 2, eff. April 2, 1942.

C.C.P. SECTION 662-b

§ 662-b. Procedure where defendant is found to be in a state of idiocy, imbecility or insanity.

1. If, after giving the district attorney and counsel for the defendant opportunity to be heard thereon, the court is of the opinion that the defendant is in such state of idiocy, imbecility or insanity as to be incapable of understanding the charge against him or the proceedings or of making his defense, the trial or proceedings must be suspended, except as hereinafter provided, until he is no longer in such state of idiocy, imbecility or insanity as to be incapable of understanding the charge against him and the proceedings and of making his defense, and the court shall commit the defendant to the custody of the commissioner of mental hygiene to be placed in an appropriate institution in the state department of mental hygiene or the state department of correction which has been approved by the heads of such departments. If the defendant is not in a hospital as defined in the mental hygiene law, the court shall direct the sheriff, if the court is located in a county outside the city of New York, and the court shall direct the department of correction of the city of New York, if the court is located in the city of New York, to hold the defendant temporarily pending such approval or designation of an appropriate institution in which the defendant shall be placed, and, when notified by the commissioner of mental hygiene of the designated institution, the sheriff or the department of correction, as the case may be, shall forthwith cause the defendant to be delivered to the head of such institution. If the defendant is in a hospital as defined in the mental hygiene law, the defendant shall be temporarily detained therein pending such approval or designation of an appropriate institution by the commissioner of mental hygiene.

2. A defendant so committed may at any time during the period

C.C.P. SECTION 662-b *continued*

of his commitment be transferred to any appropriate state institution of the department of mental hygiene or of the department of correction, as may be approved by the heads of such departments. A defendant so committed shall remain in such institution until he is no longer in such state of idiocy, imbecility or insanity as to be incapable of understanding the charge against him or of making his defense thereto except as hereinafter provided. In that event the director of the institution where such defendant is confined shall inform the court and the district attorney, or their successors, of such fact that the person so confined may be returned forthwith to the authority by which he was originally held in confinement. The court from which such defendant was committed shall cause the sheriff without delay to bring the defendant from such institution and place him in proper custody, whereupon the proceedings against such defendant shall be resumed and he shall be brought to trial or legally discharged.

3. Notwithstanding any provisions of this chapter to the contrary, any court having jurisdiction in any case heretofore or hereafter arising under this chapter may upon ten days notice to and upon consent of the district attorney dismiss the indictments or proceedings against the defendant upon its own motion or upon the motion of the district attorney or upon the motion of the defendant or of anyone on his behalf or upon the motion of the head of the institution in which the defendant is so confined with the approval of the head of the department having jurisdiction of such institution upon a showing that the defendant is a resident or citizen of another state or country and that he may be removed thereto upon the dismissal of the indictments or proceedings, and in any case at any time after two years from the date of the defendant's commitment to a mental institution upon such notice to and upon such consent of the district attorney and upon a showing that such defendant has remained continuously confined because of mental illness or mental defect. Upon the dismissal of the indictments or proceedings, the court shall direct that notice of such dismissal shall be served upon the commissioner of mental hygiene.

a. In the event of the dismissal of the indictments or proceedings as herein provided, and if the defendant shall be confined to an institution in the department of mental hygiene and shall continue to be so mentally ill or mentally defective as to require continued treatment and confinement in an institution, the head of the institution where such defendant may be confined may retain the defendant for observation, care or treatment for a period not to exceed thirty days from the date of service upon the commissioner of mental hygiene of written notice of the dismissal of the indictments or proceedings against the defendant. If the head of the institution determines that the condition of such defendant requires his retention in the institution for continued care and treatment, the head of the institution shall, before the expiration of such thirty day period, make application for an order of retention or certification in the same manner as is provided for in section seventy-three or section one hundred twenty-four of the mental hygiene law, as the case may be, for the retention of a person not

C.C.P. SECTION 662-b *continued*

in confinement on a criminal charge. The defendant may thereafter be retained pursuant to the appropriate provisions of the mental hygiene law.

b. In the event of the dismissal of the indictments or proceedings as herein provided and if the defendant shall be confined to an institution in the department of correction and shall continue to be so dangerously mentally ill or dangerously mentally defective as to require continued treatment and confinement in an institution in the department of correction, the head of such institution may retain the defendant for observation, care and treatment for a period of thirty days from the date of service upon the commissioner of mental hygiene of written notice of the dismissal of the indictments or proceedings against the defendant. If at any time prior to the expiration of such thirty days, the head of such institution finds that the defendant continues to be so dangerously mentally ill or dangerously mentally defective as to require continued treatment and confinement in an institution in the department of correction, he shall so certify to the commissioner of mental hygiene and the commissioner of mental hygiene may authorize the head of such institution to make an application to a court of record or to a judge thereof for a court order of certification to an institution in the department of correction in the same manner as is provided for in section eighty-five or section one hundred thirty-five of the mental hygiene law, as the case may be, for certification of dangerously mentally ill or dangerously mentally defective patients in a mental hygiene institution who are not in confinement on a criminal charge. Upon such application all of the applicable provisions of sections eighty-five and one hundred thirty-five of the mental hygiene law, including notice and hearing, shall apply. As amended. L. 1958, c. 705; L. 1959, c. 337; L. 1965, c. 540, § 1, eff. Sept. 1, 1965.

C.C.P. SECTION 662-c

§ 662-c. Procedure where defendant is not found insane.

If, after receiving the report of the psychiatrists and giving counsel for the defendant and the district attorney opportunity to be heard thereon, the court is of the opinion that the defendant is not in such state of idiocy, imbecility or insanity as to be incapable of understanding the charge against him or the proceedings or of making his defense, the proceedings against such defendant shall be resumed as if no examination had been ordered. Added L. 1942, c. 284, § 4, eff. April 2, 1942.

C.C.P. SECTION 662-d

§ 662-d. Return of bail or refund of deposit of money upon commitment of defendant.

The commitment of the defendant under the provisions of the preceding section exonerates his bail or authorizes the return of any money deposited instead of bail. Formerly § 662-b, added L. 1939, c. 861, § 2; renumbered 662-d, L. 1942, c. 284, § 5, eff. April 2, 1942.

C.C.P. SECTION 662-e

§ 662-e. Costs.

Outside of New York city each psychiatrist designated shall be entitled to his reasonable traveling expenses and a fee of twenty-five dollars for each examination of the defendant but not exceeding one hundred dollars in fees in any one case, except that if such psychiatrist be an employee of the state of New York he shall be entitled only to reasonable traveling expenses. Such fees and traveling expenses and the costs of sending a defendant to another place of detention or to a hospital for examination, of his maintenance therein and of returning him shall, when approved by the court, be a charge on the county in which the defendant is being tried. The county or New York city, as the case may be, may recover such cost from the estate of the defendant, if he has any, or from a relative legally responsible for his support. As amended L. 1967, c. 681, § 79, eff. Sept. 1, 1967.

C.C.P. SECTION 662-f

§ 662-f. Effect of other statutes.

The provisions of the foregoing sections shall not be deemed to be superseded by any provision of the mental hygiene law or other statute unless specifically so provided, nor shall the jurisdiction of the court to enforce its own orders be impaired. Formerly § 662-d, added L. 1939, c. 861, § 2; renumbered 662-f, L. 1942, c. 284, § 5, eff. April 2, 1942.

C.C.P. SECTION 870

§ 870. Order for examination as to sanity of a defendant.

If at any time it shall appear to a court or magistrate having jurisdiction of a defendant charged with a felony or misdemeanor but not under indictment therefor, or charged with an offense which is not a crime, or in the city of New York charged with a misdemeanor in a case where an information has not been filed, that there is reasonable ground to believe that such defendant is in such state of idiocy, imbecility or insanity that he is incapable of understanding the charge or proceeding or of making his defense, the court or magistrate upon his own motion or that of the district attorney or of the defendant may in his discretion order such defendant to be examined to determine the question of his sanity. The provisions of sections six hundred fifty-nine, six hundred sixty, six hundred sixty-one, and six hundred sixty-two-e of this code shall apply. Upon making such order the court or magistrate shall notify the district attorney thereof. If the two psychiatrists designated to examine the defendant do not agree in their findings, the superintendent of the hospital, or in the city of New York the director of the division of psychiatry of Bellevue Hospital or Kings County Hospital, shall appoint a third psychiatrist to examine the defendant, and his examination shall be deemed a part of the examination ordered by the court or magistrate.

257

C.C.P. SECTION 870 *continued*

During the time that the defendant so charged is under examination or is confined for that purpose in any hospital provided for in section six hundred fifty-nine of this code, the superintendent or person in charge of such hospital may administer or cause to be administered to such defendant, such psychiatric, medical or other therapeutic treatment as in his discretion should be administered, As amended L. 1961, c. 96; L. 1962, c. 698, § 24, eff. Sept. 1, 1962.

C.C.P. SECTION 871

§ 871. Procedure if defendant is subsequently indicted.

If, before the report of the psychiatrists is presented to the court or magistrate or proceedings are instituted for the commitment of the defendant as hereinafter provided, the defendant is indicted or, in the city of New York in the case of a misdemeanor an information is filed against him by the district attorney, the report of the psychiatrists shall be presented to the court in which the indictment or information is triable. Such court shall receive the report of the psychiatrists as if originally ordered by it and its procedure shall in all other respects be as set forth in chapter V of title XII [1] of part four of this code with regard to a person under indictment. Added L. 1943, c. 402, § 3, eff. April 8, 1943.

C.C.P. SECTION 872

§ 872. Defendant found to be in a state of idiocy, imbecility or insanity; procedure where charged with crime.

1. In the event that the defendant is not indicted, or in the city of New York in the case of a misdemeanor and information is not filed against him, and if two duly designated psychiatrists find that the defendant is in such state of idiocy, imbecility or insanity that he is incapable of understanding the charge or proceedings or of making his defense, the director or other person in charge of the hospital shall notify the court in which the charge is pending and the district attorney. If, after giving the district attorney and counsel for the defendant opportunity to be heard thereon, the court is of the opinion that the defendant is in such state of idiocy, imbecility or insanity as to be incapable of understanding the charge against him or the proceedings or of making his defense, the court shall commit the defendant to the custody of the commissioner of mental hygiene to be placed for observation, care and treatment, for a period not to exceed thirty days, in an appropriate institution in the state department of mental hygiene or the state department of correction which has been approved by the heads of such departments, and, if the defendant is not in a hospital as defined in the mental hygiene law, the court shall direct the sheriff, if the court is located in a county outside the city of New

[1] See section 658 et seq.

C.C.P. section 872 *continued*

York, and the court shall direct the department of correction of the city of New York, if the court is located in the city of New York, to hold the defendant temporarily pending such approval or designation of an appropriate institution in which the defendant shall be placed, and when notified by the commissioner of mental hygiene of the designated institution, the sheriff or the department of correction, as the case may be, shall forthwith cause the defendant to be delivered to the head of such institution. If the defendant is in a hospital as defined in the mental hygiene law, the defendant shall be temporarily detained therein pending such approval or designation of an appropriate institution by the commissioner of mental hygiene.

a. If the defendant is confined in an institution in the department of mental hygiene pursuant to such approval or designation and if the head of the institution determines that the condition of such defendant requires his retention in the institution for continued care and treatment, the head of the institution shall, before the expiration of such thirty day period, make application for an order of retention or certification in the same manner as is provided for in section seventy-three or section one hundred twenty-four of the mental hygiene law, as the case may be, for the retention of a person not in confinement on a criminal charge. The defendant may thereafter be retained pursuant to the appropriate provisions of the mental hygiene law.

b. If the defendant is confined in an institution in the department of correction pursuant to such approval or designation and the head of such institution determines that the defendant is so dangerously mentally ill or dangerously mentally defective as to require continued treatment and confinement in an institution in the department of correction, he shall so certify to the commissioner of mental hygiene and the commissioner of mental hygiene may authorize the head of such institution to make an application to a court of record or to a judge thereof for a court order of certification to an institution in the department of correction in the same manner as is provided for in section eighty-five or section one hundred thirty-five of the mental hygiene law, as the case may be, for certification of dangerously mentally ill or dangerously mentally defective patients in a mental hygiene institution who are not in confinement on a criminal charge. Upon such application all of the applicable provisions of section eighty-five and one hundred thirty-five of the mental hygiene law, including notice and hearing, shall apply.

Commitment pursuant to this section shall be made upon blanks prescribed by the commissioner of mental hygiene and shall be deemed a civil commitment.

A person so committed may at any time during the period of his commitment be transferred to any appropriate state institution of the department of correction or of the department of mental hygiene, as may be approved by the heads of such departments, or to a veterans administration institution or facility with the consent of the veterans administration.

259

C.C.P. SECTION 872 *continued*

2. Upon the commitment of the defendant all proceedings against the defendant before the court or magistrate ordering the examination shall terminate.

None of the provisions of this title shall prevent the district attorney at any time from reopening the matter and from presenting evidence against the defendant to a grand jury. If the defendant be indicted or in the city of New York in the case of a misdemeanor and information be filed against him by the district attorney, the warrant shall be lodged with the director of the institution where he is confined and all further proceedings shall be had as if he had been indicted prior to his commitment.

Provided, however, that if the district attorney has not reopened the matter or presented evidence thereon against the defendant to a grand jury prior to the expiration of six months from the date of the defendant's commitment as herein provided and shall have stated in writing his determination not to reopen the matter or present evidence thereon to a grand jury, the matter may not be reopened and the district attorney may not present evidence thereon to a grand jury. As amended L. 1960, c. 75; L. 1962, c. 698, § 25; L. 1965, c. 540, § 2, eff. Sept. 1, 1965.

C.C.P. SECTION 873

§ 873. **Defendant found insane; procedure where charged with offense not a crime and certain misdemeanors.**

Where the defendant is charged with an offense which is not a crime or outside of the city of New York with a misdemeanor of which courts of special sessions are declared in this code to have exclusive jurisdiction, if two duly designated psychiatrists who examine such defendant find that he is in such state of idiocy, imbecility or insanity that he is incapable of understanding the charge or proceedings or of making his defense, the superintendent or other person in charge of the hospital, or in the city of New York the director of the division of psychiatry of Bellevue Hospital or Kings County Hospital, shall, if he deems the condition of such person is such that it would be for his benefit to receive immediate care and treatment, notify the court or magistrate wherein the charge is pending of such fact and he shall also notify the local officers mentioned in subdivisions one and two of section eighty-one of the mental hygiene law whose duty it shall be to institute proceedings for the defendant's admission to a hospital as provided in the mental hygiene law for the admission of a person not in confinement on a criminal charge, and such local officers shall notify the court or magistrate of the result of such proceedings. Such admission shall be deemed a final disposition of the offense or misdemeanor charged. If two duly designated psychiatrists report that the defendant is in such state of idiocy, imbecility or insanity that he is incapable of understanding the charge or proceedings or of making his defense, and the defendant is not admitted to a hospital as above provided a copy of the report shall be filed with the court or magistrate and the

C.C.P. SECTION 873 *continued*

court or magistrate may in his discretion dismiss the charge and discharge such defendant or may make such order as may be appropriate and within his powers. As amended L. 1965, c. 540, § 3, eff. Sept. 1, 1965.

C.C.P. SECTION 874

§ 874. Defendant found not insane; procedure.
If the defendant is not indicted, or in the city of New York in the case of a misdemeanor an information is not filed against him, and two duly designated psychiatrists report to the court or magistrate that he is not in such a state of idiocy, imbecility or insanity as to be incapable of understanding the charge or proceedings or of making his defense or a judge or justice, at the conclusion of commitment proceedings under the mental hygiene law, shall have determined that he is not insane, the proceedings against such defendant shall be resumed before the court or magistrate as if no examination had been ordered. As amended L. 1962, c. 698, § 26, eff. Sept. 1, 1962.

C.C.P. SECTION 875

§ 875. Procedure in criminal court of the city of New York.
If at any time before final judgment it shall appear to the criminal court of the city of New York that there is reasonable ground for believing that a defendant before it is in such state of idiocy, imbecility or insanity that he is incapable of understanding the charge, information or proceedings or of making his defense, or if the defendant makes a plea of insanity to the information, instead of proceeding with the trial, the court, upon its own motion, or that of the district attorney or the defendant, may in its discretion order such defendant to be examined to determine the question of his sanity, and the procedure therefor shall be as set forth in sections six hundred fifty-nine, six hundred sixty, six hundred sixty-one, six hundred sixty-two, six hundred sixty-two-a, six hundred sixty-two-b and six hundred sixty-two-c. As amended L. 1962, c. 698, § 27, eff. Sept. 1. 1962.

C.C.P. SECTION 876

§ 876. [Inconsistent laws].
The provisions of this title shall supersede any provisions of the mental hygiene law or other statute inconsistent with the provisions hereof. Added L. 1943, c. 402, § 3, eff. April 8, 1943.